Combating Inequality

Combating Inequality

Rethinking Government's Role

Edited by Olivier Blanchard and Dani Rodrik

 PETERSON INSTITUTE FOR INTERNATIONAL ECONOMICS

The MIT Press
Cambridge, Massachusetts
London, England

This book was set in Sabon by Westchester Publishing Services. Printed and bound in the United States of America.

Library of Congress Cataloging-in-Publication Data is available.
Names: Blanchard, Olivier (Olivier J.), editor. | Rodrik, Dani, editor.
Title: Combating inequality : rethinking government's role /
    edited Olivier Blanchard and Dani Rodrik.
Description: Cambridge, Massachusetts : The MIT Press, [2021] |
    Includes bibliographical references and index.
Identifiers: LCCN 2020008513 | ISBN 9780262045612 (hardcover)
Subjects: LCSH: Income distribution—Government policy. |
    Equality—Economic aspects. | Equality—Government policy.
Classification: LCC HB523 .C644 2021 | DDC 339.2/2—dc23
LC record available at https://lccn.loc.gov/2020008513

A catalogue record of the book is available from the British Library.

10 9 8 7 6 5 4 3 2 1

Dedicated to Alan Krueger

Contents

Introduction: We Have the Tools to Reverse
the Rise in Inequality   xi
Olivier Blanchard and Dani Rodrik

I   The Landscape   1

1   Ten Facts about Inequality in Advanced Economies   3
     Lucas Chancel

2   Discussion of the Landscape   31
     Peter Diamond

II   Ethical and Philosophical Dimensions   39

3   Time for New Philosophical Foundations
     for Economic Theory?   41
     Danielle Allen

4   What Kinds of Inequality Should Economists Address?   49
     Philippe Van Parijs

5   Why Does Inequality Matter?   59
     T. M. Scanlon

III Political Dimensions   65

6   Wealth Inequality and Politics   67
     Ben Ansell

7   The Political Conditions Necessary for Addressing Inequality   75
     Sheri Berman

8   The Political Obstacles to Tackling Economic Inequality
     in the United States   85
     Nolan McCarty

IV The Distribution of Human Capital   91

9   A Modern Safety Net   93
Jesse Rothstein, Lawrence F. Katz, and Michael Stynes

10 Education's Untapped Potential   99
Tharman Shanmugaratnam

V   Policies toward Trade, Outsourcing, and Foreign Investment   107

11 Why Was the "China Shock" So Shocking—and What Does
This Mean for Policy?   109
David Autor

12 Trade, Labor Markets, and the China Shock: What
Can Be Learned from the German Experience?   117
Christian Dustmann

13 Combating Inequality: Rethinking Policies to
Reduce Inequality in Advanced Economies   125
Caroline Freund

VI The (Re)distribution of Financial Capital   135

14 How to Increase Taxes on the Rich (If You Must)   137
N. Gregory Mankiw

15 Would a Wealth Tax Help Combat Inequality?   141
Lawrence H. Summers

16 Should We Tax Wealth?   153
Emmanuel Saez

VII Policies That Affect the Rate and Direction of Technological
Change   161

17 Could We and Should We Reverse (Excessive) Automation?   163
Daron Acemoglu

18 Innovation and Inequality   171
Philippe Aghion

19 Technological Change, Income Inequality, and Good Jobs   177
Laura D'Andrea Tyson

VIII Labor Market Policies, Institutions, and Social Norms   193

20 Gender Inequality   195
Marianne Bertrand

21 Ownership Cures for Inequality   201
Richard B. Freeman

IX Labor Market Tools   211

22 Guaranteeing Employment for All   213
William Darity Jr.

23 Making Work Work   219
David T. Ellwood

24 The Importance of Enforcement in Designing Effective
Labor Market Tools   227
Heidi Shierholz

X Social Safety Net   235

25 Enhancing Micro and Macro Resilience by Building
on the Improvements in the Social Safety Net   237
Jason Furman

26 The Social Safety Net for Families with Children:
What Is Working and How to Do More   245
Hilary Hoynes

XI Progressive Taxation   253

27 Reflections on Taxation in Support of Redistributive Policies   255
Wojciech Kopczuk

28 Why Do We Not Support More Redistribution?
New Explanations from Economics Research   263
Stefanie Stantcheva

29 Can a Wealth Tax Work?   271
Gabriel Zucman

Contributors   277
Index   279

Introduction: We Have the Tools to Reverse the Rise in Inequality

Olivier Blanchard and Dani Rodrik

Inequality is widening, posing major moral, social, and political challenges to which policymakers must react. A combination of forces since the 1980s—globalization, new technologies, and institutional changes—have generated strong centrifugal effects in advanced economies, deepening existing divisions and creating new ones. Groups with the assets, skills, talents, and (sometimes) political connections needed to take advantage of these changes have benefited handsomely from the economic opportunities that were created. For many others, however, the same underlying trends have weakened employment prospects, suppressed incomes, and heightened economic insecurity.

Reacting to this evidence, we organized a major conference on inequality at the Peterson Institute for International Economics in October 2019. The conference focused on the tools that policymakers already have or could have to combat inequality.

The conference started with a statistical overview by Lucas Chancel (which he summarizes here in chapter 1) of the changes in the distributional landscape. Among the key takeaways was that, after declining for many decades, the income shares of the richest 1% in Western Europe and the United States increased from around 8% in the 1970s and 1980s to 11% and 20%, respectively, today. In 1980, the income share of the bottom 50% stood at 20% in both regions. Over the subsequent three and a half decades, this figure dropped to 12.5% in the United States and 18% in Europe.

Even though the United States and Europe have been exposed to broadly similar trends in globalization and technology, the rise in inequality has been much sharper in the United States, where the wealth share of the top 1% has risen from 25% in the late 1970s to around 40% today. Also, greater income and wealth inequality in the United States has been accompanied by reductions in key indicators of social mobility. The percentage of children in the United States earning more than their parents has fallen from 90% in the 1940s to around 50% today (reflecting in part lower underlying economic growth rates). On the positive side, gender and racial inequalities have generally come down (but remain high).

As Chancel noted, these differences suggest that countries have dealt differently with the effects of the global economic and technological forces on wealth and income distribution. Income and wealth gaps widened less in countries with more progressive tax regimes, strong labor market institutions (such as trade unions and minimum-wage laws), broad-based access to education and health services, and generous social transfers.

As striking as some of the numbers are, conventional economic measures of inequality such as the income share of top earners do not tell the entire story of the widening gaps within advanced economies. Important geographic and cultural divisions have also emerged, mainly between small towns, rural areas, and outer cities on the one hand and large cities and metropolitan zones on the other. These divisions reflect divergences in economic opportunities and cultural orientations—social conservatism versus social liberalism—that reinforce each other. They manifest themselves in reduced trust in political elites, social discontent, and support for the Far Right. This kind of social polarization along largely (but not exclusively) geographic lines has played a significant role even in countries such as France, where the income share of top earners has not risen much.

How intractable are such inequalities, and can they be fixed with the existing toolkit? The conference was aimed at answering these questions. The presentations and discussions focused on a wide range of remedies, discussed in the chapters that follow. We cannot claim that there was general consensus on the answers. To produce a detailed action plan was not our goal. Some proposals—especially wealth taxes—generated significant and heated debate. At the same time, the conference reflected a broad convergence around a multipronged attack on inequality, encompassing a wide set of tools, and the contributions to this volume reflect that.

A Growing Consensus

Importantly, there was widespread (if often implicit) agreement on many aspects of inequality that would have been more contentious some years earlier. For one thing, nobody at the conference challenged the view that inequality is a first-order problem requiring significant policy attention. (It is true that when you invite researchers and policymakers who work on inequality, they are likely to think that this is indeed an important issue, but we sensed a much stronger belief than in the past that inequality is an urgent issue and should be at the top of policymakers' agendas.)

There was widespread agreement that policies should focus on more than poverty reduction. There was not much discussion of an equity versus efficiency trade-off (i.e., a trade-off between income equality and economic performance). If anything, the implicit assumption in many of the presentations was that inequality is restraining economic growth by reducing economic opportunities for the lower and middle classes and fostering (or reflecting) monopolistic rents for the very wealthy.

Nobody proposed giving market forces freer rein by deregulating labor markets or cutting social programs as remedies for inequality. These were almost always discussed as causes of—rather than solutions to—inequality. Had our conference taken place, say, a decade ago, participants would probably have pointed to government interventions, blunted economic incentives to work, and rigid labor markets as the causes for incomes languishing at the bottom of the income distribution.

Finally, in relation to expanding social programs, nobody asked, "Can we pay for it?" There was broad agreement that taxes (at least in the United States) have to rise. The only debate here was about whether progressivity should focus on the revenue side or the expenditure side. Some would fund public spending directed at the lower and middle parts of the income distribution through broad-based taxes such as the value-added tax (VAT), which are easy to collect. Others prefer to redress inequality at the very top by using wealth taxes and more progressive income taxes. At the end of the day, most would probably agree that we need some of both.

Hence, the conference revealed widespread acceptance that we need to do something about inequality and that removing government interventions or just stimulating economic growth will not do the job. Instead, we need the government to play a more forceful direct role in closing gaps in living standards. The conversation among economists has indeed changed.

Which Policies?

Our conference covered a very wide range of policies to combat inequality. It helps to think about them by distinguishing them across two dimensions.

First, policies vary with respect to the stage of the economy they target. We organized the conference panels around three types of policies that differ along this dimension. They are shown as column headings in table 0.1 (see later in introduction).

Some policies focus on the *preproduction* stage. These policies shape the endowments with which people enter the workforce, such as educational, health, and financial access policies. Chapters by Jesse Rothstein, Lawrence F. Katz, and Michael Stynes (chapter 9), Tharman Shanmugaratnam (chapter 10), Gregory Mankiw (chapter 14), Lawrence Summers (chapter 15), and Emmanuel Saez (chapter 16) discuss these policies.

Some policies intervene directly at the *production* stage, by affecting the composition and organization of production. Such policies help determine relative prices and incentives in hiring, investment, and innovation decisions. They also affect the bargaining power of those with claims on output (workers, shareholders, managers, and suppliers). Examples are minimum wages, trade agreements, investment and research and development subsidies, place-based policies, and other types of "industrial policies." We have contributions from David Autor (chapter 11), Christian Dustmann (chapter 12), Caroline Freund (chapter 13), Daron Acemoglu (chapter 17), Philippe Aghion (chapter 18), Laura Tyson (chapter 19), Marianne Bertrand (chapter 20), Richard B. Freeman (chapter 21), William Darity Jr. (chapter 22), David Ellwood (chapter 23), and Heidi Shierholz (chapter 24) on these types of policies.

Finally, some policies focus on the *postproduction* stage, the redistribution of income and wealth. Progressive income taxation, wealth taxation, income-support policies such as the negative income tax (Earned Income Tax Credit [EITC] in the United States), and food stamps fall in this category. We have contributions here from Jason Furman (chapter 25), Hilary Hoynes (chapter 26), N. Greg Mankiw (chapter 14), Jesse Rothstein, Lawrence F. Katz, and Michael Stynes (chapter 9), Wojciech Kopczuk (chapter 27), Stefanie Stantcheva (chapter 28), Lawrence Summers (chapter 15), and Gabriel Zucman (chapter 29).

A second dimension along which policies differ is the part of the income distribution they seek to "fix." The choices here relate to the question: what kind of inequality do we care about? Some policies target the *bottom* of the distribution. Poverty-reduction policies are the key example of this type of policy. Other policies try to lift incomes in the *middle* to support the middle class. Yet others focus on reducing incomes at the *top*. These three types of policies are shown as the rows in table 0.1.

Combining the two dimensions yields a 3×3 matrix with nine different sets of possible policies. Which cells of the table should we focus on to tackle inequality more effectively? Economics provides some guidance here but is not enough on its own. Economic analysis must be combined with values and normative judgments (or a political philosophy), at least implicitly, and it must be combined with views on how the economy and polity interact.

One of the themes that emerged from our conference is the importance of policies that tackle the middle of the income distribution—in particular, policies that support the expansion of middle-class, or "good," jobs. The literature on the drivers of authoritarian populism makes it clear that the scarcity of good jobs and the economic anxieties that accompany it have played a substantial role in the rise of the Far Right. These are also the kinds of jobs that are most at risk with the spread of new technologies such as artificial intelligence, digitalization, and automation. The presentations here suggest that the requisite remedies will need to go beyond education, training, and redistribution. We need a policy environment that directly targets the creation of good jobs. The middle cell of table 0.1 is especially important and poses its own particular problems (as we discuss briefly here).

Philosophy and Politics

Consider the role of political philosophy. As Danielle Allen (chapter 3), T. M. Scanlon (chapter 5), and Philippe Van Parijs (chapter 4) remind us, what we want to do about inequality must start with answering the following questions: What is wrong with it? Do we want to reduce inequality because its consequences are bad or because it is bad in itself? If we think it is bad in itself, how do we distinguish between objectionable and unobjectionable inequality? The answers to these questions help us orient ourselves in table 0.1.

As Scanlon emphasizes, there are good reasons to promote equity beyond simply increasing the incomes of the poor. Inequality can be objectionable because of its adverse consequences or because of the unjustifiability of the institutions that generate it. In the latter case, if a high concentration of wealth is the consequence of unfair institutions, we may want to tax the top 1% regardless of the economic consequences, say, on economic growth. If not, such taxes must be otherwise justified—by appealing, for example, to the revenues they could generate to fund social programs. A Rawlsian perspective (advocated by both Scanlon and Van Parijs) would lead us to demand that any increase in inequality must improve the well-being of the worst off in society. An emphasis on political equality (supported by Allen) may require more radical interventions in markets that level the playing field among different groups and ensure equal access to rule-making (in labor markets, corporate governance, regulation, and so on).

Understanding what is achievable (and how) also requires a view on political economy. The difficulty here lies in teasing out the effect of inequality on politics and vice versa. The chapters by political scientists Ben Ansell (chapter 6), Sheri Berman (chapter 7), and Nolan McCarty (chapter 8) focus mostly on the effects of economic inequality on political outcomes. They emphasize that rising inequality does not translate directly into political demand for remedies; political parties may choose to put social and cultural elements before economics. But, clearly, *political* inequality exacerbates economic inequality as well. Even in democracies, some have more power than others. Our current policies and institutional arrangements reflect the power of prevailing coalitions of special interests and reinforce that power in turn. But if that is the case, how can we move to a different, more equitable equilibrium without the wealthy and powerful rejecting or subverting the best policy ideas? What is the implicit theory of change? Is it enough to target the worst symptoms of inequality? Or do we need a more comprehensive overhaul that tackles the root causes in the political system? If the latter, what is the relationship between specific sets of interventions, as shown in table 0.1, and the operation of the political system?

If the very wealthy exert too much political influence, what is the more effective (and feasible) strategy, preventing wealth accumulation by taxing it (as Saez and Zucman advocate) or reforming corporate governance, antitrust, and labor markets that thwart winner-take-all and superstar effects (which Summers pointed at)? If the poor are disenfranchised and therefore have little voice in determining the economic policies that affect them, is improving their economic circumstances adequate? Or should we also contemplate changes in political rules, such as making it easier to vote or restricting campaign financing? While our conference did not discuss political reforms, one implication of our discussions is that they may well be needed to alter the political-economic equilibrium in a more equitable direction.

Urgency, Ambition, and Evidence

A further question has to do with the scope of our ambition. Do we only pursue policies for which there is good evidence, or are we willing to be bolder and to experiment? Do we seek a gradual evolution of our policies or a more wholesale revolution? This is perhaps at least as much a question of temperament as of economics. Of course, it makes sense to prioritize reforms for which there is good evidence. But a high evidentiary threshold also restricts us to the margins of existing policies and small scale changes. We necessarily have good evidence only on policies that have been tried. Policies that are fundamentally innovative are, well, untested.

Franklin D. Roosevelt famously called for "bold, persistent experimentation" during the New Deal. Even John Maynard Keynes, whose ideas on fiscal stimulus were revolutionary at the time, thought FDR's more structural policies—for example, facilitating labor unions and increasing their bargaining power via the National Industrial Recovery Act of 1933 (NIRA) or introducing massive regulation of businesses (a measure later declared unconstitutional by the Supreme Court)—were "crack-brained and queer" (as he wrote in a letter to FDR in late 1933). There was little prior evidence on how these new rules would work. If New Deal policies had been subject to the "evidence-based" test, few of them would have been implemented. Yet many, if not most, eventually became commonplace elements of modern economies and are credited with saving capitalism from its excesses.

The extent to which policies should be experimental is a question that is especially germane for policies in the middle cell of table 0.1, those that address middle-class incomes at the production stage. As many contributors to this volume emphasize, an adequate response to inequality will require policies that aim to influence the direction of technological change and the employment practices of firms. Many of the potential remedies are untested, and their effects are unclear. Daron Acemoglu (chapter 17) and Laura Tyson (chapter 19) both suggest that the structure of taxation should be amended to remove (or reduce) subsidies to capital (and to automation) and strengthen rewards for the use of labor. This makes intuitive sense: innovators and employers presumably respond to price incentives. But will the effects on the direction of technological change be large enough, or do we also need more ambitious government programs that integrate innovation policy with job creation policies and require government collaboration with firms? In all likelihood, we will need a range of new instruments and programs and are largely in uncharted territory.

Successful experiences in other countries can sometimes provide useful guidance. For example, Christian Dustmann (chapter 12) describes how German industrial-relations arrangements moderated the impact of the China shock on German labor markets. The trade shock was accommodated partly by wage reductions but also partly by firms taking an active role in retraining their workers for different jobs. The presence of apprenticeship programs and labor unions both motivated firms to take labor interests on board and facilitated the requisite adjustments. If they can be generalized, such firm-level strategies may be a model for how to ameliorate the future employment consequences of new technologies. But the German example is also a reminder that copy and paste rarely works in the absence of more thorough institutional reengineering encompassing training, labor relations, and other arrangements.

Reforms in specific segments of the economy can also shed insight. Perhaps we can take heart from David Ellwood's brief example in chapter 23 of how a broken child-care system in the military was fixed after the 1980s. Once reform of the system became a priority, the US military embarked on some dramatic changes, including new standards, improved facilities, expanded training, and significantly higher pay. Even though an economy runs on different principles than the military, the case illustrates the possibilities of systemic change. In related work, one of us (Rodrik) has proposed a general set of iterative, cooperative public-private arrangements for building a good jobs economy (Rodrik and Sabel 2019). Where there is political will, there may be a way.

Similar considerations come into play in policies addressing other segments of the income distribution as well. Are joblessness and low incomes best addressed through the expansion of existing (and well-tested) programs such as the EITC, or do we need a more fundamental restructuring of labor laws and a federal job guarantee (as advocated by Darity)? Should wealth concentration at the very top be addressed by a wealth tax, which has never been implemented in the United States and may not even be constitutional (as advocated by Saez and Zucman but opposed by Mankiw and Summers)? How well can the universal basic income (UBI) work?

The more deep-seated we think the drivers of inequality are, the more radical the surgery needed. There is general agreement among the contributors that the playing field of our market economies has tilted away from the poor and the middle class. Corporations and the wealthy exercise too much power and have excessive influence on determining the rules of the game. At the conference, Angus Deaton laid out the harrowing consequences of corporate power blunting sensible regulation of painkillers and promoting "deaths of despair" in the American heartland. In his presentation, Philippe Aghion described how big tech platforms such as Facebook may reduce innovation and productivity in the long run, both trough political lobbying and foreclosing entry by new innovators. David Autor's presentation made it clear that the terms under which the United States allowed China to accede to the World Trade Organization were detrimental to workers in many regional labor markets (even as China's accession generated significant benefits for US workers and investors in the export sector). Others mentioned declining trade unions and growing monopsony power of a handful of firms controlling local labor markets as important factors behind the stagnation of median wages. "Monopsony power" of employers was indeed a recurring theme in many of the presentations.

Any stable social order reflects an underlying social contract. As Peter Diamond puts it in chapter 2, "Corporations have limited liability because the government gives it to them." The privileges corporations are given—legal personhood—entail a quid pro quo with society. In the old days, the sovereign chartered companies so they could enrich the crown's—and its cronies'—coffers. Today, presumably the goal is loftier and entails social well-being. Looming large is the question of how the social contract has frayed and what it will take to patch it up.

The Path Ahead

Our discussions yielded a large set of policy proposals, leaving no blank cells in table 0.1. We are either all over the map or have a lot of good ideas! We believe it is the latter. The conference demonstrated that there is no shortage of ideas and policy instruments to combat inequality. No

Table 0.1
A taxonomy of policies affecting inequality

		At what stage of the economy does policy intervene?		
		Pre-production	Production	Post-production
What kind of inequality do we care about?	Bottom	Endowment policies (health care, education); universal basic income	Minimum wage; job guarantees	Social transfers (e.g., Earned Income Tax Credit); full-employment macro policies
	Middle	Public spending on higher education	"Good jobs" policies; industrial relations and labor laws; sectoral wage boards; trade agreements; innovation policies; employee ownership	Safety nets; social insurance policies
	Top	Inheritance/estate taxes	Regulations; antitrust laws	Wealth taxes

specific proposal will do the job by itself. But we have different margins to work with, and many areas have low-hanging fruit: expansion of EITC-type programs, increased public funding of both prekindergarten and tertiary education, redirection of subsidies to employment-friendly innovation, greater overall progressivity in taxation, and policies to help workers reorganize in the face of new production modes.

The conference that led to this volume gives us hope that economists will be at the vanguard of policy reform rather than playing their habitual role of naysayer ("we can't afford it," "we don't have enough evidence," "incentives will be distorted," and so on). We both came out of this conference more optimistic about the economics profession's capacity to contribute to reducing inequality.

Acknowledgments

We are very grateful to David Xu at the Peterson Institute for International Economics and Hal Henglein at Westchester Publishing Services for a masterful job of editing the contributions in this volume.

Reference

Rodrik, Dani, and Charles F. Sabel. 2019. "Building a Good Jobs Economy." Unpublished paper. https://drodrik.scholar.harvard.edu/publications/building-good-jobs -economy.

I

The Landscape

1

Ten Facts about Inequality in Advanced Economies

Lucas Chancel

Introduction

Inequality in high-income countries has attracted a large amount of attention among academics, policymakers, and the general public in recent years. To be sure, the opacity of the international financial system and the shortcomings of standard tools to track inequality still hinder our ability to properly measure income and wealth in the twenty-first century. Nevertheless, there has been a "quantum leap" in the realm of inequality research over the past two decades, in part resulting from the production of historical income and wealth inequality series (Atkinson and Harrison 1978; Piketty and Saez 2003).

This chapter reviews recent findings on inequality dynamics in rich countries, discusses them in the broader context of educational, intergenerational, gender, and racial inequalities, and provides insights on the policy implications of this burgeoning literature. It is organized around 10 key facts that have structured recent debates on inequality: (1) inequality data remain scarce in the digital age; (2) income inequality has risen at different speeds since the 1980s, after a historical decline; (3) nations have become richer and governments poorer; (4) capital is back, for a few; (5) the Great Recession during the first decade of this century did not halt the rise of inequality; (6) global inequality is now more about class than about nationality; (7) higher inequality is associated with lower social mobility; (8) gender and racial income inequalities declined in the twentieth century but remain high; (9) equal access to education, health, and high-paying jobs lifts pretax incomes for those at the bottom of the distribution; (10) progressive taxation is key to curbing inequality at the top of the distribution.[1]

Inequality Data Remain Scarce in the Digital Age

Standard measures to track income and wealth inequality face serious comparability issues across countries and over time. Inequality data published by statistical institutions essentially rely on household surveys, which provide a rich source of socioeconomic data on individuals' standard of living, giving information on the various faces of socioeconomic inequalities. However, surveys have known limitations when it comes to measuring inequality, particularly at the top end of the distribution (Atkinson and Bourguignon 2000). Income and wealth levels reported in household surveys generally do not add up to national account aggregates and hence to macroeconomic growth estimates. Changes in household survey methodologies also make it challenging to compare inequality levels across countries and over time (UNECE 2011). In Europe, Blanchet, Chancel, and Gethin (2019) find that annual pretax incomes of the top 1% of Europeans recorded in household surveys are about €220,000, 60% below the value of €340,000 measured when mobilizing tax data and national accounts.

The use of tax data to track income and wealth dynamics builds on the pioneering work of Kuznets (1953) and Atkinson and Harrison (1978), who mobilized tax tabulations to monitor top income and wealth dynamics. The first decade of this century witnessed a renewed interest in this methodology, with historical series produced for several high-income countries (Piketty and Saez 2003; Atkinson and Piketty 2007, 2010). Thanks to the contributions of dozens of researchers collaborating on the World Top Incomes Database, top fiscal income series were initially produced for over 70 countries and contributed to a flourishing global inequality debate.

Top income series based on fiscal data are not immune from limitations. Comparability between countries and time periods is challenging because of differences in national tax legislation, which also changes over time. In the United States, about two-thirds of capital income is included in macroeconomic growth statistics but is generally missing from survey data as well as from tax statistics (Piketty, Saez, and Zucman 2018). These income sources (which include imputed rents, undistributed profits, and income paid to pensions and insurance) gained importance over the past two decades in the United States and many other rich countries.[2] Tax data are also known to suffer from evasion practices at varying degrees across nations. In Russia, the wealth share of the top 0.01% recorded without tax evasion is 5%, but it turns out to be higher than 12% when offshore assets are (at least partly) taken into account. In the United Kingdom, the figure rises from less than 3% to 4.5%, and in France it rises from 3.5% to 5.5% (Alstadsæter, Johannesen, and Zucman 2018).

The more recent development of the distributional national accounts methodology (DINA; see Alvaredo et al. 2016) seeks to address the limitations of existing data sources via the systematic combination of survey, tax, and national accounts data—and, to the extent possible, of tax-evasion information (see Zucman 2019). This methodology has been applied to several high-income and emerging countries, providing novel comparable results on global income and wealth inequality dynamics (see, for instance, Piketty, Saez, and Zucman 2018; Alvaredo, Chancel, Piketty, Saez and Zucman 2018; Blanchet, Chancel, and Gethin 2019). The results of these collaborative and cumulative efforts by the research community are available online in the World Inequality Database (at WID.world).[3] The DINA methodology makes it possible to produce historical pretax and posttax income and wealth estimates, as well as tax rates by income or wealth group. Producing such series requires setting conventions in order to ensure comparability across countries and over time. Some of these conventions can and should be debated, as has been the case (and as has been the case with key national accounts concepts since their creation). The most obvious way to move forward would be for the statistical community, under the auspices of the United Nations, to agree on new international standards for the distribution of income and wealth growth. The next revision of the UN System of National Accounts (around 2022–2023) may include new standards to guide national statistical organizations in the production of such statistics—but it is too early to know exactly what can be expected from this lengthy process. In the meantime, publicly available and comparable *official* data on income, wealth, or tax inequality remain particularly scarce.[4]

Income Inequality Has Risen at Different Speeds since the 1980s, after a Historical Decline

The systematic combination of available survey, tax, and national accounts data reveals that income inequality has been rising since the 1980s in most advanced economies, after a historical decline in the twentieth century. The richest 1% of Western Europeans and North Americans captured around 17%–20% of national income a century ago. This value decreased to 8% in the 1970–1980s before returning to 10%–20% in the late 2010s (figure 1.1). Other advanced economies (Australia, New Zealand, and Japan) followed broadly similar trajectories.

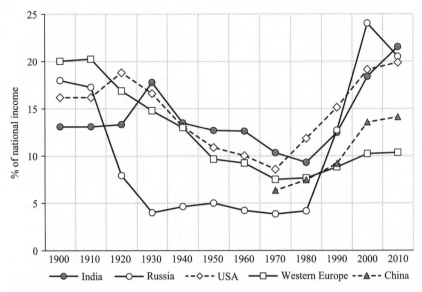

Figure 1.1
Income inequality rises at different speeds after a historical decline. Western Europe is the average of France, the United Kingdom, Germany, and Sweden. Distribution of pretax national income per adult. *Source*: Author based on WID.world (2019). See www.wid .world/methodology for data series and notes.

The historical decline of inequality in advanced economies in the mid-twentieth century was mainly driven by the fall of capital incomes. The role of the two world wars, the economic crisis in the wake of the 1929 stock market crash, and decolonization processes in the reduction of top capital incomes via capital losses and the destruction of physical capital has been amply discussed (see Piketty 2014; Alvaredo, Chancel, Piketty, Saez and Zucman 2018). The importance of peacetime policies implemented in the interwar period and in the aftermath of World War II should not be underestimated: high tax progressivity, nationalizations, and capital control policies (rent controls, lease regulations, and limitation of shareholders' rights in governance boards) also had strong impacts on income inequality.

Since the early 1980s, income inequality trajectories have diverged in Europe and the United States.[5] Between 1980 and 2017, the income share of the bottom 50% in the United States collapsed (from 20% to 12.5%) (figure 1.2). The income share of the top 1% followed an almost exactly inverse trajectory (rising from nearly 10% in 1980 to over 20% in 2017). In Europe, the income share of the top 1% rose much less rapidly over

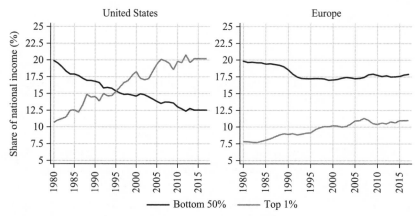

Figure 1.2
Inequality in the United States and the European Union, 1980–2017: the Great Divide.
Source: Blanchet, Chancel, and Gethin (2019), combing surveys, tax data, and national accounts for Europe. US series are based on Piketty, Saez, and Zucman (2018). See Blanchet, Chancel, and Gethin (2019) for data series and notes.

the same period.[6] The income share of the bottom 50% was reduced but maintained a relatively high level. Over this period, the income of the poorest 50% of Europeans rose by 40%, while the bottom 50% of the US distribution was de facto shut off from economic growth (with 3% overall income growth over a nearly 40 year time span). At the very top of the distribution, incomes skyrocketed in the United States, where the income share of the top 0.001% grew by more than 650% over the period (vs. 200% in Europe). The rise in inequality in rich countries is not driven by population aging: focusing on working-age individuals only, income growth has actually been negative for the bottom 50% of Americans since 1980. Changes in family structure do not explain the trends either.

Rich Countries Have Become Richer but Their Governments Have Become Poorer

A basic way to think about the dynamics of wealth inequality is to focus on the decomposition of net national wealth into net private wealth (total assets held by private actors, net of debts) and public wealth (net assets held by governments).[7] Why does such adecomposition matter for inequality analysis? A given level of wealth concentration does not have the same meaning in countries where private wealth is low and where wealth is preponderant in the economy. Low (or negative) public wealth levels tend to be associated with less room for governments to invest in public goods that matter for inclusive and sustainable growth (e.g., education, health, or climate protection). Relatively high private wealth levels tend to be associated with higher wealth inequality between individuals because of the cumulative and multiplicative nature of wealth accumulation processes.

A key fact about wealth in advanced economies in the twenty-first century is that capital is back, after collapsing during the twentieth century (Piketty and Zucman 2014). National wealth-to-income ratios (the sum of net private and net public wealth divided by national income) were 500%–700% in the early twentieth century in rich countries. They fell to 200%–350% after World War II and then stabilized around 400% until the early 1980s before returning to 400%–600% in the late 2010s (with significant country variations). The decline in national wealth in the twentieth century echoes the dynamics of income inequality: the military shocks of the two world wars and the loss of assets by wealth owners resulting from the decolonization process and capital control policies of the interwar and postwar periods contributed to deflating wealth-to-income ratios in the long run.

Another important finding about aggregate wealth dynamics is that capital is back because private wealth is back. Private wealth-to-income ratios were around 200%–300% in the late 1970s and have risen to 400%–600% in the late 2010s. On the other hand, public wealth-to-income ratios have declined from 50%–100% of national income to nearly 0% in most advanced economies (see figure 1.3). The secular decline of public wealth was driven by the rise of public debt and the sale of public assets, particularly in infrastructure.

Some countries (including the United States and the United Kingdom) now have negative public wealth positions. Negative public wealth implies that total public debt is greater than the total value of public assets (schools, roads, hospitals, etc.). In other words, the owners of public debt (essentially held by nationals in rich countries)[8] possess, via their financial assets, the totality of public infrastructure and financial assets in their country. Such a situation tends to give private owners of public debt more political leverage to influence fiscal and budgetary policies.

Capital Is Back, for a Few

The return of private wealth since the 1980s has been accompanied by a return of high wealth concentration in rich countries (Alvaredo, Chancel, Piketty, Saez and Zucman 2018; Zucman 2019). In the United States, the

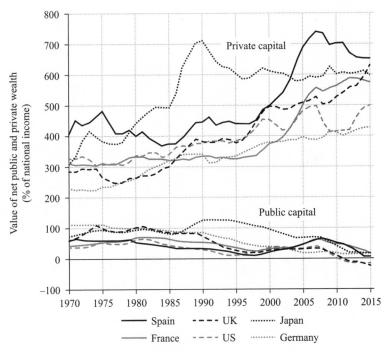

Figure 1.3
The rise of private wealth and the fall of public wealth in rich countries, 1970–2015.
Source: Alvaredo, Chancel, Piketty, Saez and Zucman (2018). See wir2018.wid.world for data series and notes.

wealth share of the top 1% culminated at around 45% during the Gilded Age and fell after the 1930s and 1940s. By the late 1970s, the wealth share of the top 1% had dropped to about 25%. The wealth share of the top 1% rose back to 40% (figure 1.4) recently. In the United States, the rise has been almost entirely driven by the top 0.1% of the distribution—whose wealth share grew from 7% in 1979 to around 20% today (Saez and Zucman 2016).

Western European countries experienced a larger decline than the United States in wealth inequality throughout the twentieth century and a slower increase since the 1980s. The wealth share of the top 1% in France, the United Kingdom, and Sweden culminated at around 55%–70% of national wealth in the early twentieth century—levels significantly higher than in the United States at the time. Interestingly enough, in France, despite the French Revolution and the self-proclaimed meritocratic Third Republic, wealth concentration remained extremely high throughout the nineteenth and early twentieth centuries (Piketty 2014).

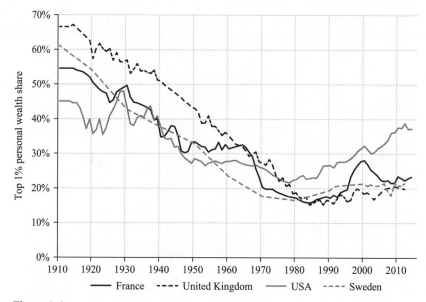

Figure 1.4
Top 1% personal wealth share in rich countries, 1910–2014. *Source*: Author, based on data from WID.world (2019). See www.wid.world/methodology for data series and notes.

Under the combined effects of military, policy, and economic shocks, the wealth share of the top 1% fell to around 15% in Western Europe by the late 1970s before rising to 20%–25% recently. In Europe, the twentieth century was marked by the appearance and the persistence of a patrimonial middle class, which had not existed before.

In the long run, wealth concentration is determined by the inequality of rates of return on wealth and the growth rate of average income, as well as by the inequality of savings rates (Piketty and Saez 2014). Rates of return available for large financial portfolios usually have little do with those open to small deposits. Between 1987 and 2017, the wealth of *Forbes* 500 Europeans and North Americans grew at an average annual rate of 8.9%—significantly faster than the average rate of wealth growth (2.7%). In comparison, average incomes grew at 1% per year over the period (see table 1.1).

The dynamics of savings rate inequality played a large role in the collapse of the wealth share of the bottom 90% in the United States. The savings of the bottom 90% of the population collapsed from 10% to 0% from the 1970s to the 2010s. On the contrary, the savings rate of the top 1% increased from 30% to 35% during that time. Had the savings rate

Table 1.1
Annual wealth growth by wealth group in the United States and Europe,
1987–2017

Wealth group	US + EU
Top 1/100 million (*Forbes*)	8.9%
Top 1/20 million (*Forbes*)	8.8%
Top 0.01% (WID.world)	6.1%
Top 0.1% (WID.world)	4.9%
Top 1% (WID.world)	4.0%
Average wealth	*2.7%*
Average income	*1.0%*

Note: Real growth of net personal wealth per adult. Top 1/100 million corresponds to the top 0.000001%, the top 1/20 million corresponds to the top 0.000005%.
Source: Author, based on Alvaredo, Chancel, Piketty, Saez and Zucman (2018) and Blanchet (2017). See www.wid.world/methodology for data series and notes.

for the poorest 90% of the population held constant, Saez and Zucman (2016) find that the wealth share of the bottom 90% would have been roughly stable between the mid-1990s and the early 2010s. In Europe and France in particular, similar dynamics hold. Garbinti, Goupille-Lebret, and Piketty (2018) find that the continuation of current inequalities in savings rates and rates of return in France will gradually bring levels of wealth concentration back to the values observed in the early twentieth century.

No Sign a of New Normal after the Great Recession

The 2008 financial crisis was immediately followed by a drop in income and wealth shares at the top of the distribution across the world and by several policy initiatives seeking to embed stricter regulatory frameworks in financial markets. Did the Great Recession and the subsequent policy responses alter the long-run inequality trends? Evidence from 10 years of data provides little support for this view.

The secular rise of private wealth in high-income countries seems to have been broadly unaffected by the financial crisis, suggesting a strong structural element to the rise in private wealth, beyond cyclical fluctuations. Similarly, long-term trends in wealth inequality have been broadly unchanged. In the United States, the total net wealth of the top 1% in 2014 was 10% above its 2006 value and 20% above its 2000 value, whereas the bottom 99% still hasn't recovered to its precrisis wealth levels. In France and the

United Kingdom, the secular rise in wealth share of the top 1% does not seem to have been significantly affected by the crisis either. In Spain, where the destruction of wealth was particularly strong after the housing bubble burst, top wealth groups were left relatively unaffected, as they were able to shift their investment portfolios from real estate to financial assets at the right time (Alvaredo, Chancel, Piketty, Saez and Zucman 2018).

Income inequality dynamics across countries since the crisis are relatively more diverse. In Germany and France, income shares of the top earners have declined slightly from their precrisis level and incomes of top earners still have not recovered from their 2008 values. In Italy, Japan, Australia, and New Zealand, income shares of the top earners have been broadly stable since 2007. In the United States, Spain, and Northern Europe (Denmark and Sweden in particular), income shares of the top 1% have more than recovered from their precrisis values.[9] Looking at wealth or at income inequality, there is no clear sign of a new normal after the Great Recession.

Global Inequality Is Now More about Class Than about Nationality

The rise in income inequality in high-income countries as well as in large emerging economies, combined with the reduction of average income inequalities between countries, transformed the geography of global inequality over the past few decades.[10] While incomes grew rapidly at the bottom of the global income distribution (over 100% growth since 1980 for the bottom 50%), incomes of top global earners rose even faster (over 200% growth for the top 0.001%). Low- and middle-income groups in rich countries were squeezed in between, with total income growth rates of less than 50% over the period. Overall, distributional national accounts estimates reveal that the top 1% captured close to twice as much growth as the bottom 50% of the world population since 1980 (Alvaredo, Chancel, Piketty, Saez and Zucman 2018).

The geography of global income inequality has modified profoundly since 1980. Forty years ago, nationality mattered more than class in accounting for global inequality. Today, class matters more than nationality. The Theil index of pretax national income inequality accounted for slightly more than half of global inequality in the early 1980s and only about a quarter today (figure 1.5). Put differently, in order to predict the position of an adult in the global distribution of income, it is more useful to know her income group rather than her nationality. This finding may have important implications for global inequality policy debates on the relative importance of migration, between-country transfers, and national-level inequality policies (see also Milanovic 2019).[11]

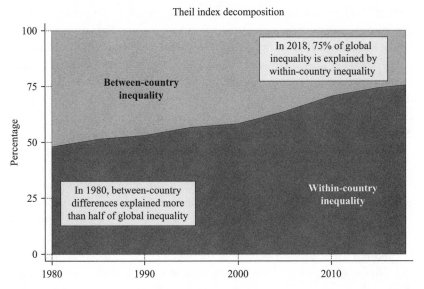

Theil index decomposition

Figure 1.5
Global income inequality between countries versus within country, 1980–2018. Distribution of pretax income per adult measured at purchasing power parity. *Source*: Author, based on WID.world (2019) and own updates. See wir2018.wid.world/methodology for sources and notes.

Despite persistent income inequalities between countries, income distributions of rich countries are now spread across the global inequality spectrum. In 1980, the bottom 20% of the distribution in Germany and in the United States stood between the sixtieth and eightieth percentiles of the global income distribution. In Germany, the bottom two deciles now belong to the fiftieth to seventieth percentiles of the global distribution, whereas the bottom 20% in the United States belongs to the thirtieth to fiftieth global percentiles. In other words, there are now global poor in rich countries.[12]

Higher Inequality Is Associated with Lower Mobility Rates

Has the rise of inequality in most high-income countries since the early 1980s been counterbalanced by an increase in social mobility? There are two broad ways to think about mobility: mobility across generations (intergenerational mobility) and mobility during individuals' lifetimes (intragenerational mobility).

Countries with higher inequality at a given point in time tend to have lower intergenerational mobility rates. Among rich countries, those that record low levels of income inequality (e.g., Scandinavian countries, with the income share of the top 10% around 25%–30%) tend to have relatively high levels of mobility (the intergenerational earnings elasticity[13] in these countries is low, around 0.15–0.2). Countries with moderate income inequality (e.g., France or Germany, with the income share of the top 10% around 30%–35%) have moderate mobility levels (elasticity of 0.3–0.4), and countries with high income inequality (e.g., the United States, with the income share of the top 10% around 45%) have a relatively high elasticity (around 0.5) (Corak 2013; Solon 2002). This relationship, dubbed the "Great Gatsby curve,"[14] reveals that countries with high income inequality do not compensate for that by having higher intergenerational mobility rates.

Chetty et al. (2014) find that relative mobility in the United States has been stable over the past two decades, at low levels. The probability that a child born in the bottom 20% of the income distribution will reach the top 20% is only 10%, whereas the probability that a child born in the top 20% will remain in the top 20% is three times higher. Absolute mobility in the United States (measured by the percentage of children earning more than their parents) fell from about 90% in the 1940s to around 50% today (figure 1.6). The decline in absolute mobility concerned all income groups, but the middle class was hit hardest. Absolute mobility dropped while relative mobility remained stable, because the bottom half of Americans have been nearly shut off from economic growth since the 1980s. This implies that higher average growth rates, keeping the distribution of growth unchanged in the United States, would be insufficient to return the country to the absolute mobility rates observed in the 1940–1960s. In Europe, available data are scarcer, but evidence points toward declining or stable intergenerational educational mobility since the 1980s (World Bank 2018).

Inequality of lifetime earnings has also risen in rich countries. In the United States, Kopczuk, Saez, and Song (2010) find that all the increase in "snapshot" inequality of earnings since the 1980s results from an increase in the inequality of lifetime earnings. Focusing on 24 OECD countries, Garnero, Hijzen, and Martin (2019) reach a similar conclusion. It has been argued that countries with high inequality levels have relatively higher intragenerational mobility rates, but this assertion has received only mixed empirical support.[15] Other measures of intragenerational mobility (e.g., probability of moving from bottom to top groups) have been broadly stable in the United States since the early to mid-1970s but mask heterogeneous trajectories among men and women. Lifetime mobility among males has actually worsened since the mid-1970s in the

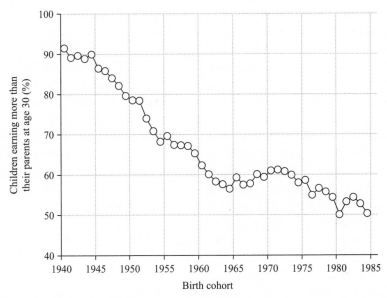

Figure 1.6
Absolute mobility in the United States, 1970–2014. Child income is measured at age 30, while parent income is measured as the sum of the spouses' incomes for families in which the highest earner is between ages 25 and 35. *Source*: Chetty et al. (2017, figure 1B).

United States (and even more so since the 1950s). On the contrary, lifetime mobility of women has dramatically increased since the 1970s (and even more so since the 1950s), driven by the rise of females in the workforce and the secular reduction of the gender pay gap (Kopczuk, Saez, and Song 2010)—as discussed in the next section.

Gender and Racial Income Inequalities Were Reduced in the Twentieth Century but Remain High

Thanks to rising labor participation rates for women (now above 46% in the United States, the United Kingdom, France, Germany, and Canada) and a reduction in the earnings gap, the male to female pretax income ratio was significantly reduced in the second half of the twentieth century. In the United States, it fell from over 350% in the 1960s to 200% in the 1980s. Since the 1980s, however, progress has been much slower: the ratio was still close to 180% in 2014 in the United States (Piketty, Saez, and Zucman 2018). The ratio of male to female earnings for full-time workers decreased from around 170% in 1980 to 130% in 2014, revealing the persistence of both composition effects and "pure" pay discrimination effects.[16] Gender differences in occupations and industries are found to account for about half the gender pay gap among full-time workers in the United States (Blau and Kahn 2016).

Women remain strikingly underrepresented among top income and wealth groups. Only about a quarter of top 10% earners in the United States are women (Piketty, Saez, and Zucman 2018), and the representation gap increases the further one goes up the income distribution. Among the top 0.1%, only 10% of individuals are females. Similar values are found in France and other European countries, including Norway, Italy, and Denmark (Garbinti, Goupille-Lebret, and Piketty 2018; Atkinson, Casarico, and Voitchovsky 2018). In France, it will take about a hundred years to reach parity among top income groups should progress continue at current rates (figure 1.7).

Turning to racial wealth inequalities, evidence shows that they also decreased in the second half of the twentieth century in the United States. The ratio of average earnings of whites divided by that of blacks was 250% in the 1960s. This value decreased to around 130% in the 1980s, in part because of the extension of the minimum wage in the 1960s (Derenoncourt and Montialoux 2018). However, the earnings gap has

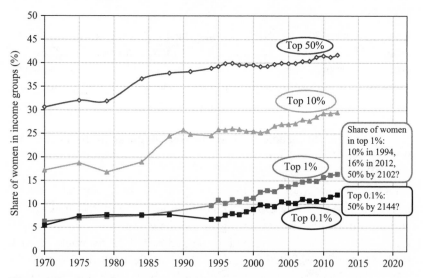

Figure 1.7
Share of women by fractiles of labor income for top groups in France, 1970–2012.
Source: Garbinti, Goupille, and Piketty (2018). See www.wid.world/methodology for data series and notes.

shown no sign of further reduction since the 1980s. Discrimination at the entry level of the labor market tends to perpetuate such levels of income inequality in the United States (Bertrand and Mullainathan 2004).

The racial wealth gap (measured as the average wealth of whites divided by that of blacks) in the United States has widened over the past decade: it was around 500%–600% in the 1980–1990s and rose to over 700% more recently (see Wolff 2017). The rise in the racial wealth gap is driven not only by a surge in wealth inequality levels at the top of the distribution; it dramatically increased between median black and white households as well.

Evidence points toward persistent racial inequalities in other high-income immigration countries, but data are scarce. In the United Kingdom, the earnings ratio of South Asians to whites was found to be broadly stable over the 2012–2018 period, at around 120% (ONS 2019). Official inequality data on race are still missing in many rich countries, such as France, Germany, and Italy, because of administrative regulations. Discrimination in the job market is nevertheless found to be large in countries such as France, with evidence of a strong racial and religious bias in the labor market. Candidates with Muslim names have four times less chance of being selected for an interview than candidates with non-Muslim names having the same qualifications (Valfort 2018).

Equal Access to Education, Health, and High-Paying Jobs Is Key to Lifting Pretax Incomes at the Bottom of the Distribution

Given the large variations in inequality trajectories across rich countries, it is important to understand not only the general rise in inequality but also (and perhaps most importantly) what explains such variations. Indeed, the drivers of inequality and growth differentials across countries might also differ depending on which segment of the distribution is looked at (e.g., the bottom 50%, the middle class, or the top 1%).

One of the standard explanations for the rise in inequality has been the impacts of technological change and openness. According to this line of explanation, technology and trade increased the relative productivity of skilled labor relative to unskilled labor in rich countries, thereby increasing the demand—and hence relative pay—for skilled workers. This line of explanation has several limitations. Rising income inequality is a broad-ranging phenomenon that also involves capital income and wealth dynamics, not only the distribution of labor income. In addition, the supply of skilled labor is determined by education, which depends on policy.

The expansion of education increases the supply of skills, while technological change and globalization may increase the demand for skills. Depending on which process occurs faster, the inequality of labor income will either fall or rise. This idea has been described as the race between education and technology (Goldin and Katz 2008).

While trade and technology are likely to explain part of the general rise in inequality observed in rich countries, they mostly fail to explain the large variations in growth trajectories at the top or at the bottom of the distribution. Western Europe and the United States had similar population sizes and technological development levels in the 1980s as well as relatively similar penetration rates of goods from low-income and emerging countries since then (from about 1.5% of GDP in the late 1980s to around 7% today). The two regions were also exposed to similar penetration rates of new technologies.[17] However, they followed radically divergent inequality pathways.

Another way to think about divergence in inequality trajectories across rich countries is to focus on the level and the dynamics of redistribution policies. However, Europe managed to generate faster income growth than in the United States at the bottom of the distribution, not mainly because of the effect of the tax and transfer system but essentially thanks to policies and institutional settings that determine pretax incomes (figure 1.8). Pretax incomes grew by 40% for the bottom 50% in Europe between 1980 and 2017 versus only 3% in the United States. To understand the US-EU inequality gap, one must thus look at policies impacting pretax income growth.

Inequality differences in access to higher education and training are likely to have played an important role in pretax income growth differentials between the United States and EU countries for the bottom 50%. Access to higher education remains notably unequal in the United States. Chetty et al. (2014) show that children whose parents are within the bottom 10% of income earners only have a 30% probability of attending college, while those whose parents are within the top 10% of earners have a 90% probability (figure 1.9).[18] The probability gap for Ivy League colleges is even more stark, as children whose parents belong to the top 1% of the income distribution have a 77 times better chance of attending an Ivy League college than children of the bottom quintile (Chetty et al., 2017). Available evidence suggests that the influence of parental background in educational outcomes is lower in Europe than in the United States and also relatively well correlated with levels of pretax income inequality among European countries (Causa and Chapuis 2009).

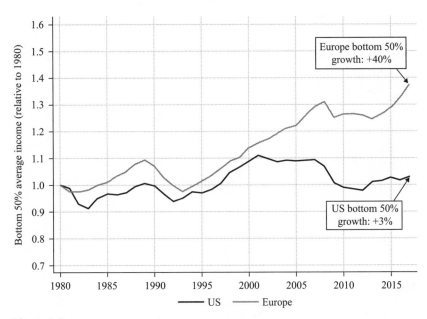

Figure 1.8
Pretax income growth of the bottom 50% in the United States and Western Europe, 1980–2017. Distribution of pretax income per adult. *Source*: Blanchet, Chancel, and Gethin (2019). See www.wid.world/methodology for data series and notes.

Universal access to higher education systems tends to be associated with lower educational inequalities (Martins et al., 2010). In the United States, the share of private expenditures on tertiary educational institutions is over 65%, whereas this value is around 60% in other Anglo-Saxon countries, 30% in France, Spain, and Italy, and as low as 8% in Germany and Scandinavian countries (Piketty 2019). Recent research points toward strong positive impacts of highly subsidized higher education on intergenerational mobility and college attendance in the United States (Chetty et al. 2017).[19]

Differences in the organization of health systems across countries are also likely to drive differences in pretax income inequality outcomes. Case and Deaton (2015) show that, after a historical decline, morbidity rates among white men have increased in the United States since the late 1990s, contrary to rates in other high-income countries. Chetty et al. (2016) find that there is a 14-year gap in life expectancy between males in the top and bottom 1% in the United States and that this gap has widened since 2001. Poor health is associated with reduced capabilities for the worse off as well as lower incomes and mobility chances (Marmot 2003; Case, Lubotsky,

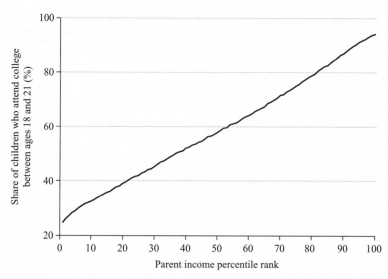

Figure 1.9
College attendance rate and parent income rank in the United States for children born in 1980–1982. *Source*: Chetty et al. (2014). See www.equality-of-opportunity.org/ for data series and notes.

and Paxson 2002), fueling a broader cycle of socioeconomic inequality. One of the most salient differences between the US and Western European health systems is that the latter are characterized by public universal access, which tends to limit inequalities in access to health care.

Beyond education and health, labor market institutions are found to play an important role in determining pretax growth rates, particularly at the bottom. While an increase in the minimum wage contributed to reducing inequalities in the United States in the 1960s (as discussed earlier), its later decline reversed the dynamics. The US minimum wage went from 42% of average earnings in 1980 to 24% today (in real terms, it decreased from more than $10 per hour in the 1960s to $7.25 in 2018). In many European countries, the movement was in the opposite direction. In France, the minimum wage was kept at approximately 50% of the average wage (in real terms, it rose from 5.5€ to 10€ per hour between 1980 and today). In the United Kingdom and in Germany, a minimum wage was introduced after 1990.

European countries with low pretax income inequality and without a minimum wage have powerful trade unions and collective bargaining agreements to set wages at the sectorial level. In Scandinavian countries, union density is around 50%–70%, the highest rate among OECD countries, where union density has been falling dramatically over the past forty years. Variations in union density across rich countries are found to be relatively well correlated with pretax income inequality dynamics (Jaumotte and Osorio Buitron 2019). The distribution of power in corporate governance bodies can also matter for pretax income growth at the bottom of the distribution. In Sweden, the Netherlands, and Germany, for instance, workers are represented on corporate governance boards and can influence corporate decisions on wages and other strategic issues.

To summarize, the large growth differences observed in the United States and Europe since the 1980s—when the two regions had broadly similar levels of inequality—do not appear to be mainly caused by trade or technological change, but neither do they result from cash redistribution. The gap results largely from different policies and institutional setups, which impact pretax incomes. The opposition between "predistribution" (or "preproduction") policies on the one hand and redistribution (or "postproduction") policies on the other should be nuanced: the public provision of higher education or universal health coverage (which fall in the realm of "predistribution" policies) requires government resources—and hence redistribution. So far, many European countries have succeeded in maintaining a relatively high level of public spending, guaranteeing broad access to public higher education and health care. Yet, European countries have also increasingly relied on flat taxes to finance public services and government expenditures.[20] These dynamics have raised concerns about the political sustainability of the financing of public services among European countries and suggest that redistribution (and progressive taxation in particular) and predistribution cannot be discussed independently.

Tax Progressivity Has Shaped the Dynamics of Inequality at the Top

One explanation for rising labor incomes at the top is the "superstar effect" (Rosen 1981). Technological change and globalization surely made it easier for those who make it to the top to reap a higher share of growth thanks to a rising market size. Tiny differences in talent—or sometimes in bargaining power and other attributes—may translate into very large income and wealth differences. This effect likely accounts for the common trends in inequality observed across rich countries, but stark divergences in rates of pretax income growth at the very top of the distribution in rich countries again suggest that other factors were at play.

Higher educational attainment and higher productivity of top income groups have also been presented as forces driving rising shares of income and wealth for those at the top (Mankiw 2013). However, remuneration levels of earners in the top 0.01% across rich countries show large variations and little or no correlation with productivity. The remunerations of CEOs of Germany's largest companies are on average about 50% below the remunerations of top CEOs in the United States, with little evidence that such pay differentials reflect significant differences in productivity between firms on both sides of the Atlantic (Alvaredo, Chancel, Piketty, Saez, and Zucman 2018).

Taxation dynamics are an important determinant of posttax income trends at the top of the distribution. One often-neglected role of progressive taxation is its ability to reduce not only posttax but also pretax income inequality. With high top marginal tax rates, top earners have less money to accumulate wealth and, all else being equal, less capital income in the long run. In addition, a high top marginal tax rate may also discourage top wage earners from negotiating pay increases, as bargaining becomes relatively less rewarding (Piketty, Saez, and Stantcheva 2014).

Top income tax rates were reduced significantly in several rich countries after the 1970s (figure 1.10), and their variations are relatively well associated with changes in the share of pretax income for those at the top across rich and emerging countries. Countries such as Germany, Spain, Denmark, and Switzerland, which did not experience any significant cut in tax rates for those at the top, did not experience significant increases in income share for those at the top. Conversely, the United States, United Kingdom, and Canada implemented important reductions in their top

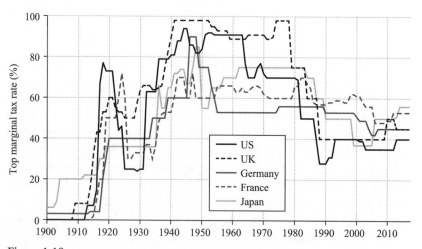

Figure 1.10
Top income tax rates in rich countries, 1900–2017. *Source*: Alvaredo, Chancel, Piketty, Saez, and Zucman (2018). See wir2018.wid.world for data series and notes.

marginal tax rates and saw strong increases in their income shares for the top 1% (Piketty, Saez, and Stantcheva 2014).

Since the 1980s, top marginal estate tax rates have also declined in the United States and the United Kingdom. All taxes considered, the effective tax rate applicable to individuals at the top of the distribution has declined significantly in the United States. Piketty, Saez, and Zucman (2018) find that the overall tax rate on the top 0.01% fell from 50% in the 1950s to less than 40% after the 1980s. The tax rate on the top 400 Americans declined from 60% in the 1960s to slightly over 30% today (Saez and Zucman 2019).

The strong decline of progressive taxation at the top of the income distribution in the United States resulted not only from the movements of income tax rates but also largely from the joint dynamics of income and corporate tax rates. The huge fall in the corporate tax since the 1960s in the United States allowed top business owners to shift their compensation in order to reduce taxes. Around 1.3% of US GDP accruing to S-corporation business owners corresponds to disguised salary (Smith et al. 2019).

The reduction in tax rates at the top was associated with an increase in the tax rate of the middle class. Egger, Nigai, and Strecker (2019) show that since the mid-1990s, the labor income tax of the middle class rose in high-income countries, while the top 1% of workers and employees faced a reduction in their total tax rates. In the United States, taxes on the bottom 90% grew from less than 10% in the 1910s to 1920s to around 30% today (Saez and Zucman 2019).[21]

Is low tax progressivity better than high tax progressivity for overall growth and capital accumulation? Historical data show that the era of high tax progressivity from the 1940s to the 1980s did not prevent high rates of income growth in the European Union and the United States, whereas the post-1980 era of low tax progressivity has been associated with lower rates of income growth—particularly at the bottom of the distribution. The dynamics of capital accumulation over the past hundred years also appear to be disconnected from relatively large variations in capital taxation (Saez and Zucman 2019).

The data at our disposal to properly measure the full impact of changes in tax progressivity on inequality and welfare are still imperfect. A combination of historical trends and econometric evidence cannot replace public deliberation and political decision-making on these complex issues, but there is sufficient evidence suggesting that shifts in progressivity contributed to the rise in income and wealth inequality in rich countries to reopen the discussion about progressive income and wealth taxation. Such a discussion is all the more important given the current needs for additional public resources to be invested in education, health care, and infrastructure that is resilient to climate change.

Concluding Remarks: While Designing Policy Responses to Current Inequality Trends, Future Inequality Drivers Must Also Be Factored In

Perhaps one of the most salient findings of recent research on inequality is the importance of policies and institutions in explaining the large differences in inequality trajectories across advanced economies. In other words, there is room for a much more equitable distribution of growth in the decades to come. Without significant policy changes (in terms of equal access to education, health care, and well-paid jobs as well as in progressive taxation), it is likely that current trends could be prolonged throughout the twenty-first century. Factors such as climate change and the pursuit of automation could also exacerbate such trends.

To limit the impact of automation on inequality, policies seeking to increase universal access to high-quality and high-skill education at all stages of life will become all the more important (Acemoglu and Restrepo 2017), yet educational policies alone are unlikely to mitigate the potential disruptive effects of automation and other innovations (e.g., artificial intelligence and biogenetics) on inequality. Policies can also seek to guide future innovations (Mazzucato and Semieniuk 2017) as they have done in the past. The question of the impact of machines and innovation on inequality is indeed also an issue of property rights: who owns the machine (or the algorithm) is as important as who the machine is replacing in the production chain.

Climate change is also expected to worsen inequalities between countries (Diffenbaugh and Burke 2019) as well as within countries. Groups with low income and wealth tend to be particularly exposed to environmental damage and are also particularly sensitive to environmental shocks (Chancel 2020a, 2020b). Without proper strategies to protect these groups, the increased occurrence of extreme climate-related events will exacerbate existing inequality levels. Carbon taxes are necessary (though not sufficient) policy tools to tackle climate change. However, they can also enhance inequality levels in the short run (Grainger and Kolstad 2010). In order to limit their impacts on inequality, their distributional consequences must be factored into their policy design. When coupled with low-carbon infrastructure investments and progressive tax reforms (as done successfully in some countries and much less so in others), climate policies can become powerful instruments for a more equitable and sustainable economy.

Let us end with a simple question with no easy answer: how do we make the most of facts in inequality debates? Researchers measure inequality as they measure carbon emissions: not only for statistical recording but also to help identify potential policy options to address current trends. The elephant in the room is what is missing, beyond more systematic inequality data, in order to tackle inequality effectively? What is our theory of change? What is wrong with it? Today, the case for inequality reduction is not as strong as the evidence of rising inequality. In that regard, efforts to systematically monitor inequalities have not yet been matched by equivalent efforts to systematize their impacts. In addition, there have been only a few attempts to identify the ideological, institutional, and political conditions under which policies affecting inequality have been successfully implemented in the past and could be implemented in the future.

Notes

1. A longer version of this paper, containing additional figures and an appendix, is available online at www.lucaschancel.info/10-facts.

2. That is, profits retained by the corporation rather than, for example, being paid out as dividends. Recent work has found that the choice to keep profits within a company largely depends on tax incentives. Failing to include them in inequality estimates thus makes the income share of top earners artificially volatile and would leave a share of macroeconomic growth unaccounted for—see Blanchet, Chancel, and Gethin (2019).

3. Other highly complementary inequality databases contributing to global efforts toward better distributional statistics include the Luxembourg Income Study (LIS), the database of the Commitment for Equity Institute (CEQ), or the PovCalNet database of the World Bank, for instance.

4. See WID.world/transparency.

5. See Piketty, Saez, and Zucman (2018) for the United States and Blanchet, Chancel, and Gethin (2019) for Europe.

6. The income share of the top 1% of Europeans rose from 7.5% to around 11%. The share for the bottom 50% dropped from 20% in 1980 to to 17.5% in the late 1980s and later stabilized at this level. The Gini coefficient for US pretax income per adult increased from 0.46 in 1980 to 0.6 in 2016. In Western Europe, it increased from 0.37 to 0.43 over the same period.

7. The notions of private and public property take different meanings depending on the country or the period considered. Their study must be coupled with a deeper understanding of the countries' institutions and how they affect political and social inequality; see, for example, Piketty (2019).

8. The net foreign wealth position of Japan, Europe, and the United States is positive, implying that wealth owners in these countries hold more wealth abroad than foreign wealth owners hold at home. See Piketty (2019).

9. Data from WID.world (2019) and Blanchet, Chancel, and Gethin (2019).

10. We build, in particular, on Lakner and Milanovic (2015).

11. These results confirm the trend observed in earlier work but provide novel insights with respect to the level of within-country inequality today. According to Lakner and Milanovic (2015), the global within-country Theil index increased over the past few decades, but between-country inequality remained more important in 2011 than within-country inequality. The use of new datasets of national-level inequality in line with the DINA (see also the first section of this chapter) account for a large part of the difference. The use of a single concept (pretax national income per adult) rather than a mixture of income and consumption distributions per capita as in earlier studies also contributes to explaining the gap (see Chancel 2019).

12. See the online appendix at www.lucaschancel.info/10-facts.

13. The intergenerational elasticity is the elasticity of parental income on the income of their children at adulthood (see Corak 2013).

14. See Corak (2013).

15. See, for instance, Flinn (2002) and Garnero et al. (2019), who find that countries that are more unequal tend to have higher intragenerational mobility rates, and Burkhauser et al. (2002) and Gottschalk and Spoalore (2002), who find the opposite.

16. Ratios computed using values from Blau and Kahn (2016). The median earnings gap of male and female full-time workers in the United States and the United Kingdom decreased from 35% to around 20% between 1980 and 2015, and from 20% to 15% in Denmark (Kleven, Landais, and Søgaard 2018).

17. In most industrial sectors, robot penetration appears to be lower in the United States than in Western European countries (see Acemoglu and Restrepo 2017).

18. See also Bratberg et al. (2017) and Deutscher and Mazumder (2019).

19. Top to bottom quintile intergenerational mobility is found to be the highest in midtier public colleges in the United States (Chetty et al. 2017).

20. Indeed, the average top corporate income tax rate in the European Union decreased from 50% in 1980 to 25% today. Conversely, the average VAT rate increased over the period (by 4%, from 17.5% to 21.5%, from 1980 to 2017).

21. At the bottom of the distribution, should tax credits to low-income individuals (such as the Earned Income Tax Credit in the United States) be treated as in Saez and Zucman (2019) or should they be seen as negative taxes? Tax credits fall in a gray area, and no choice is likely to be fully satisfactory. Focusing on corporate taxes, Saez and Zucman (2019) and the DINA methodology in general attribute them to shareholders, who pay these taxes. To the extent that corporate taxes might be partly passed on to workers' wages (Fuest, Peichl, and Siegloch 2018), one might argue that they should be partly attributed to workers. Doing

so would temper the fall in top tax rates in the United States, but the drop would remain important. This choice would also increase the regressivity of the current US tax system. Attributing part of corporate taxes to workers shifts the analysis away from the static study of tax rates at a given point in time to the study of the dynamic effects of taxation on growth. Both types of analyses are useful and complementary and should be carried out by tax authorities and statistical offices to allow informed debates on taxation (see also the first section of this chapter).

References

Acemoglu, D., and P. Restrepo. 2017. "Robots and Jobs: Evidence from US Labor Markets." NBER Working Paper 23285, National Bureau of Economic Research, Cambridge, MA.

Alstadsæter, A., N. Johannesen, and G. Zucman. 2018. "Who Owns the Wealth in Tax Havens? Macro Evidence and Implications for Global Inequality." *Journal of Public Economics* 162: 89–100.

Alvaredo, A., A. B. Atkinson, L. Chancel, T. Piketty, E. Saez, and G. Zucman. 2016. "Distributional National Accounts (DINA) Guidelines: Concepts and Methods Used in the World Wealth and Income Database." WID.world Working Paper 2016/2.

Alvaredo, A., L. Chancel, T. Piketty, E. Saez, and G. Zucman. 2018. *World Inequality Report 2018*. Cambridge, MA: Harvard University Press.

Atkinson, A. B., and F. Bourguignon. 2000. *Handbook of Income Distribution*. Amsterdam: Elsevier.

Atkinson, A. B., A. Casarico, and S. Voitchovsky. 2018. "Top Incomes and the Gender Divide." *Journal of Economic Inequality* 16(2): 225–256.

Atkinson, A. B., and A. J. Harrison. 1978. *Distribution of Personal Wealth in Britain*. Cambridge: Cambridge University Press.

Atkinson, A. B., and T. Piketty, eds. 2007. *Top Incomes over the Twentieth Century: A Contrast between Continental European and English-Speaking Countries*. Oxford: Oxford University Press.

Atkinson, A. B., and T. Piketty, eds. 2010. *Top Incomes from a Global Perspective*. Oxford: Oxford University Press.

Bertrand, M., and S. Mullainathan. 2004. "Are Emily and Greg More Employable than Lakisha and Jamal? A Field Experiment on Labor Market Discrimination." *American Economic Review* 94(4): 991–1013.

Blanchet, T. 2017. "Estimates of the Global Distribution of Wealth." WID.world Technical Note 2017/7.

Blanchet, T., L. Chancel, and A. Gethin. 2019. "How Unequal Is Europe? Evidence from Distributional National Accounts, 1980–2017." WID.world Working Paper 2019/06.

Blau, F. D., and L. M. Kahn. 2016. "The Gender Wage Gap: Extent, Trends, and Explanations." NBER Working Paper 21913, National Bureau of Economic Research, Cambridge, MA.

Case, A., and A. Deaton. 2015. "Rising Morbidity and Mortality in Midlife among White Non-Hispanic Americans in the 21st Century." *Proceedings of the National Academy of Sciences* 112(49): 15078–15083.

Case, A., D. Lubotsky, and C. Paxson. 2002. "Economic Status and Health in Childhood: The Origins of the Gradient." *American Economic Review* 92(5): 1308–1334.

Causa, O., and C. Chapuis. 2009. *Equity in Student Achievement across OECD Countries*. Paris: OECD.

Chancel, L. 2020a. "Clarifying the Muddle of Global Inequality Data." WID.world Working Paper 2020/5 (forthcoming).

Chancel, L. 2020b. *Unsustainable Inequalities*. Cambridge, MA: Harvard University Press.

Chetty, R., D. Grusky, M. Hell, N. Hendren, R. Manduca, and J. Narang. 2017. "The Fading American Dream: Trends in Absolute Income Mobility since 1940." *Science* 356(6336): 398–406.

Chetty, R., N. Hendren, P. Kline, E. Saez, and N. Turner. 2014. "Is the United States Still a Land of Opportunity? Recent Trends in Intergenerational Mobility." *AEA Papers and Proceedings* 104(5): 141–147.

Chetty, R., M. Stepner, S. Abraham, S. Lin, B. Scuderi, N. Turner, and D. Cutler. 2016. "The Association between Income and Life Expectancy in the United States, 2001–2014." *Journal of the American Medical Association* 315(16): 1750–1766.

Corak, M. 2013. "Income Inequality, Equality of Opportunity, and Intergenerational Mobility." *Journal of Economic Perspectives* 27(3): 79–102.

Derenoncourt, E., and C. Montialoux. 2018. "Minimum Wages and Racial Inequality." Working paper.

Diffenbaugh, N. S., and M. Burke. 2019. "Global Warming Has Increased Global Economic Inequality." *Proceedings of the National Academy of Sciences* 116(20): 9808–9813.

Egger, P. H., S. Nigai, and N. M. Strecker. 2019. "The Taxing Deed of Globalization." *American Economic Review* 109(2): 353–390.

Flinn, C. J. 2002. "Labour Market Structure and Inequality: A Comparison of Italy and the US." *Review of Economic Studies* 69(3): 611–645.

Fuest, C., A. Peichl, and S. Siegloch. 2018. "Do Higher Corporate Taxes Reduce Wages? Micro Evidence from Germany." *American Economic Review* 108(2): 393–418.

Garbinti, B., J. Goupille-Lebret, and T. Piketty. 2018. "Income Inequality in France, 1900–2014: Evidence from Distributional National Accounts (DINA)." *Journal of Public Economics* 162: 63–77.

Garnero, A., A. Hijzen, and S. Martin. 2019. "More Unequal, but More Mobile? Earnings Inequality and Mobility in OECD Countries." *Labour Economics* 56:26–35.

Goldin, C., and L. Katz. 2008. *The Race between Education and Technology*. Cambridge, MA: Belknap Press.

Gottschalk, P., and E. Spolaore. 2002. "On the Evaluation of Economic Mobility." *Review of Economic Studies* 69(1): 191–208.

Grainger, C. A., and C. D. Kolstad. 2010. "Who Pays a Price on Carbon?" *Environmental and Resource Economics* 46(3): 359–376.

Jaumotte, F., and C. Osorio Buitron. 2019. "Inequality: Traditional Drivers and the Role of Union Power." Oxford Economic Papers, Oxford University.

Kleven, H., C. Landais, and J. E. Søgaard. 2018. "Children and Gender Inequality: Evidence from Denmark." NBER Working Paper 24219, National Bureau of Economic Research, Cambridge, MA.

Kopczuk, W., E. Saez, and J. Song. 2010. "Earnings Inequality and Mobility in the United States: Evidence from Social Security Data since 1937." *Quarterly Journal of Economics* 125(1): 91–128.

Kuznets, S. 1953. *Shares of Upper Income Groups in Income and Savings*. New York: National Bureau of Economic Research.

Lakner, C., and B. Milanovic. 2015. *Global Income Distribution: From the Fall of the Berlin Wall to the Great Recession*. World Bank Economic Review. Washington, DC: World Bank.

Mankiw, N. G. 2013. "Defending the One Percent." *Journal of Economic Perspectives* 27(3): 21–34.

Marmot, M. G. 2003. "Understanding Social Inequalities in Health." *Perspectives in Biology and Medicine* 46(3): S9–S23.

Martins, J. O., R. Boarini, H. Strauss, and C. De La Maisonneuve. 2010. "The Policy Determinants of Investment in Tertiary Education." *OECD Journal: Economic Studies* 2010 (1): 1–37.

Mazzucato, M., and G. Semieniuk. 2017. "Public Financing of Innovation: New Questions." *Oxford Review of Economic Policy* 33(1): 24–48.

Milanovic, B. 2019. *Capitalism, Alone: The Future of the System That Rules the World*. Cambridge, MA: Harvard University Press.

ONS. 2019. UK Office for National Statistics. "Annual Population Survey, Ethnicity Pay Gaps Reference Tables." https://www.ons.gov.uk/employmentandlabourmarket /peopleinwork/earningsandworkinghours/datasets/ethnicitypaygappreferencetables.

Piketty, T. 2014. *Capital in the Twenty-First Century*. Cambridge, MA: Harvard University Press.

Piketty, T. 2019. *Capital et idéologie: Le Seuil*. Cambridge, MA: Harvard University Press.

Piketty, T., and E. Saez. 2003. "Income Inequality in the United States, 1913–1998." *Quarterly Journal of Economics* 118(1): 1–41.

Piketty, T., and E. Saez. 2014. "Inequality in the Long Run." *Science* 344(6186): 838–843.

Piketty, T., E. Saez, and S. Stantcheva. 2014. "Optimal Taxation of Top Labor Incomes: A Tale of Three Elasticities." *American Economic Journal: Economic Policy* 6(1): 230–271.

Piketty, T., E. Saez, and G. Zucman. 2018. "Distributional National Accounts: Methods and Estimates for the United States." *Quarterly Journal of Economics* 133(2): 553–609.

Piketty, T., and G. Zucman. 2014. "Capital Is Back: Wealth-Income Ratios in Rich Countries 1700–2010. *Quarterly Journal of Economics* 129(3): 1255–1310.

Rosen, S. 1981. "The Economics of Superstars." *American Economic Review* 71(5): 845–858.

Saez, E., and G. Zucman. 2016. "Wealth Inequality in the United States since 1913: Evidence from Capitalized Income Tax Data." *Quarterly Journal of Economics* 131(2): 519–578.

Saez, E., and G. Zucman. 2019. *The Triumph of Injustice: How the Rich Dodge Taxes and How to Make Them Pay*. New York: W. W. Norton.

Smith, M., D. Yagan, O. M. Zidar, and E. Zwick. 2019. "Capitalists in the Twenty-First Century." NBER Working Paper 25442, National Bureau of Economic Research, Cambridge, MA.

Solon, G. 2002. "Cross-Country Differences in Intergenerational Earnings Mobility." *Journal of Economic Perspectives* 16(3): 59–66.

United Nations Economic Commission for Europe (UNECE). 2011. *Canberra Group Handbook on Household Income Survey*. 2nd ed. Geneva: United Nations Economic Commission for Europe.

Valfort, M. 2018. *Anti-Muslim Discrimination in France: Evidence from a Field Experiment*. Bonn: IZA Publications.

WID.world. 2019. World Inequality Database. www.wid.world.

Wolff, E. N. 2017. "Household Wealth Trends in the United States, 1962 to 2016: Has Middle Class Wealth Recovered?" NBER Working Paper 24085, National Bureau of Economic Research, Cambridge, MA.

World Bank, Development Research Group. 2018. *Global Database on Intergenerational Mobility (GDIM)*. Washington, DC: World Bank.

Zucman, G. 2019. "Global Wealth Inequality." *Annual Review of Economics* 11: 109–138.

2

Discussion of the Landscape

Peter Diamond

In chapter 1 of this volume, Lucas Chancel did a terrific job of presenting inequality data, going beyond basic income and wealth measures, including life expectancy, mobility, and education. Comparing US data with data from elsewhere sheds light on both causes and possible responses. Chancel identified groups that have done very badly over the last 40 years compared to other groups or times.

In planning this volume, Olivier Blanchard and Dani Rodrik assembled a juicy list of policy topics, asking for concrete proposals. This chapter discusses steps in going from analysis to policy but limited to a public economics setting, particularly proposals to raise and spend federal revenue. A key issue is the social cost of financing. As calls for more public investment are widespread, the chapter focuses on tax revenue to finance it—the difficulty of getting more revenue and the connection (or lack thereof) between deadweight burdens of taxation and optimal levels of public goods. The chapter also touches on climate change and Social Security, two topics significantly affecting the future of inequality and that raise important issues of taxation.

Too Little Tax Revenue and Too Little Investment

I share the widely held view that for lots and lots of people economic outcomes over the last 40 years have been really disappointing. These outcomes reflect both some policies that have been followed and some policy issues that have been inadequately addressed. Overall, tax revenue has been far too low and there has been far too little public investment. The latter is visible as needs that are not adequately addressed and reflects a decline in investment spending relative to GNP. I support the familiar litany of investment targets—education, from preschool through college, infrastructure, and basic research. Some analysts have called for debt-financed investments, given how low interest rates are and how unlikely a near-term bond market default or inflation is. However, I focus on having more revenue to finance more investment. Not discussed are effects from too few resources for government agencies such as the Internal Revenue Service and, strikingly, the Federal Aviation Administration. Too little spending on government activities is bound to lower the quality of government services.

Chancel (chapter 1, this volume) reported large growth in private capital and shrinking public capital. Rich countries have become richer (a doubling in wealth-to-income ratios), but their governments have become poorer, with many ratios near zero, and indeed negative in the United States. Both politically and financially, low or negative public wealth tends to limit government investments that can add to growth and help to reduce inequalities.

Of course, tax increases have long faced political difficulty, although I don't expect a repeat of Shay's Rebellion of 1786–1787. Consider James Madison's 1782 letter referring to the fighting in the War of Independence: "We have shed our blood in the glorious cause in which we are engaged; we are ready to shed the last drop in its defense. Nothing is above our courage, except only (with shame I speak it) the courage to TAX ourselves."

The need for more taxation influenced the 1787 Constitutional Convention, which looked to replace the Articles of Confederation. We have come a long way since then, but attitudes toward taxation seem similar. Consider the July 14, 1978, statement by Alan Greenspan at a Senate Finance Committee hearing. Greenspan, previously chairman of the Council of Economic Advisers under President Ford, was endorsing the Kemp-Roth bill with this explanation: "Let us remember that the basic purpose of any tax cut program in today's environment is to reduce the momentum of expenditure growth by restraining the amount of revenues available and trust that there is a political limit to deficit spending."

Commonly referred to as "starve the beast," this strategy is likely to make investment a prime victim of less spending, as the effects of reduced investments are seen less quickly and less clearly than those from much other spending.

Equity, Efficiency, and Public Good Expenditures

This focus on new revenue for investment differs from this volume's primary focus on inequality per se. Of course, a key part of tax design is the impact on inequality. It matters who is paying to provide additional revenue, as well as who benefits from additional spending. Concern about inequality is a central part of public economics and, vice versa, the standard public economics approach is a central part of the analysis of inequality—or at least should be. Consider Tony Atkinson's famous 1970 paper on inequality (Atkinson 1970), where he states: "The conventional approach in nearly all empirical work is to adopt some summary statistic of inequality such as the variance, the coefficient of variation or the Gini coefficient with no very explicit reason being given for preferring one measure rather than another. As, however, was pointed out by Dalton 50 years ago in his pioneering article [Dalton 1920], underlying any such measure is some concept of social welfare and it is with this concept that we should be concerned. He argued that we should approach the question by considering directly the form of the social welfare function to be employed." Atkinson argued that inequality should be considered in terms of a social welfare function, and he looked at the sum of identical utility functions, with utility function curvature being a critical element.

Public economics does not view equity and efficiency as separate categories but instead focuses on overall social value when considering government taxing and spending. It is common to see claims that the cost of tax-financed resources should be multiplied by a factor above 1, for example 1.5, in order to reflect the efficiency cost of marginal deadweight burdens. But tax structures reflect concerns about income distribution as well as concerns about incentives. In selecting a revenue cost multiplying factor that reflects only marginal deadweight burdens, equity is not being considered. That is, excluding the equity dimension of the tax structure in this way is not appropriate.

Since the 1927 analysis of optimal commodity taxes by Ramsey, it has been common to analyze models with a single consumer (or a set of identical consumers). By omitting complications from the income distribution, this simplification helps to clarify the role of deadweight burdens of taxation. Such modeling does not allow reliance on a lump-sum tax, as that would leave no reason for using distorting taxes. Derivation of a rule for the optimal scale of a public good in a one-consumer model excludes this option. Extending the analysis to a diverse population of workers can allow a lump-sum tax that is the same for everyone (a poll tax or subsidy, as with a universal basic income or a negative income tax). Such a tax or subsidy does not fully resolve concerns about income distribution and therefore preserves a role for distorting taxes. A key conclusion is that even with a poll subsidy, social welfare maximization calls for distorting taxes with deadweight burdens. And the first-order conditions for public goods need to reflect both those incentive distortions and the equity effects of marginal financing. In contrast, lump-sum taxes set separately for each person do address distributional concerns, thereby yielding rules for first-best allocations, not second-best ones.

A relatively simple case is the joint optimization of a linear income tax (with a flat benefit) along with the level of a public good. Optimal taxation in the presence of individuals with little or no earning ability calls for a positive benefit at zero income. Phasing out the benefit is part of the (negative) income tax structure. In this setting, one can examine multiplying the marginal resource cost by a factor larger than 1 in response to the presence of distorting taxes (see Lundholm 2005; Jacobs 2018). However, with joint optimization of public expenditures and income taxation, including the possibility of a uniform basic income, the optimal multiplying factor is 1—there is no role for such a multiplier. If overall taxes are not optimized, the multiplying factor may be different from 1—it may be larger or smaller. Also part of the first-order conditions are the tax revenue implications from the direct effects on labor supply of both the provision of the public good and changes in lump-sum income.

The basic logic can be seen in a competitive market, three-good setting, with labor, a private consumption good, and a pure public good, with workers differing in labor efficiency. For simplicity, assume the level of the public good does not affect the labor supply and that labor supply has a zero income effect. The government sets the level of the public good, a poll subsidy, and a linear income tax to maximize a social welfare function of individual utilities. The optimal level of the public good equates the sum of the social values of marginal utility from the public good to the marginal resource cost. There is no need for an explicit adjustment for a change in deadweight burdens. Applying the underlying logic of the envelope condition, there is the same social value from any marginal tax change considered to cover the marginal resource cost. Lowering the basic income is one such option; with no effect on labor supply, there is no role for a change in deadweight burden. Thus, from the envelope condition, at the optimum, changing the income tax rate to cover the marginal resource cost has a distributional impact that exactly balances the deadweight burden change. If there is an income effect for labor supply or an impact of the public good on labor supply, these impacts on income tax revenue need to be factored in, but they do not change the basic logic of omitting a separate multiplier of the resource cost for the marginal deadweight burden.

Such social welfare optimization calculations are inputs into policy discussions, intended to help shape decision-making, but they are only part of the story. Unlike in the simple model given earlier, policy discussions do not consider everything in the economy all at once, and policies set previously will generally not be consistent with overall welfare maximization. Often, increased program spending is bundled with a particular source of revenue as part of the policy discussion, the rest of the tax structure being left unchanged. Proponents of new spending are regularly asked how to pay for the spending they favor, and legislation may raise revenue to limit the impact on the budget deficit. Paying attention to income distribution issues when choosing a revenue source brings in a roughly similar underlying logic as in the full optimization calculations. Thus, for any particular revenue source, the weighting of resource costs in the first-order condition may be larger than 1 or may be smaller than 1, depending on the effects of the chosen financing on both income distribution and efficiency. Paying attention to the deadweight burdens of marginal taxation while ignoring distributional effects is not assisting good policy decision-making.

Faced with a broad policy agenda like the one in the conference that led to this book, political outcomes may depend on which taxes are bundled with which spending. Supporters of different spending categories will naturally compete to be paired with the least politically painful tax increases. Perhaps the more popular programs, such as Social Security, should consider other program needs and go light on the less strongly opposed taxes.

Climate Change and Social Security as Future Drivers of Inequality

The final section of Chancel's chapter calls for factoring in future drivers of inequality. He singles out climate change, which is not among the concrete policy issues that were on the program agenda at the conference. Yet, in the paper circulated for the conference, he noted: "Climate change will further exacerbate inequalities between countries but also within countries. Low income and wealth groups tend to be particularly exposed to environmental damage, and are also more sensitive to environmental shocks (such as hurricanes, floods, or heat waves) than the rest of the population." (For more, see, for example, Hallegatte et al. 2016; Islam and Winkel 2017.) To this, I would add that poor groups have fewer resources to help them adapt, both before and after environmental shocks. As an example, consider the October 9, 2019, *New York Times* headline "Rich Counties Get More Help to Escape Climate Risk, New Data Show" (Flavelle 2019).

The need for revenue is likely to rise as additional government spending accompanies both the bad impacts of climate change, such as from larger hurricanes, and the costs of adapting, trying to limit both climate change and the vulnerability to it. Another part of the climate discussion is the possibility of a carbon tax, which would raise significant revenue. This might be used to significantly impact inequality (and policy popularity), for example, by financing a uniform basic income.

Social Security is another future driver of inequality. Without new legislation, Social Security benefits will be cut by roughly 20% in about 15 years. Although there are advantages to acting sooner rather than at the last minute, that does not seem likely to happen. The eventual outcome, presumably last-minute legislation, will come from the dueling political approaches, with one party favoring primarily (or fully) benefit cuts, while the other calls for significantly more revenue. Influencing the details of this future legislation will matter for future inequality.

The United States does have substantial sovereign financial funds in Social Security—asset reserves of $2.9 trillion as of the end of 2018. Of course, the reserves are currently invested in Treasury debt, passing up higher expected returns while receiving a level of liquidity not needed for this pension program. In contrast to the 1983 US reform, which built up a large trust fund to be run down as baby boomers aged, both Canada and Sweden have national pension plans with targets of preserving significant funding for the long run, with those funds invested worldwide, like typical sovereign wealth funds. And both plans have automatic adjustments intended to help preserve the funds. I like both policy approaches.

If a standard sovereign wealth fund portfolio goes too far for US politics, a step in the right direction would be Social Security Trust Fund investment in a diverse portfolio relying on the Thrift Savings Plan. This is a very low-cost 401(k)-like pension for federal employees, using privately supplied index funds. Contrary to the worry when the plan was created, there has been no congressional meddling with the Thrift Savings Plan. If holding of the Wilshire 5000 stock index had started in 1984 and then slowly phased in to reach 40% (with no change in the type of bonds being held) the ratio of the trust fund balance to expenditures in 2016 would have been 4.2 compared to the actual ratio of 3.0 (Burtless et al. 2017). Access to the Thrift Savings Plan could also be made available for 401(k) plans, 403(b) plans, and individual IRAs. As financial literacy correlates with income, easier and better retirement investing would help with inequality.

Of course, the conference included discussion of progressive taxation, including personal income taxes, wealth and estate taxes, and corporate taxes. I think all these need major overhauls with considerable fundamental rethinking. There was also discussion about antitrust policies. We should remember that corporations get limited liability because the government gives it to them. If the government wants to tie more strings to its availability, that would have efficiency implications and income distribution implications, but it doesn't seem to relate to fundamental rights. As Earl Warren said in a 1952 address: "Many people consider the things government does for them to be social progress but they regard the things government does for others as socialism."

Acknowledgment

I am grateful to Nick Barr, Olivier Blanchard, and Bob Solow for valuable comments, all responsibility for this chapter remaining with me.

References

Atkinson, Anthony B. 1970. "On the Measurement of Inequality." *Journal of Economic Theory* 2:244–263.

Burtless, Gary, Anqi Chen, Wenliang Hou, and Alicia H. Munnell. 2017. "What Are the Costs and Benefits of Social Security Investing in Equities?" Issue Brief Number 17–10, Center for Retirement Research, Boston College.

Dalton, Hugh. 1920. "The Measurement of the Inequality of Incomes." *Economic Journal* 30:348–361.

Flavelle, Christopher. 2019. "Rich Counties Get More Help to Escape Climate Risk, New Data Show." *New York Times*, October 9, 2019. https://www.nytimes.com/2019/10/09/climate/disaster-flood-buyouts-climate-change.html.

Hallegatte, Stephane, Mook Bangalore, Laura Bonzanigo, Marianne Fay, Tamaro Kane, Ulf Narloch, Julie Rozenberg, David Treguer, and Adrien Vogt-Schilb. 2016. *Shock Waves: Managing the Impacts of Climate Change on Poverty*. Climate Change and Development Series. Washington, DC: World Bank.

Islam, S. Nazrul, and John Winkel. 2017. "Climate Change and Social Inequality." DESA Working Paper 152, United Nations, New York. https://www.un.org/development/desa/publications/working-paper.

Jacobs, Bas. 2018. "The Marginal Cost of Public Funds Is One at the Optimal Tax System." *International Tax and Public Finance* 25(4): 883–912.

Lundholm, Michael. 2005. "Cost-Benefit Analysis and the Marginal Cost of Public Funds." Research Papers in Economics, Department of Economics, Stockholm University.

Ramsey, F. P. 1927. "A Contribution to the Theory of Taxation." *Economic Journal* 37: 47–61.

Warren, Earl. 1952. Address presented to National Press Club as quoted in *Freedom and Union*, Washington, DC, April 1952.

II
Ethical and Philosophical Dimensions

3

Time for New Philosophical Foundations for Economic Theory?

Danielle Allen

To contribute as a philosopher to a collection of pieces by economists feels a bit like coming as a third cousin thrice removed to a family reunion. Once upon a time, thousands of years ago, we were all Aristotle. Following in the wake of Socrates and Plato, he systematized the study of political philosophy and included within it focus on management of the household, or *oikonomikos*, the original meaning of "economics." He or a student of his wrote a related treatise on economic matters, *Oikonomika*. Despite this shared ancestry, we've become people whose vocabularies are very different.

Nonetheless, there is a family resemblance among political philosophers and economists: we are all concerned with the well-being of humankind, yet differences creep in again. The picture of well-being that occupies our imaginations comes from different sources. The ghosts of Adam Smith, John Stuart Mill, John Maynard Keynes, Friedrich Hayek, Milton Friedman, and John Rawls flit in and out of the shadows at economic meetings, often unacknowledged. Their basic pictures of what human beings and social relations are like, and of what economies should be for, frame the questions economists ask about economic models and behavioral realities.

Political philosophers, however, have continued to adjust these background pictures about the basic content of human well-being. John Rawls continues to populate our imagination, but so does more recent work by figures such as Philip Pettit, Amartya Sen, and Elizabeth Anderson (see Rawls 1971; Pettit 1999; Sen 1999a, 1999b; Anderson 1999, 2017). It's important for economists to stop now and again and to revisit those basic questions about human beings, social relations, and the purposes of coordinated activity, for instance in the economy. Is the picture that any given economist uses as the basic backdrop to their work, deriving from another historical period, still the one to keep? Or are there fresh pictures that might now be more useful and have more traction in reality, helping us better meet our goal of advancing the well-being of humankind? Let me first propose an alternative picture, building on Pettit, Sen, Anderson, and my own previous work (Allen 2004, 2014, 2016, 2017, 2020) and then explore what that picture would mean for policy-making.

Rather than seeing human beings as being driven by rational self-interest, we might adopt a picture of human beings as being driven by purposiveness. Purposiveness incorporates rational self-interest, but it's a bigger concept. Human purposiveness describes the effort of human beings to ascertain their own best path toward flourishing. In order to pursue their own path toward flourishing, they need freedom to make their own choices, and that's the element of purposiveness that we typically associate with rational self-interest. But human beings live under constraints, social norms, laws, and institutions, and those constraints are always the product of collective action. At the end of the day, if human beings are going to exercise purposiveness fully, then in addition to having private autonomy or personal freedoms or liberties, they also need public autonomy or participatory rights. They need rights that place them among the people who are coauthoring the norms, whether social or legal, that set the constraints within which they make their decisions. In other words, human purposiveness depends on the transactions of individual autonomous figures who, an economist might say, are acting with rational self-interest, but it also depends on the opportunity to exercise that direction of choice through political participation. Moreover, the interaction between participation in social choice and individual choice-making also contributes to shaping the preferences acted on via private autonomy and personal freedom. Even as autonomous actors, human beings are social animals whose choices connect to the horizons of value of particular communities and typically must be justified within them.

The supports needed for the two parts of human purposiveness are often described by means of the distinction between negative liberties and positive liberties, derived from Benjamin Constant's nineteenth-century juxtaposition of the liberties of the ancients with the liberties of the moderns (Constant 1819). The liberties of the ancients were the rights to participate in collective decision-making; that is, political rights and rights to social participation. The liberties of the modern consisted of rights to be left alone, that conventional idea of having freedom from governmental interference so that one can pursue commercial transactions and wealth. Constant's argument was that industrialization was bringing new possibilities for wealth and economic growth of such immense value that human beings would pick those modern liberties and be eager to leave behind the time-consuming ancient liberties. His distinction was later crystallized by Isaiah Berlin's distinction between negative liberties and positive liberties.

For more than two centuries, liberalism, whether classical or neo-, has been continuously afflicted by a split between these two categories of liberties, attending primarily to the negative liberties, as though they suffice to deliver human well-being. In being relatively neglectful of the positive liberties and of the value of public autonomy to human beings, liberalisms of most varieties have shortchanged recognizable, documentable human needs. John Rawls intended to resist and undo the distinction between negative and positive liberties, labeling them coequal and co-original, yet for reasons I won't go into here, he, too, failed to treat not only the negative liberties but also the positive liberties as nonsacrificeable.

In my book-in-progress, *Justice by Means of Democracy*, and in related essays (Allen 2016, 2020), I argue that human purposiveness is what economists should be supporting as they pursue human well-being. This requires gluing together the negative liberties that are connected to our being creatures with rational (but socially pliable) self-interest and positive liberties, which are upheld through political participation and democratic forms of governance. If you glue together these two kinds of liberties as equally nonsacrificeable, then the goal of supporting political equality becomes the overarching objective for policy-making. The question becomes, do you have a set of institutional, social, and economic structures that achieve egalitarian empowerment of the citizenry? Egalitarian empowerment of the citizenry requires protecting the basic negative liberties, so if you pursue political equality, you will seek to build in the whole package of rights necessary to support human purposiveness. The same is not true the other way around. One can aim to protect personal autonomy (negative liberties) and turn one's back on positive liberties. Liberalism has often done this.

What follows from this rough sketch of the bases of human well-being for economic and social policy? If you protect the basic liberties, both negative and positive, social difference will emerge, and difference is another word for inequality. As T. M. Scanlon puts it in chapter 5 of this volume, the important question is whether the emergent differences are justified or not. To make this determination, I rely on a principle I've named "difference without domination." If the relevant inequality subjects individuals or groups to the arbitrary reserve control of others, or in other ways undermines political equality, then that inequality is problematic and needs to be redressed, undone, or mitigated, depending on the circumstances. The goal is a world in which social difference is not articulated as domination of any one person, or any group, by any other person or group.

Scanlon (chapter 5, this volume) identifies six kinds of inequalities to which we might object: inequality of status, unacceptable control of some by others, interference with equality of opportunity, interference with the fairness of political institutions, unequal provision of benefits owed to all, and institutions that generate unequal incomes without adequate justification. Notably, the first four objections capture problems of political or social inequality, whereas the last two problems address material inequality. This underscores how important political equality is within a picture of human flourishing. The goal of economic policy, or political economy, should be to treat political empowerment or equality as what we're aiming for and then ask how we also work toward social and economic egalitarianism in support of political empowerment. To reiterate, the reason to prioritize institutional, social, and economic bases for political equality or empowerment is that this concept fully captures human purposiveness.

Importantly, the success of political institutions, and especially the capacity to have functioning democratic institutions, depends on social cohesion and forms of connectedness and mutual commitment within the citizenry. Those things are affected by economic questions, but they are not reducible to them. To the degree that human purposiveness requires sound political institutions for its fulfillment, the measure of whether an economy supports human purposiveness cannot be merely income or money. Consequently, you cannot reduce human well-being to growth. My argument is captured by figure 3.1.

Respecting and responding to human moral equality means (a) respecting human purposiveness as having both the individual, autonomous, rational, self-interest actor component and the social and political component that requires both negative rights and positive rights, and (b) treating political equality as the thing that we are after above all. The pursuit of political equality is supported by the pursuit of economic fairness and social equality. Again, I use the principle of difference without domination to make assessments about what policies are preferable in these spaces. The arrows go both ways, so if you fail to build a fair economy, you will undermine political equality, as Larry Bartels and Nolan McCarty have pointed out (Bartels 2008; McCarty 2006). The same is true with social equality. Segregation, it should be remembered, was an economic system. It allocated property value; it established patterns of wealth aggregation and accumulation over time. Race has always been an economic question in this country, not merely a social question.

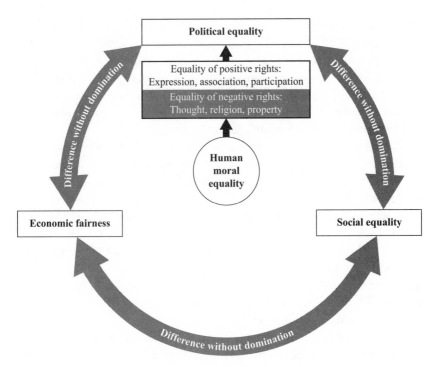

Figure 3.1
A virtuous circle: political equality as the basis of justice.

What does this focus on political equality, and the characterization of the economy and society as supports for the achievement of an empowered citizenry, mean for political economy? In introducing the post–World War II Marshall Plan, George Marshall said, "Our policy is directed not against any country or doctrine, but against hunger, poverty, desperation and chaos. Its purpose should be the revival of a working economy in the world so as to permit the emergence of political and social conditions in which free institutions can exist" (Marshall 1947). In this vision of human well-being, the goal established for economists is not that they should build democracy but that they should understand the economic and social supports for democracy or, as I say, for political equality.

What do policies that meet these criteria look like? First, those features of the current structure of the economy that leave people subject to domination require redress. We need labor markets without job lock, which in the United States means universal access to a health care system with portability. It also means things such as housing and transportation policies to restore labor mobility, and perhaps mortgage insurance. We need immigration policies designed to maximize labor mobility but without undercutting pathways to citizenship. Possibly the sponsorship models used in Canada could be scaled up to support simultaneously both more effective immigrant integration and, eventually, increased levels of immigration into the United States. We need democratic forms of governance in the operations of corporations and employers, for instance a seat at the decision-making table for labor as in Germany.

Second, those features of the economy that undercut the empowerment of the citizenry need to be redesigned. For instance, as we race against technology with education, we need to ensure that the forms of education we deploy support civic participation instead of suppressing it, as evidence suggests science, technology, engineering, and mathematics (STEM) education as currently configured does. We need a "good jobs" economy (as Dani Rodrik and Charles Sabel have sketched out) that focuses on the structure of production, so that the economy itself delivers the bases of well-being, in the form of a sufficient number of good, purpose-sustaining jobs rather than leaving significant portions of the citizenry highly exposed to the political dynamics determining the level of progressive taxation.

Third, we need to restore practices of governance that permit societies to steer their economies in the direction of their purposes as defined by the circumstances of their era. The anti-inflation strategy was the right response to the structure of the real economy in the 1970s and 1980s. It is no longer the right strategy. But as central banks seek to adjust, they should do that with governance practices that establish democratic accountability and restore to legislatures the capacity to set objectives for the national economy. Relatedly, national legislatures need to rebuild their capacity to meaningfully superintend fiscal policy.

Progressive taxation should be part of the conversation, yet it's also the part of the story we already know well. Given the quantity of work that has been done on taxation, it seems important to turn attention, at least for a time, to some of the other tools at our disposal, at least long enough to let a genuine preproduction and production agenda emerge.

Along this path we are for more likely than along the redistributive path to find economic policies that deliver material well-being that supports rather than undermines political empowerment.

References

Allen, Danielle. 2004. *Talking to Strangers*. Chicago: University of Chicago Press.

Allen, Danielle. 2014. *Our Declaration: A Reading of the Declaration of Independence in Defense of Equality*. New York: Norton/Liveright.

Allen, Danielle. 2016. "Toward a Connected Society." In *Our Compelling Interests: The Value of Diversity for Democracy and a Prosperous Society*, edited by Earl Lewis and Nancy Kantor, 71–195. Princeton, NJ: Princeton University Press.

Allen, Danielle. 2017. "What Is Education For?" *Boston Review*.

Allen, Danielle. 2020. "Difference without Domination: Toward a New Theory of Justice." In *Difference without Domination: Pursuing Justice in Diverse Democracies*, edited by Danielle Allen and R. Somanathan. Chicago: University of Chicago Press.

Anderson, Elizabeth S. 1999. "What Is the Point of Equality?" *Ethics* 109(2): 287–337.

Anderson, Elizabeth S. 2017. *Private Government: How Employers Rule Our Lives (and Why We Don't Talk about It)*. Princeton, NJ: Princeton University Press.

Bartels, Larry M. 2008. *Unequal Democracy: The Political Economy of the New Gilded Age*. Princeton, NJ: Princeton University Press.

Berlin, Isaiah. 1961. Two Concepts of Liberty. Oxford: Clarendon Press.

Constant, Benjamin. 1819. "The Liberty of the Ancients Compared with That of the Moderns." Speech given at the Athéné Royale in Paris.

Marshall, G. 1947. "The Marshall Plan Speech." https://www.marshallfoundation .org/marshall/the-marshall-plan/marshall-plan-speech/.

McCarty, Nolan, Keith T. Poole, and Howard Rosenthal. 2006. *Polarized America: The Dance of Ideology and Unequal Riches*. Cambridge, MA: MIT Press.

Pettit, Philip. 1999. *Republicanism: A Theory of Freedom and Government*. Oxford: Oxford University Press.

Rawls, John. 1971. *A Theory of Justice*. Cambridge, MA: Harvard University Press.

Rodrik, Dani and Charles Sabel. Under review. "Building a Good Jobs Economy." In *Political Economy and Justice*, edited by Danielle Allen, Yochai Benkler, and Rebecca Henderson. Chicago: University of Chicago Press.

Sen, Amartya. 1999a. "Democracy as a Universal Value." *Journal of Democracy* 10(3): 3–17.

Sen, Amartya. 1999b. *Development as Freedom*. New York: Knopf.

4

What Kinds of Inequality Should Economists Address?

Philippe Van Parijs

"I think that in no country in the civilized world is there less interest in philosophy than in the United States," Alexis de Tocqueville (1835) wrote in the opening sentence of the second volume of *Democracy in America*. Assuming that this is still the case today, it is a very special honor but also a special responsibility for our little team of philosophers to be invited by our economist colleagues in this unphilosophical yet civilized country to help identify the kind(s) of inequality they should address against the background of robust convictions about why one should care about inequality.

The Criterion: Strict versus Lax

I will respond to this request by addressing three questions in quick succession. First, is it economic inequality as such that is objectionable or is it objectionable because of its consequences? In particular, should we say that economic inequality is objectionable if and only if (a) it does not contribute to or (b) it prevents (1) an increase in the level of material welfare of the worse off, (2) an increase in the overall level of material welfare, or (3) a sufficient level of material welfare for all?[1] In a static context, where total material welfare is given, economic inequalities are unobjectionable under (2b) and also, in circumstances in which all have enough, under (3), while being objectionable under the other criteria.[2] In a real-life context, the total is not given but is affected by inequalities that, if anticipated, may affect incentives and also affect the distribution of the capacity to invest. It is then the *sustainable* achievement of (1), (2), or (3) that provides the criterion for distinguishing justifiable economic inequalities (if any) from objectionable ones. Philosophers disagree on which version makes the most sense. Against the less egalitarian (2) and (3) and the more egalitarian maximin (a) version of (1), I side with John Rawls (1971) in opting for its leximin version (1b). This leaves room for justifiable economic inequalities, namely those that do not make the worse off worse off than they could (sustainably) be. Needless to say, conjectures about the short- and long-term consequences of economic inequalities on the situation of the worse off are unavoidably complex and speculative. When assessing whether inequalities are justifiable, it is important to consider not only their impact on material incentives and the distribution of the capacity to invest but also possible effects on the media and on political power. Even more important, neither the individual agents' motives nor the potential for tax evasion and tax competition should be taken as parameters immune to institutional reform. Unlike strict egalitarians, maximin and leximin egalitarians will allow for significant economic inequalities, but far less than a narrow focus on economic incentives would suggest.[3]

The Scale: Domestic versus Global

Next comes the question of scale. Are the inequalities that economists should address local, national, or global? Some philosophers, such as John Rawls (1999) and Thomas Nagel (2005), hold the view that the demands of egalitarian distributive justice are only triggered within the framework of a nation or a state. Distributive justice between countries is less demanding—in Rawls's approach, it reduces to a duty of assistance to "burdened societies"—and economic inequalities that would be unjustifiable within countries are unobjectionable between countries. Other philosophers, such as Peter Singer (2002) and Simon Caney (2005), maintain that egalitarian distributive justice today must be understood as applying globally, even though many of the instruments to be used in its pursuit operate at the national or even the local level.[4] However, some of those who hold the latter view—as I do—may be willing to concede that more equality is demanded at the domestic level than at the global level, to the extent that justice is a matter not only of distribution but also of recognition: even if it benefits the worst off in material terms, some level of inequality may damage their self-respect and thereby violate justice as equal dignity if it obtains within a community, while being innocuous if it obtains between people so distant that they will never meet.

The Distribuendum: Snapshot Outcome versus Lifetime Opportunity

Third and less summarily, let us turn to the question of the distribuendum, This is the familiar question "Equality of what?,"[5] but I want to approach it from an unfamiliar angle. I take as my point of departure what I found the most surprising statement in Lucas Chancel's (chapter 1, this volume) very instructive background overview. One of the facts he highlights relates to the within- and between-country components of global inequality: "Forty years ago, nationality mattered more than class in accounting for global inequality. Today, class matters more than nationality. The Theil index of pretax national income inequality accounted for slightly more than half of global inequality in the early 1980s and only about a quarter today. Put differently, in order to predict the position of an adult in the global distribution of income, it is more useful to know her income group rather than her nationality." This claim contrasts sharply with earlier assessments, for example by Branko Milanovic (2016, 133): "It turns out that we can 'explain' (in a regression sense) more than two-thirds of the variability in incomes across country-percentiles by only one variable: the country where people live."

Per Adult Primary or Per Capita Disposable Income?
The difference no doubt results partly from Chancel's use of more recent and richer data,[6] but it has two more causes, which provide us with useful food for our reflection on the distribuendum of social justice and hence on what inequalities economists should address and therefore try to measure. First, Chancel's estimates are formulated on a per adult basis, whereas Milanovic's are per capita. As many of the poorest countries have a number of children per adult far above the world average, shifting to per capita estimates is bound to increase the contribution of between-country inequality. Second, Milanovic's estimates are about disposable (posttax, posttransfer) income, not primary income. Because taxation and transfers reduce inequality within countries but hardly at all between countries, shifting from primary to disposable income will again substantially diminish the relative contribution of within-country inequality.[7] If one were to include in a household's disposable income the value of education and other public services provided free of charge or at a highly subsidized rate, this relative contribution would shrink even further. Focusing on inequalities in per adult primary income is no doubt useful for various descriptive and explanatory purposes, but surely the inequalities that may be objectionable in themselves, rather than as proxies or causal factors, must be inequalities in people's actual material welfare and hence in their per capita disposable income rather than in their per adult primary income. However, this is not the end of the story. Even when opting for the former, as Milanovic does, one may still be underestimating the between-country relative share in *objectionable* inequalities—those that should be addressed—for four reasons.

Nominal Income or Purchasing Power Parity?
First, take the role played by purchasing power parity (PPP). Using this amounts to scaling down between-country inequalities on the grounds that the same income, expressed in nominal terms and using official exchange rates between currencies, can buy more goods and services in countries where the cost of living is lower. However, there are also large differences in housing and other real estate prices, and hence in the cost of living generally, between different parts of the same country. Indeed, the ongoing process of metropolization can be expected to deepen these differences. If PPP is used to correct downward between-country inequalities, does consistency not require that it should also be used to correct downward within-country inequalities? It can legitimately be objected that there is a reason why people choose to live in expensive places when nothing prevents them from moving to cheaper ones. The amenities and opportunities offered by an urban environment are deemed to offset the additional cost. Consequently, it would be wrong to lower the estimates of within-country inequality by using PPP to correct for internal differences in cost of living. But should this conclusion not apply just as much, if not more, to between-country inequality? True, mobility is generally more difficult between countries than within countries. It cannot therefore simply be said that those who continue to live in a country with a high cost of living do so because it is good value for the money. However, the obstacles to free movement are generally much greater in the other direction: for those wanting to move from a poorer country to a richer country. These obstacles prevent those confined to a poor country from sharing the many advantages of living in a richer one. Correcting their incomes upward on the grounds that they can be fed and housed more cheaply where they live is therefore at least as illegitimate as doing so for people who choose to live in a cheaper part of a particular country. So, at the very least, consistency requires that if PPP is not used within countries, it should not be used between countries either.[8]

Snapshot or Lifetime Income?
Suppose next that the income inequality between two parts of a population correlates perfectly with their ages: young people earn less than older people not by virtue of the cohort to which they belong but by virtue of the stage in life they are at. This inequality is no doubt less objectionable than if both parts of the population have the same income at each stage in their lives but the income of one of them is at a higher level than the other's. Because they capture snapshot incomes, not lifetime incomes,

inequality indices will yield the same results whether the inequality is of the first or the second type. If, in contrast to within-cohort and between-cohort lifetime inequalities, one regards age-related inequalities as unobjectionable, the component of within-country inequality we should be concerned with is bound to shrink considerably. The component of between-country inequality that should concern us will also be affected. The higher a country's proportion of people who are too young or too old to work, the more its snapshot per capita income underestimates its lifetime per capita income. Because of higher birthrates and lower life expectancies, many poorer countries have a lower proportion of elderly people and a higher proportion of children. The latter difference suggests that between-country inequality in lifetime per capita income will be lower than in snapshot per capita income and closer to inequality in snapshot per adult income. But how should the former difference—following from a shorter average life span—be taken into account? Presumably by trying to approximate not lifetime per capita average *annual* income but rather lifetime per capita *total* income. Being, on average, alive rather than dead when reaching a particular age is no doubt an important component of objectionable economic inequality that is not captured by estimates of snapshot income inequality, and one that is likely to weigh more heavily between countries than within them.

Annual or Hourly Income?

Third, consider a case in which the inequality between the incomes of two parts of a population correlates perfectly with their working time. Some choose to work part-time and others full-time, and incomes vary accordingly. Again, this inequality is bound to be regarded as less objectionable, if at all, than the same level of inequality, however measured, between two groups of people working the same amount of time with one earning double the income of the other. Hence, bundles of income and leisure, or income per hour worked, would be more appropriate than incomes alone in capturing objectionable inequalities. Within countries, inequality scores will necessarily shrink as a result. Between countries, there are certainly differences in average working time—for example, between the United States and Western Europe—which would neutralize at least part of the inequality in per capita income. But how can one obtain a reliable measure of average working time in countries with a large informal economy. Especially if due attention is paid, as it must, to the voluntariness of leisure and the intensity of work, estimates can only be offered with the greatest caution. While it is clear that objectionable within-country inequality would shrink once working time is taken into account, it is less clear that objectionable between-country inequality would shrink, too, and, if so, whether it would do so more than objectionable within-country inequality.

Outcome or Opportunity?

Fourth and finally, consider two parts of a population that grew up in similar circumstances and went to the same schools. However, one part went for a consultant career and is earning a lot of money, while the other opted for an artistic life and is earning just enough money to get by while working just as many hours. Again, we find this inequality far less objectionable, if at all, than one between two parts of a population that, owing to different social backgrounds, attended different schools, one preparing all its pupils to become well-paid consultants and the other producing future street cleaners with a far lower income for the same amount of work. Inequality indices will detect no difference, but our normative evaluations will differ greatly. Even those most inclined to emphasize the role of unchosen circumstances in causing within-country economic inequalities will need to recognize that individual choice is unavoidably even less significant as a factor in between-country inequality.[9] Once again, the assessment of the latter's relative share in objectionable worldwide inequality will need to be adjusted upward.

Policy Implications?

What follows from this sequence of considerations? Certainly not that indices of snapshot income inequality—whether primary or disposable, per adult or per capita—are of no use. Rather, their usefulness for the sake of defining a sensible objective and guiding our policies depends on their being able to track inequalities in lifetime per capita disposable income that cannot be justified by their boosting the opportunities of some of the worse off.[10]

To illustrate this, consider just one question: Should we choose an immigration policy that favors the entry of highly skilled people in sectors in which there are shortages in the domestic labor market or should we favor the entry of low-skilled people facing poverty in their own country? If we want to improve our Gini index and look good in international comparisons as an egalitarian country, there should be little room for hesitation: we should open our doors to the highly skilled so that they can compete with local professionals in high demand, whose earnings would otherwise skyrocket, while keeping out the low skilled, who would not only push the Gini index upward by virtue of their sheer presence but also keep down the wages of the lower strata of the domestic workforce. Moreover, by attracting some of the better paid, such a policy may well have the unintended effect of reducing inequality in the country of origin. If within-country snapshot income inequality is identified as the inequality economists should address, this is the way to go.

If instead we want to pursue egalitarian justice understood as a global sustainable maximin or leximin of opportunities, welcoming those fleeing from poverty in their own country is at least prima facie far more commendable than further contributing to the brain drain, even if this means boosting within-country inequality. There may be decisive reasons for adopting more restrictive and more selective immigration policies, but they cannot be presented as following directly from the objective of "combating inequality" once duly subjected to philosophical scrutiny.

Notes

1. See Scanlon (2018) for a far more comprehensive critical exploration of the many reasons for being, in some sense, an economic egalitarian.

2. Assuming that there is no "leaky bucket" effect (i.e., no economic waste in the redistribution process). If there is such an effect, inequalities can also be justified under (2a) and, if it is sufficiently strong, even under (1b). Then only (1a) converges with strict egalitarianism.

3. Van Parijs (2003) explores a number of interpretations of Rawls's difference principle that differ according to their sensitivity to these various considerations.

4. Van Parijs (2007) provides a systematic overview of the different variants of the "nationalist" and "globalist" views.

5. See Dworkin (1981), Sen (1982), Cohen (1989), Anderson (1999).

6. Chancel's data are from 2017 and Milanovic's from 2008, and the earlier data already suggested "a decreasing importance of the locational element in the last decade" (Milanovic 2016, 131). Chancel's data are based not only on household surveys but also on tax records, which are better at tracking very high incomes, and between-country inequality is less pronounced among the rich than among the poor (Milanovic 2016, 134).

7. Taking remittances into account would shrink between-country inequality somewhat, just as taking donations into account would shrink within-country inequalities somewhat. But voluntary transfers are presumably best interpreted as a use one makes of one's disposable income rather than as a reduction of it, and resources one owes to discretionary generosity should presumably not be given the same status as market earnings or benefits to which one is legally entitled.

8. Here I am leaving out the difficulties raised by many of the assumptions that enter into the construction of PPP coefficients (see the lucid discussion in Deaton 2010) and will not question their use, duly qualified, for the purpose of estimating real GDP per capita and poverty rates, as opposed to between-country inequality.

9. There are no doubt countries whose cultures and institutions are less favorable to material prosperity than others. It could be said that it is up to them to change them, and if they do not, it is their responsibility. But this cannot be said to individual members of these societies, whose opportunities are shaped by a culture and institutions they did not and cannot choose. Normatively relevant global inequality is not between personified societies but rather between individual human beings.

10. Chancel (chapter 1, this volume) also noted: "This finding may have important implications for global inequality policy debates on the relative importance of migration, between-country transfers, and national-level inequality policies." The underlying suggestion is presumably that one should concentrate policy efforts on the component of inequality, as measured, that is now dominant. Along the same lines, after having shown that three-quarters of overall inequality between European citizens, as they measure it, is explained by within-country inequality, Blanchet, Chancel, and Gethin (2019) conclude that, "this suggests that social and fiscal policies in the European Union (and even more so in the US) seeking to reduce income inequality should primarily focus on within-country (or within-state) measures, rather than by organizing transfers between countries (or states)."

References

Anderson, Elizabeth S. 1999. "What Is the Point of Equality?" *Ethics* 109(2): 287–337.

Blanchet, Thomas, Lucas Chancel, and Amory Gethin. 2019. "How Unequal Is Europe? Evidence from Distributional National Accounts, 1980–2017." WID. world Working Paper 2019/06. https://wid.world/wid-world.

Caney, Simon. 2005. *Justice beyond Borders: A Global Political Theory*. Oxford: Oxford University Press.

Cohen, G. A. 1989. "On the Currency of Egalitarian Justice." *Ethics* 99(4): 906–944.

Deaton, Angus. 2010. "Prince Indexes, Inequality and the Measurement of World Poverty." Presidential address, American Economic Association, Atlanta, January 2010.

Dworkin, Ronald. 1981. "What Is Equality?" *Philosophy and Public Affairs* 10(3):185–246 and 10(4): 283–345.

Milanovic, Branko. 2016. *Global Inequality: A New Approach for the Age of Globalization*. Cambridge, MA: Belknap Press.

Nagel, Thomas. 2005. "The Problem of Global Justice." *Philosophy and Public Affairs* 33(2): 113–147.

Rawls, John. 1971. *A Theory of Justice.* Cambridge, MA: Harvard University Press.

Rawls, John. 1999. *The Law of Peoples.* Cambridge, MA: Harvard University Press.

Scanlon, T. M. 2018. *Why Does Inequality Matter?* Oxford: Oxford University Press.

Sen, Amartya. 1982. "Equality of What?" In *Choice, Welfare and Measurement,* by A. Sen, 353–369. Oxford: Blackwell.

Singer, Peter. 2002. *One World: The Ethics of Globalization.* New Haven, CT: Yale University Press.

Tocqueville, Alexis de. 1835. *De la Démocratie en Amérique (Democracy in America),* Vol.2, Online Library of Liberty, 2012, https://oll.libertyfund.org/titles/democracy-in-america-english-edition-vol-2.

Van Parijs, Philippe. 2003. "Difference Principles." In *The Cambridge Companion to John Rawls,* edited by Samuel Freeman, 200–240. Cambridge: Cambridge University Press.

Van Parijs, Philippe. 2007. "International Distributive Justice." In *The Blackwell Companion to Political Philosophy,* Vol. 2, edited by Robert E. Goodin, Philip Pettit, and Thomas Pogge, 638–652. Oxford: Blackwell.

5

Why Does Inequality Matter?

T. M. Scanlon

Why does inequality matter? In other words, what reason do we have for being concerned with the *difference* between what some have and what others have, as opposed to just trying to make the poor better off? My idea in asking this question is not that inequality is more important than poverty. Often it is not. The fact that millions have been lifted out of extreme poverty in recent decades matters more than the increased inequality among people in rich countries. I am interested in inequality not because it is more important than poverty but because it is more puzzling. People have obvious reasons for wanting to be better off and particularly strong reasons for wanting to escape from poverty, but it is less clear what reason they have for being concerned with the difference between what they have and what others have. Why isn't this just envy, as critics of egalitarianism often claim?

Some philosophers, called *prioritarians*, think we should be concerned only with improving the welfare of the poor.[1] In their view, the fact that there are some who have more than the poor is relevant only for the reason that bank robber Willy Sutton is said to have given when asked why he robbed banks: "That's where the money is." Other philosophers think that inequality is bad in itself unless it results simply from the free choices of those who have less.[2]

I disagree with both arguments. I think that there are a number of reasons for objecting to inequality, which arise either from its effects or from the unjustifiability of the institutions that produce it. The plurality of these objections matters for the purposes of this book, since different objections to inequality call for different policies to combat it. In this chapter, I will summarize this pluralist view.[3]

Inequality is not always objectionable. The fact that people in Scandinavia live longer than people in the United States indicates that we could do better in this regard, but the inequality involved is not what is troubling. The fact that women live longer than men is also not a troubling inequality, but if men in the United States lived longer than women, this would be worrisome because it could result from male babies getting better nourishment or men getting better medical care.

This illustrates one way in which inequality can be objectionable because of the institutions that produce it. An inequality is objectionable if it results from the fact that an individual or institution that has the same obligation to provide a certain benefit to each member of a group provides this benefit at a higher level for some than for others, without special justification (Scanlon 2018, chapter 2). It is objectionable in this way, for example, if a municipality (without justification) provides better street paving, sanitation, or other conditions of public health to some residents than to others. This objection depends on the existence of a specific obligation to provide the benefit to those people. It is not a case of objectionable inequality if I give more to one charity than to some other that is equally worthy. I have no general account of when such obligations exist. My point is only that this particular objection to inequality depends on there being an obligation of this kind.

To illustrate some different objections to inequality, imagine two societies in which 99% of the residents of each have the same quite tolerable level of income. In society A, 1% of the people are much poorer than this, and in society B 1% are much richer, by the same amount. Since these societies are mirror images of one another, they may have the same Gini coefficient, but there are different objections to the forms of inequality that they involve.

One thing that comes to mind about society A is what it would be like to be one of the poor people in this society—not just what it would be like to have so little money, but what it would be like to be so much poorer than almost everyone else. As Adam Smith observed (Smith 1910, 351–352), it is a serious objection when a society forces some to live and dress in such a way that they cannot go out in public without shame. Whether having so little money is an occasion for shame depends, of course, on the prevailing attitudes of the society: on whether being poor involves being regarded as inferior, less desirable as a friend or neighbor, or unsuitable for positions of authority (Ci 2014). Where such attitudes exist, poverty is an objectionable form of status inequality, like race and gender (Scanlon 2018, chapter 3).

This particular objection would not apply to the inequality in society B, since it is unlikely that members of the 99% in that society have reason to feel ashamed for not living in the way that the rich do. If the rich are just a few entertainers and athletes with no political power, this inequality might not matter very much, but things are different if the rich own the factories where everyone else has to work or can dominate the political process. Economic inequality is objectionable it if gives some an unacceptable degree of control over the lives of others or if it undermines the fairness of a society's political institutions. The inequality in society A may be objectionable in these ways as well if the 99% control the political process and the opportunities available to the poor.

Inequality is also objectionable when it interferes with equality of opportunity (Scanlon 2018, chapters 4 and 5) Equality of opportunity involves two requirements. Procedural fairness requires that individuals should be selected for positions of advantage on the basis of relevant criteria. Substantive opportunity requires that all individuals should have the opportunity to develop the capabilities required to be successful candidates and to decide whether to do so. Economic inequality can interfere with both requirements. In the case of university admissions, for example, procedural fairness is violated if the rich bribe admissions officers to give preference to their children or if the need to raise money leads universities to give preference to children from rich families. Substantive opportunity is violated if children from rich families have much better opportunities to develop the abilities that make them good candidates for admission.

It is important to note that equality of opportunity is not actually achieved in the contemporary United States and that even if it were achieved it would not in itself justify the unequal outcomes that it leads to. Rather, equality of opportunity is merely a necessary condition for the justice of these unequal outcomes. They are just only if there is some other justification for the unequal positions involved. The "relevant" criteria for selection that define procedural fairness depend on this justification: they are the properties that those who are selected for positions of advantage need to have in order for those positions to serve the purposes that are supposed to justify them.

Inequality in income and wealth can be objectionable not only because of its consequences but also because of the unjustifiability of the institutional mechanisms that produce it. Discussions of inequality often focus on "redistribution" as the main means for reducing it. But in considering inequality of income and wealth we should look first at what produces inequality in pretax income in the first place, treating redistributive taxation as a secondary matter. Many institutional mechanisms that generate inequality, such as intellectual property laws, laws governing limited liability corporations and various forms of financial instruments, and laws making it difficult to form unions and engage in collective bargaining, could be changed without infringing on anyone's liberty. So, in the case of the two societies I mentioned, we should ask where the money of the rich in society A comes from and what keeps the poor in society B down.

The basic egalitarian idea here is that institutional mechanisms that generate large-scale economic inequality in either of these ways need to be justified. They cannot merely be arbitrary. Commonly heard objections to "the one percent" may be based in part on the consequences of this inequality for equality of opportunity and political fairness, but I believe that these objections also reflect the sense that these large holdings are unjustifiable.

How, then, might the institutional mechanisms that produce such differences be justified? I argue that they cannot be justified by appealing to property rights or to ideas of desert. Property rights are important, but they are the creatures of economic institutions, which need to be justified in some other way (Scanlon 2018, chapter 7). And the only forms of desert that are relevant to economic distribution are, again, dependent on institutions (Scanlon 2018, chapter 8).

Transactions that generate inequality can sometimes be justified on the grounds that restricting them would involve unacceptable interference with individual liberty. For example, we could not prevent Wilt Chamberlain from becoming rich, in the way Robert Nozick (Nozick 1974) imagined him doing, by telling people that they could not spend their money on basketball tickets if they wished to do so. But this covers only a few cases. Today, even the large incomes of sports figures depend on institutional mechanisms such as television licensing and antitrust law rather than on individual fans putting an extra dollar into a box for the pleasure of watching Wilt play, as Nozick imagined they might do.

Mechanisms that generate inequality cannot be justified simply on the grounds that they lead to increases in GDP, independent of how these increases are distributed. How, then, can such institutions be justified? I suggest that it is only by the fact that they are to the benefit even of those who receive smaller shares and therefore could not be eliminated in a way that would leave those in this position better off.

We thus arrive at Rawls's difference principle (Rawls 1971) by means of a direct moral argument rather than by appealing to the idea of rational choice behind a veil of ignorance. (Although the basic elements of this argument are ones that Rawls mentions.)

So far, I have been considering inequality in pretax income. Taxation can be justified in a number of ways, including as a fair way to fund benefits owed to all, such as the provision of education and other conditions that are required by substantive opportunity; as a way of reducing inequality in order to ward off its ill effects; and as a way of restraining the growth of inequality by reducing the reasons individuals have to demand higher incomes.

To summarize, I have identified six reasons for objecting to inequality. Some of these objections are based on its consequences: inequality of status, unacceptable control of some by others, and interference with equality of opportunity and with the fairness of political institutions. Other objections arise from the way the inequality is produced, through the unequal provision of benefits owed to all or by institutions that generate unequal incomes without adequate justification.

Some implications of this pluralist view include:

1. There is no specific degree of inequality that should obtain in complex society (no "pattern" or Gini coefficient that must be maintained). A degree of inequality is acceptable if it is not open to objections of these kinds (or perhaps others).
2. Since there are many reasons for taxation, the appropriate rate of taxation depends on many factors.
3. There is no single answer to the question "equality of what?" The kind of inequality that is objectionable varies, depending on the objection to inequality that is in question.

Notes

1. Parfit (2000). For a discussion, see O'Neill (2008).
2. Cohen (1989). For a critical discussion, see Anderson (1999) and Scheffler (2003).
3. For a fuller statement, see Scanlon (2018).

References

Anderson, Elizabeth S. 1999. "What Is the Point of Equality?" *Ethics* 109(2): 287–337.

Ci, Jiwei. 2014. "Agency and Other Stakes of Poverty." *Journal of Political Philosophy* 21(2): 125–150.

Cohen, G. A. 1989. "On the Currency of Egalitarian Justice." *Ethics* 99(4): 906–944.

Nozick, Robert. 1974. *Anarchy, State, and Utopia*. New York: Basic Books.

O'Neill, Martin. 2008. "What Should Egalitarians Believe?" *Philosophy and Public Affairs* 36(2): 119–156.

Parfit, Derek. 2000. "Equality or Priority?" In *The Idea of Equality*, edited by Michael Clayton and Andrew Williams, 81–125. New York: Palgrave Macmillan.

Rawls, John. 1971. *A Theory of Justice*. Cambridge, MA: Harvard University Press.

Scanlon, T. M. 2018. *Why Does Inequality Matter?* Oxford: Oxford University Press.

Scheffler, Samuel. 2003. "What Is Egalitarianism?" *Philosophy and Public Affairs* 31(1): 5–39.

Smith, Adam. 1910. *An Inquiry into the Nature and Causes of the Wealth of Nations*. London: Home University.

III
Political Dimensions

6

Wealth Inequality and Politics

Ben Ansell

We live in an era of both rising economic inequalities and heightened political polarization. Is this mere coincidence? If not, exactly how are inequality and politics related? And, in particular, is there something distinct about growing inequalities in wealth and housing separate from the more widely discussed inequalities in labor market incomes? After all, the rise in house prices, in both absolute terms and relative to income, across the industrialized world since the 1990s is both unprecedented in magnitude and intimately connected to the global credit crisis of a decade ago. It would have been surprising if the surge, collapse, and revival of asset prices over the past two decades, or indeed the widening of regional and generational divides in wealth, had not had political effects. Yet we know rather little about how wealth, particularly residential wealth, affects political life.

Why is wealth inequality, as opposed to income inequality, important for political scientists to look at? We should be cautious in assuming their effects on political life would be different—after all, wealth inequality could emerge mechanically from income inequality, as savings from earnings compound in stocks of assets. Indeed, people with higher incomes tend to have higher levels of wealth, oftentimes in a snapshot and certainly over their lifetimes. So we face an empirical challenge in separating out the effects of wealth and income at the individual level on, say, voting. We also know that wealth can be harder to measure both individually and in the aggregate.

For example, voters do not typically know how wealthy they are. They may be unaware that they have a private pension. They do not receive a paycheck every month telling them what their wealth is in the way that they do with their income. They probably know roughly how much their house is worth, but that only really manifests when they try and sell their house or when their neighbors do. On the aggregate side, how we measure wealth in the national accounts affects how countries vary in terms of their wealth inequality. For example, if you include wealth held in pensions, Denmark, Sweden, and Norway look like they have extremely high wealth inequality, mirroring that of a country, such as the United States, that we would more typically associate with high levels of inequality. This happens because public pensions are very high in Scandinavian countries, but even if someone is entitled to a public pension in the future, that entitlement is not counted as their current wealth in the way that private retirement assets vested in a fund are.

Thus, thinking about how wealth and wealth inequality matter for politics runs up against some serious measurement issues. We have very little evidence for the effects of financial wealth on political behavior because those surveys that do include questions about political and social preferences typically do not include questions about financial wealth, which in any case may be seriously misestimated by respondents.

What surveys do often include, however, is information about housing. The British Household Panel Survey, for example, asks people to estimate how much their house is worth and how much it cost when they bought it. It also asks respondents where they live at quite a low level of aggregation. In recent years, most industrialized countries have provided comparable local data on house prices, which means we can both match survey respondents to where they live and draw conclusions about inequality in residential wealth with much greater certainty. Accordingly, even though for measurement reasons it is hard to connect wealth in its entirety to political behavior, we can say a good deal about the effects of differences in residential wealth. This focus on residential wealth aligns with the fact that growth in residential wealth explains a good deal of the "return of capital" identified by Thomas Piketty (2014), as Matthew Ronglie's (2015) important rejoinder to Piketty shows. Residential wealth is also important politically because it is visible and because it is, for most people, the substantively largest and sentimentally most important part of their wealth portfolios.

In order to connect residential wealth to political behavior, we need to think about how political behavior is organized. Crudely, political preferences are structured across two dimensions. The first dimension, the economic dimension, is very familiar: support for the welfare state—support for taxation and redistribution. This is territory in which political economists are very comfortable. However, they are rather less comfortable with something that appears to be increasingly important: the second dimension, political preferences, a cultural dimension, between cosmopolitanism and nationalism or populism and liberalism. As we will see, wealth inequality is deeply connected to the structure of political preferences and behavior across both dimensions.

How should we think about how wealth, particularly embodied in housing, should matter for people's preferences? Our first expectation is that wealth ought to play out like labor market income. People with more expensive houses are likely to behave more or less like people with higher incomes in the sense that their tax preferences and their demand for social insurance rise and fall with their wealth. In many countries, when housing rises in value, individuals become liable for paying higher property taxes. Higher property values also lead to higher tax payments when houses are bought or sold; for example, stamp duty in the United Kingdom. And, when people die, a more expensive house typically leads to higher inheritance taxes paid by their descendants. Thus, higher house prices might inculcate more antitax attitudes, even when controlling for income effects. In terms of public spending preferences, people may use their housing as a nest egg, as a form of social insurance that they can fall back on in tough times or in retirement. Thus, on both the tax and spending sides, we might expect an association between people having more expensive property and wanting the state to do less redistribution.

Indeed, this is what we find in those surveys that do allow us to extract wealth from income. Using the British Household Panel Survey, we can examine the period between 1991 and about 2008, in which a series of questions were asked about what respondents thought their house was currently worth, its price upon purchase, and their location. Thus, we can either take subjective estimates of individuals' house prices or take objective measures of median house prices at the local level for homeowning respondents and use either of these as measures for individual wealth. Ansell (2014) shows that changes in house prices—both increases and decreases—appear to affect social policy preferences. As an example, a £100,000 increase in house prices is associated with about a 10% decline in support for full employment policies. The American National Election Survey panel between 2000 and 2004 only provides information about home ownership status and location (and hence no subjective estimates of house prices, unlike the British Household Panel Survey), but we also see patterns similar to the British case when we examine homeowners in metropolitan statistical areas that had higher or lower house price growth and their support for changes in funding Social Security over the panel. Homeowners who experienced greater house price appreciation became less supportive of Social Security spending over that period.

Cross-nationally, we can look at the International Social Survey Program, which surveyed citizens across 19 countries in 2009 and asked them about how much equity they would have left if they had to sell their house tomorrow. This permits us to obtain a measure of how much equity people have in their house, and we see that this is strongly negatively associated with supporting government redistribution of income from rich to poor.

On average, we find that rising house prices appear to reduce demand for the welfare state, but there is an intriguing wrinkle to this finding. This effect is largely concentrated in center-right voters. Left-wing voters broadly like high redistribution regardless of their personal residential wealth, but people on the right do appear to react to changes to their wealth, both positive and negative. From a tactical point of view, this means Margaret Thatcher and George W. Bush's emphasis on the importance of an ownership society was a good political strategy. If conservative voters could be incentivized to support cuts to the welfare state if house prices were rising, then stimulating home ownership and the housing market coalesced with plans to shrink the size of the state. The flip side of this is that an era of booming housing markets may be one of declining support for redistribution, even when that might appear to be the most effective way of narrowing inequality.

The effect of wealth on the first—material—dimension of politics is unsurprising for political economists. But what is the connection between wealth and inequality and changes on the second—cultural—dimension? One way to think about this is to focus again on residential wealth and note that it is largely defined by relative location; that is, the price of housing reflects the relative demand for land in different locations. That demand in turn comes from how well local economies have performed and how attractive a location is to move to. Much has been made of the connection between "left behind" locations and support for populist parties or causes—from Brexit, to Donald Trump, to Marine Le Pen. Those left behind places are ones that are in economic decline or considered low-status locations by the housing market. Indeed, much scholarship shows that both direct material economic effects and subjective perceptions of status shape support for populist movements. House prices therefore provide an excellent proxy for relative geographical support for populism and attitudes toward the political establishment and consensus economic policies of the past few decades. Lower house prices correlate strongly with support for populism. Bluntly, what's a better measure of the value that society has for the place that you live than the value that it attaches financially to the place where you live? There is a further potentially causal effect of differences across housing markets. Expensive places are hard to move to from less expensive places. Housing inequality therefore locks people into the communities they live in. It segregates the country economically. It means that friends and family do not move away and people get locked into different communities that talk past one another and don't agree with one another. In other words, housing polarization can underpin political polarization.

We can see this pattern across a number of different countries. Figure 6.1 shows the overall pattern for voting to leave the European Union in the 2016 Brexit referendum. This figure shows the bivariate relationship between logged median house prices at the local authority level (a unit with an average of 100,000 inhabitants) and support for Remain (i.e., remaining in the European Union) in England and Wales. House prices are a strong predictor of support for Remain, explaining around half the variance in voting. Importantly, this relationship is robust to controlling for demographic factors, including ethnicity, immigration, and age, and to economic factors, including wages and industrial structure, as well as to dummy variables for each region in England and Wales. On average, in England and Wales we're looking at about 100,000 people. This

Figure 6.1
House prices in 2015 and support for Remain (remaining in the European Union) in the 2016 EU referendum.

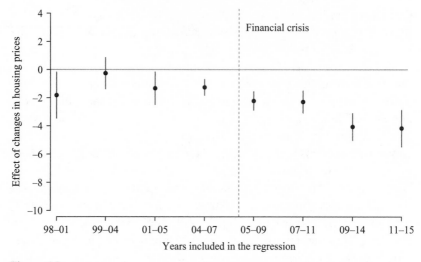

Figure 6.2
Changes in house prices and support for the Danish People's Party.

result even holds up within local authorities. When we examine wards, which have 1,000 or 3,000 people in them, and add a dummy for each local authority, we see the same relationship (Adler and Ansell 2019).

We see a similar pattern with time-series data at a very low level of analysis in Denmark. Figure 6.2 uses Danish registry data at the electoral precinct level (500 to 1,000 people) to examine the relationship between election-to-election changes in housing prices and support for the Danish People's Party (DPP; Ansell et al. 2019). We see a consistently negative relationship: rising house prices are associated with less support for the DPP, and this pattern became steeper after the Great Recession. In both the British and Danish cases, these regional divides, which are at least manifest in house prices, appear to be strongly related to differences in support for populist causes.

Housing then appears to be closely connected to the two key dimensions of political life—preferences and voting along the material dimension and along the group-identity dimension. Rising house prices in some regions push regions toward low-tax, low-spending, antipopulist preferences, whereas house price declines push other regions toward a greater demand for both redistribution and populism. Unsurprisingly, then, the housing booms and busts of the past few decades have cut across traditional divides, breaking apart old political cleavages but galvanizing new ones.

References

Adler, David, and Ben Ansell. 2020. "Housing and Populism." *West European Politics* 43(20): 344–365.

Ansell, Ben. 2014. "The Political Economy of Ownership." *American Political Science Review* 108(2): 383–402.

Ansell, Ben, Frederik Hjorth, Jacob Nyrup, and Martin Vinæs Larsen. 2019. "Sheltering Populists?" Working paper.

Piketty, Thomas. 2014. *Capital in the Twenty-First Century*. Cambridge, MA: Harvard University Press.

Ronglie, Matthew. 2015. "Deciphering the Fall and Rise in the Net Capital Share: Accumulation or Scarcity?" *Brookings Papers on Economic Activity* 46(1): 1–69.

7

The Political Conditions Necessary for Addressing Inequality

Sheri Berman

Thanks to a "quantum leap in the realm of inequality research," we now have a better understanding of the nature and consequences of inequality in the West. In the United States, for example, during the early part of the twentieth century, the richest 1% of Americans captured around 17%–20% of national income and about 45% of national wealth (see Chancel, chapter 1, this volume). After 1945, these shares fell, reaching 8% and 25%, respectively, by the 1970s to 1980s. They began rising again during the late twentieth century, and today income inequality is at its highest point since the Census Bureau began tracking it (Telford 2019) and the top 1% control more of the nation's wealth "than the entire American middle class" (Tankersley 2019).

Inequality's consequences go far beyond increasing the distance between society's "haves" and "have nots." Rising inequality is correlated with slower growth: growth was faster during the period after World War II, when inequality was dropping, than it is today, and over the past few decades countries with high levels of inequality have grown more slowly than countries with lower levels (OECD 2014). Rising inequality is also associated with declining social mobility, particularly in the United States.[1]

Making matters worse, inequality's negative effects are not limited to the economic sphere. Those at the bottom of our increasingly unequal society lead shorter lives, suffer more from physical and mental health problems, and are more likely to fall prey to alcoholism and addiction and to live in broken communities (Case and Deaton 2020; Wilkinson and Picket 2009; Putnam 2016; US GAO 2019). Inequality has also impacted our democracy, increasing polarization, shaping the types of candidates that run for office, skewing which voters' preferences are heeded by politicians, and more (McCarty, Poole, and Rosenthal 2006; Gilens 2012; Page and Gilens 2017; Schlozman, Verba, and Brady 2012; Phillips 2002; Bartels 2016).

In addition to better understanding the extent of inequality and its consequences, we also know that it can be mitigated. Despite experiencing similar levels of trade and automation, inequality has risen less in Western Europe than in the United States, because of more expansive welfare states and other forms of government intervention in the former (Chancel, chapter 1, this volume; WID.world 2020). More generally, as the chapters in this volume make clear, in recent years scholars have increasingly turned their attention to examining policies addressing inequality (e.g., Kenworthy 2019; Hacker and Pierson 2017; Baramendi et al. 2015).

Given what we know about inequality and its negative consequences, why hasn't there been a more sustained effort to address it? If economic conditions and interests were translated relatively straightforwardly into policy preferences and political outcomes, as economists and political economists assume (Alesina et al. 2011; Iversen and Soskice 2001; Rehm 2009, 2011; Meltzer and Richard 1981), this would indeed be a puzzle, since with the exception of a relatively small elite that has flourished in recent years, policies to address inequality should be in the economic self-interest of most voters. Unfortunately, however, problems, even when accompanied by significant suffering and injustice, do not directly lead to demands for change. As one of history's great revolutionaries, Leon Trotsky, once put it, "The mere *existence* of privations is not enough to cause an insurrection; if it were, the masses would always be in revolt" (Trotsky 1930; emphasis mine).

A sustained campaign to combat inequality will emerge only if voters pressure politicians to pursue such an effort. For such pressure to emerge, several conditions would need to be met. Most obviously, citizens would need to believe that politicians are capable of and interested in responding to their economic concerns. Years of being told during the late twentieth and early twenty-first centuries by conservative and sometimes even centrist politicians that, to paraphrase Ronald Reagan, "government was the problem, rather than the solution," and more recent insistence by populists that "elites" and the "establishment" use political power to thwart the interests of "the people," has clearly led many voters to doubt the ability and willingness of politicians to respond to their needs (e.g., Cramer 2016).

Alongside a belief in the ability and willingness of politicians to respond to their needs, two other crucial political prerequisites for a sustained campaign against inequality are that voters prioritize economic issues and interests and are mobilized on the basis of them. Understanding why this has not occurred requires examining the actions of politicians and political parties. Politicians and political parties critically shape the interests and identities that dominate political life, and over the past years they have de-emphasized economic interests and identities.

Scholars have shown that as inequality rises, parties of the Right increasingly emphasize noneconomic issues and interests (Huber 2017; Roemer et al. 2007). This is particularly true for the Populist Right. The best predictor of voting for the Populist Right is views on immigration, racial anxieties, concerns about national identity, and other related concerns (Dennison and Geddes 2019; Bonikowski, Feinstein, and Bock 2019; Sides, Vavreck, and Tesler 2018; Mutz 2018). Populists do best, in short, when these issues dominate political competition, which is why they spend so much time demonizing immigrants and minorities, blaming them for rising crime, eroding national values, and other problems (e.g., Financial Times 2019; Deutsche Welle 2019). Relatedly, populist voters are divided in their economic preferences but united in having conservative social and cultural preferences. As a result, when economic issues dominate political competition, populists' voting constituencies will be divided, but when social and cultural issues dominate, they are united (Ivarsflaten 2008; Kriesi 2014). This pattern is particularly clear in Europe, where populists achieve disproportionate support from workers and small business owners (groups with widely divergent economic preferences). As one study of the interplay between rising inequality and political competition in Europe concluded, "Inequality ... often make[s] it more difficult for electoral competition to elect parties committed to addressing economic disparities. Rather than encouraging redistributive class politics, inequality often fosters the success of parties that focus on creating electoral coalitions based on noneconomic identities, such as ethnicity. And when winning electoral coalitions are based on such noneconomic identities, democracy does less to redress inequality than would be the case if class politics could prevail" (Huber 2017, 3).

A similar but less pronounced dynamic exists in the United States with the Republican Party and among Trump voters in particular, since white workers tend to be more left-wing economically than other Republican voters (Kitschelt and Rehm 2019). Shrewd Republicans understand this[2] and that it therefore makes sense for them to keep social and cultural rather than economic grievances front and center. As Steve Bannon infamously put it, as long as Democrats focus on identity politics, "I got 'em. If the left is focused on race and identity ... we can crush the Democrats."

This brings us to the Left. During the postwar period, political competition, particularly in Europe, pivoted primarily around economic policy differences, but by the late twentieth century, economic differences between left and right diminished as the former moved to the center economically, accepting much of the neoliberal agenda, including less state regulation, welfare state cutbacks, an embrace of globalization, and so on (Berman and Snegovaya 2019).

This shift weakened the Left's ability to mobilize discontent about inequality and other economic problems. This became particularly clear during the financial crisis, when such discontent exploded. As *The Economist* noted in 2009, "Parties of the left have been unable to capitalize on an economic crisis tailor made for critics of the free market." In the United States, Democratic pollster Stanley Greenberg similarly mused that "during this period of economic crisis and uncertainty, voters are generally turning to ... right wing political parties.... When unemployment is high and the rich are getting richer, you would think that voters of average means would flock to progressives, who are supposed to have their interests in mind" (New York Times 2011).

In addition to rendering the Left unable to mobilize economic discontent, economic convergence with the Center-Right led to an increasing stress on social and cultural issues by Left parties. As one set of scholars noted, as left and right converged on questions of economic policy, politicizing noneconomic issues became an attractive survival strategy insofar as shifting competition to a new issue domain allows parties to better distinguish themselves from one another and thereby avoid losing voters to indifference" (Ward et al. 2015; see also Gerring 2001; Rydgren 2013; Schaffner, Macwilliams, and Nteta 2018; Ivarsflaten 2005: Spies 2013; Bonikowski 2017). Accompanying the Left's shifting economic policy profile was a decreasing emphasis on class and a leadership increasingly drawn from a highly educated elite (Bovens and Wille 2017; Mudge 2018). With the mainstream Left and Right offering similar economic policies, and the Left moving away from its traditional identification as the champion of the working class, it is not surprising that fewer people voted on the basis of their economic preferences and interests.

An instructive, if extreme, example of this dynamic is the late twentieth-century Labour Party. Under the leadership of Tony Blair, the party adopted a technocratic, centrist economic profile. (Reflecting this, when asked to name her greatest achievement, Margaret Thatcher is said to have replied "Tony Blair.") Labour's 1997 manifesto reflected this, declaring that the party aimed "to put behind us the bitter political struggles of left and right that have torn our country apart for too many decades. Many of these conflicts have no relevance to the modern world—public versus private, bosses versus workers, middle class versus working class. It is time for this country to move on and move forward" (Labour Party 1997).

In addition to a new economic profile, Labour's appeal and rhetoric also shifted during the late twentieth century. Whereas during the post-war decades the party "regularly referred to the working class in both speeches and policy documents," by the late twentieth century "there was little recognition of class." In addition, during the postwar decades, Labour politicians were often drawn from the labor movement, but by the late twentieth century, they came mostly from "a pool of highly edu-cated, upper middle-class people." The result was that by the late 1990s voters increasingly viewed Labour as having "similar economic policies" and "representing similar people" as the Conservatives. Not surprisingly, as fewer people recognized the parties as differing on economic policy or as being associated with particular classes, "fewer people voted on these bases" (Evans and Tilly 2017, 163, 193).

The American Democratic Party was never as far left economically nor as focused on class as Labour, but a similar if less-pronounced trend occurred. During the late twentieth century, the Democratic Party adopted an increasingly centrist, technocratic economic profile and stressed social and cultural issues. These trends emerged particularly clearly during the 2016 presidential campaign. Hillary Clinton talked less about economic policy and class "and more about race, immigration and gender" than her predecessors. Alongside Trump's emphasis on these issues, the result was a campaign that was particularly focused on these issues and candidates who were particularly divided on them, raising their salience and thus impact "at the ballot box" (Sides, Vavreck, and Tesler 2018, 169; see also Grossman 2018; Mutz 2018).

Conclusion

During the last few decades, inequality has risen dramatically, generating profoundly negative economic, social, and political consequences. Recog-nizing a problem, however, is merely the first step in addressing it. Politi-cians will focus on combating inequality only if confronted with electoral incentives to do so. Such electoral incentives, in turn, will only emerge if voters prioritize economic issues and interests and are mobilized on the basis of them.

Parties of the Right, particularly populist parties, have an incentive to avoid these conditions emerging. Reflecting this, during the late twentieth and early twenty-first century, such parties worked to shift political attention away from inequality and economic class and mobilized voters on the basis of social and cultural grievances and identities instead.

During the postwar decades, parties of the Left, on the other hand, particularly in Europe, emphasized economic issues in their policy platforms and mobilized voters on the basis of their economic interests and class identities. During the late twentieth century, however, the traditional Left shifted to the center economically, increasingly stressed social and cultural issues, and deemphasized class, making it harder for voters to vote on the basis of their economic preferences and identities. In other words, cumulatively, the actions of politicians and parties—particularly on the right but also on the Left—helped create conditions that made it harder to generate a sustained campaign to combat inequality.

Notes

1. What Alan Krueger referred to as the Great Gatsby curve. See https://krugman.blogs.nytimes.com/2012/01/15/the-great-gatsby-curve/ and https://www.americanprogress.org/events/2012/01/12/17181/the-rise-and-consequences-of-inequality/.

2. For example, Lee Atwater, the 1988 campaign manager for George H. W. Bush, once said, "The way to win a presidential race against the Republicans is to develop the class welfare issue [as 1988 nominee Michael Dukakis belatedly did at the end]. To divide up the haves and have nots and to try to reinvigorate the New Deal coalition." Quoted in Phillips (2002, xiii).

References

Alesina, Alberto, Paola Giuliano, A. Bisin, and J. Benhabib. 2011. "Preferences for Redistribution." In *Handbook of Social Economics*, edited by Jess Benhabib, Alberto Bisin, Matthew O. Jackson, 93–131. San Diego: Elsevier.

Baramendi, Pablo, Silja Häusermann, Herbert Kitschel, and Hanspeter Kriesi. 2015. *The Politics of Advanced Capitalism*. New York: Cambridge University Press.

Bartels, Larry M. 2016. *Unequal Democracy: The Political Economy of the New Gilded Age*. Princeton, NJ: Princeton University Press.

Berman, Sheri, and Maria Snegovaya. 2019. "Populism and the Decline of Social Democracy." *Journal of Democracy* 30(3): 5–19.

Bonikowski, Bart. 2017. "Ethno-nationalist Populism and the Mobilization of Collective Resentment." *British Journal of Sociology* 68:181–213.

Bonikowski, Bart, Yuval Feinstein, and Sean Bock. 2019. "The Polarization of Nationalist Cleavages and the 2016 U.S. Presidential Election." *SocArXiv*, August 16, 2019.

Bovens, Mark, and Anchrit Wille. 2017. *Diploma Democracy: The Rise of Political Meritocracy*. New York: Oxford University Press.

Case, Anne, and Angus Deaton. 2020. *Deaths of Despair*. Princeton, NJ: Princeton University Press.

Cramer, Katherine. 2016. *The Politics of Resentment: Rural Consciousness in Wisconsin and the Rise of Scott Walker*. Chicago: University of Chicago Press.

Dennison, J., and A. Geddes. 2019. "A Rising Tide? The Salience of Immigration and the Rise of Anti-immigration Political Parties in Western Europe." *Political Quarterly* 90:107–116.

Deutsche Welle. 2019. "Germany's Far-Right AfD Fuels Xenophobia with D. Sistorted Crime Figures—Study." *Deutsche Welle*, August 5, 2019.

Evans, Geoffrey, and James Tilly. 2017. *The New Politics of the Working Class: The Political Exclusion of the British Working Class*. Oxford: Oxford University Press.

Financial Times. 2019. "Homegrown 'Junk News' on Migrants and Islam Surges, Studies Find. Far-Right Parties Shift Focus from Leaving EU to Divisive Social Issues." *Financial Times*, May 27, 2019.

Gerring, John. 2001. *Party Ideologies in America*. New York: Cambridge University Press.

Gilens, Martin. 2012. *Affluence and Influence*. Princeton, NJ: Princeton University Press.

Grossman, Matt. 2018. "Racial Attitudes and Political Correctness in the 2016 Presidential Election." Niskanen Center. https://www.niskanencenter.org/racial-attitudes-and-political-correctness-in-the-2016-presidential-election/.

Hacker, Jacob, and Paul Pierson. 2017. *American Amnesia*. New York: Simon and Schuster.

Huber, John. 2017. *Exclusion by Elections: Inequality, Ethnic Identity, and Democracy*. New York: Cambridge University Press.

Ivarsflaten, E. 2005. "The Vulnerable Populist Right Parties: No Economic Realignment Fueling Their Electoral Success." *European Journal of Political Research* 44: 465–492.

Ivarsflaten, Elisabeth. 2008. "What Unites Right-Wing Populists in Western Europe? Re-examining Grievance Mobilization Models in Seven Successful Cases." *Comparative Political Studies* 41(1): 3–23.

Iversen, Torben, and David Soskice. 2001. "An Asset Theory of Social Policy Preferences." *American Political Science Review* 95(4): 875–893.

Kenworthy, Lane. 2019. *Social Democratic Capitalism*. New York: Oxford University Press.

Kitschelt, Herbert, and Philip Rehm. 2019. "Secular Partisan Realignment in the United States: The Socioeconomic Reconfiguration of White Partisan Support since the New Deal Era." *Politics & Society* 47(3): 425–479.

Kriesi, Hanspeter. 2014. "The Populist Challenge." *West European Politics* 37(2): 361–378.

Labour Party. 1997. "Labour Party Manifesto." http://www.labour-party.org.uk/manifestos/1997/1997-labour-manifesto.shtml.

Lord Ashcroft. 2020. "Diagnosis of Defeat." https://lordashcroftpolls.com/wp-content/uploads/2020/02/DIAGNOSIS-OF-DEFEAT-LORD-ASHCROFT-POLLS-1.pdf.

McCarty, Nolan, Keith T. Poole, and Howard Rosenthal. 2006. *Polarized America: The Dance of Ideology and Unequal Riches.* Cambridge, MA: MIT Press.

Meltzer, Allan H., and Scott F. Richard. 1981. "A Rational Theory of the Size of Government." *Journal of Political Economy* 89(5): 914–927.

Mudge, Stephanie. 2018. *Leftism Reinvented: Western Parties from Socialism to Neoliberalism.* Cambridge, MA: Harvard University Press.

Mutz, Diana. 2018. "Status Threat, Not Economic Hardship, Explains the 2016 Presidential Vote." *Proceedings of the National Academy of Sciences* 115(19): E4330–E4339.

New York Times. 2011. "Why Voters Tune Out the Democrats." *New York Times*, July 31, 2011. https://www.nytimes.com/2011/07/31/opinion/sunday/tuning-out-the-democrats.html.

Organization for Economic Cooperation and Development (OECD 2014). "Inequality Hurts Economic Growth." http://www.oecd.org/newsroom/inequality-hurts-economic-growth.htm.

Page, Benjamin, and Martin Gilens. 2017. *Democracy in America?* Chicago: University of Chicago.

Phillips, Kevin. 2002. *Wealth and Democracy.* New York: Broadway Books.

Putnam, Robert. 2016. *Our Kids.* New York: Simon and Schuster.

Rehm, P. 2009. "Risks and Redistribution: An Individual-Level Analysis." *Comparative Political Studies* 42(7): 855–888.

Rehm, P. 2011. "Social Policy by Popular Demand." *World Politics* 63(2): 271–299.

Roemer, John E., Woojin Lee, and Karine Van der Straeten. 2007. *Racism, Xenophobia, and Distribution: Multi-issue Politics in Advanced Democracies.* New York: Russell Sage Foundation.

Rydgren, Jens, ed. 2013. *Class Politics and the Radical Right.* New York: Routledge.

Schaffner, B. F., M. Macwilliams, and T. Nteta. 2018. "Understanding White Polarization in the 2016 Vote for President: The Sobering Role of Racism and Sexism." *Political Science Quarterly* 133:9–34.

Schlozman, Kay Lehman, Sidney Verba, and Henry E. Brady. 2012. *The Unheavenly Chorus: Unequal Political Voice and the Broken Promise of American Democracy.* Princeton, NJ: Princeton University Press.

Sides, John, Lynn Vavreck, and Michael Tesler. 2018. *Identity Crisis: The 2016 Presidential Campaign and the Battle for the Meaning of America.* Princeton, NJ: Princeton University Press.

Spies, Dennis. 2013. "Explaining Working-Class Support for Extreme Right Parties: A Party Competition Approach." *Acta Politica* 48(3): 296–325.

Tankersley, Jim. 2019. "Warren Health Plan Tightens Democrats' Embrace of Tax Increases." *New York Times*, November 2, 2019. https://www.nytimes.com/2019/11/02/business/elizabeth-warren-health-care-plan.html.

Tedford, Taylor. 2019. "Inequality in America Is at the Highest It's Been since Census Bureau Started Tracking It, Data Shows." *Washington Post*, September 26, 2019. https://www.washingtonpost.com/business/2019/09/26/income-inequality-america-highest-its-been-since-census-started-tracking-it-data-show/.

Trotsky, Leon. 1930. "Introduction to Volumes 2 and 3." In *The History of the Russian Revolution*. Marxists.org. https://www.marxists.org/archive/trotsky/1930/hrr/intro23.htm.

United States Government Accountability Office (USGAO 2019). "Income and Wealth Disparities Continue through Old Age." https://www.gao.gov/assets/710/700836.pdf.

Ward, Dalston, Jeong Hyun Kim, Matthew Graham, and Margit Tavits. 2015. "How Economic Integration Affects Party Issue Emphases." *Comparative Political Studies* 48(10): 1227–1259.

WID.world. World Inequality Database 2020. www.wid.world/.

Wilkinson, Richard, and Kate Picket. 2009. *The Spirit Level: Why Greater Equality Makes Societies Stronger*. London: Bloomsbury.

8

The Political Obstacles to Tackling Economic Inequality in the United States

Nolan McCarty

In chapter 1 of this volume, Lucas Chancel presents two very important facts that are essential for framing the politics of inequality in the United States. The first is the substantial variation in the levels and trajectories of economic inequality across a wide variety of advanced democracies. Importantly, these variations do not seem to be reducible to purely social, demographic, and economic factors, as many of these transformations are common to all rich countries. This unexplainable variation leaves open the possibility that politics and policy play an important role in determining levels and trends in economic inequality.

The second fact is one that I will call "American exceptionalism." As Chancel demonstrates, the level and trajectory of income inequality in the United States were comparable to those of other countries in the 1950s and 1960s, but beginning in the 1970s, income inequality began rising in the United States at a rate far exceeding that of other OECD countries. This suggests that there may be important features of the contemporary American political economy that are especially conducive to high levels and trends in inequality.

In *Polarized America: The Dance of Ideology and Unequal Riches*, Keith Poole, Howard Rosenthal, and I examine several of these political factors behind rising income inequality in the United States (McCarty, Poole, and Rosenthal 2010, chapter 8; see also Bonica et al. 2013). Our primary argument is that there is a strong association between economic inequality in the United States and the rise of political polarization.[1] Figure 8.1 shows the basic pattern that we explored in this research. The solid line represents a measure of polarization of the roll call voting in the US House of Representatives. Using congressional roll call voting is a useful way to measure polarization because we can measure partisan conflict over very long periods of time in a way that allows reasonable comparisons. The solid line is essentially the differences in the voting

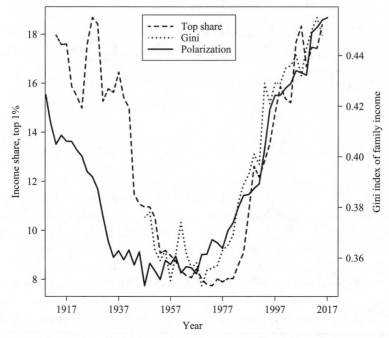

Figure 8.1
Political polarization and economic inequality. The figure plots the measure of polarization in the US House of Representatives from McCarty, Poole, and Rosenthal (2016)
against the Gini index of family income and the Piketty and Saez (2003, updated) measure
of the income share of the top 1% of taxpayers. The Gini index is a measure of inequality
that ranges from 0 (pure equality) to 1 (complete concentration of income).

behavior of Democratic and Republican legislators, and higher numbers
mean less bipartisanship and more polarization.[2]

Measures of polarization based on roll calls obviously include some
combination of ideological differences and pure partisanship, but they
also include important information about the ideological patterns of elite
politicians in the country. The basic facts of polarization are that it was
very high early in the twentieth century, stabilized at a low level at mid-
century, and has grown fairly dramatically over the past 40 years.

The other measures included in figure 8.1 are more familiar to scholars of inequality. The first is the income share of the top 1% computed
by Piketty and Saez (2003, updated), and the second is the Gini index of
family income, computed by the US Census Bureau. The main takeaway
point is that all these time series tend to move together.

Without making any strong causal claims, I think it is important to
note that periods of high income inequality in the United States tend to be

associated with high levels of political polarization. Periods of low political polarization tend to be associated with periods of low income inequality.

There is substantial evidence for a causal link between economic inequality and polarization, but the causality runs in both directions. First, income inequality has a polarizing effect that generates differences across voters at different income levels in terms of how they feel about economic policy choices and how much state intervention they prefer, and these differences have tended, over time, to map onto partisan alignments.

The second, equally important, causal link comes from the ways in which polarization paralyzes politics, especially in a political system like that of the United States, which depends on many veto players and the checks and balances between the House and Senate and the president. Political polarization produces a type of political paralysis that can make it more difficult for the government to respond to those economic and social changes that are likely to be producing the rising levels of income inequality. Of most concern regarding hopes for a policy response to income inequality is how it appears that economic inequality and political polarization form a positive feedback loop that may be hard to break.

A second important feature of the American political economy is that the polarization discussed is asymmetric in partisan terms. It is not a reflection of the Democratic Party moving as far to the left as it is the Republican Party moving to the right on economic issues. It turns out that by these measures each Republican cohort over the past 40 years has compiled a more conservative voting record on economic matters than each previous cohort. On the Democratic side, the story is much more mixed. Some new cohorts are more liberal or progressive than outgoing cohorts and vice versa. Part of the problem is that the Democratic Party has been more heterogeneous in terms of its economic policy positions. There has been a great deal of tension between the money wing of the Democratic Party, which the constituencies cater to in order to be competitive financially, and the voter wing, the consistency of lower-income voters around which we would expect a center-left party to organize. And, of course, there is a constituency that supports the Democratic Party for noneconomic reasons related to the environment and social issues. Many of these voters have relatively high incomes and are not particular supporters of redistribution.

A second factor worth noting is that part of the reason why the Democratic Party has not moved to the left as strongly as the Republican Party has moved to the right arises from the difficulty of mobilizing low-income residents. This is a long-standing problem in the United States, given its localized administration of elections and winner-take-all electoral system. The problem has become worse because of the increased number of non-citizen residents. Thus, as Danielle Allen points out in chapter 3 of this volume, a very large component of the working-class population does not have political or civic rights, and therefore the Democratic Party is unable to mobilize them electorally.

The second story about the United States is about the relationship between political inequality and economic inequality. The most striking manifestation of this relationship is the inequality in participation in the campaign finance system. Dramatic changes in this relationship are shown in figure 8.2. The solid line in the figure plots the estimated percentage of contributions to federal campaigns made by the top 0.1% of the US voting-age population. The dashed line is an estimate of the percentage of federal campaign contributions made by the top 400 contributors.

In the 1980s, a substantial fraction of federal campaign contributions, ranging from 10% to 15%, was funded by the top 0.01%, but currently that percentage is staggering, reaching nearly 40%.[3] Thus, there has been almost a fourfold increase in the share of contributions to federal campaigns coming from the wealthiest Americans.

But these figures represent only the tip of the iceberg because they do not include campaign contributions to state and local races, where we would expect a similar skew. Moreover, they do not include expenditures for policy advocacy or lobbying, where we would expect an even greater skew.

One might ask whether figure 8.2 represents greater efforts by the wealthy to mobilize in politics. The evidence points in a different direction, toward an incidental effect of increasing wealth inequality. Adam Bonica and Howard Rosenthal (Bonica and Rosenthal 2015) have estimated the elasticity of campaign contributions to wealth for the Forbes 400 richest Americans. They find that campaign contributions for the wealthy are a normal good in that contributions rise proportionate to wealth. The elasticity of contributions to wealth is approximately 1.0. Since the elasticity of campaign contributions to wealth is 0 for most nonwealthy people, wealth inequality almost mechanically produces the skew of figure 8.2.

So one of the major implications of both wealth and income inequality in the United States has been a massive shift in the proportion of support of candidates coming from wealthy individuals. No doubt, contributors contribute for lots of reasons. They are not all economically motivated. Campaign contributions of the wealthy are not always motivated by support for lower taxes or a deregulatory agenda. Moreover, many wealthy donors are on the political left and contribute for progressive causes. But very few of the campaign dollars of the very richest people are donated in

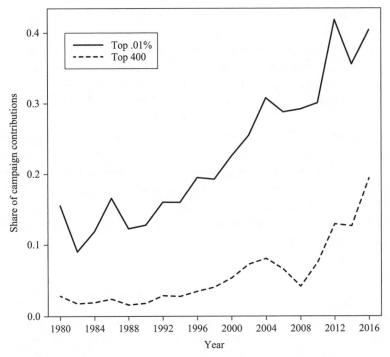

Figure 8.2
Concentration of federal campaign contributions. Contribution data updated from Bonica et al. (2013). The solid line tracks the share of campaign contributions in all federal elections donated by the top 0.01% of the voting-age population. The dashed line tracks the share of contributions from the top 400 donors.

support of expanded redistribution or the strengthening of labor unions. Thus, many politicians on the left have donor bases that are indifferent at best to the sorts of policies that reduce economic inequality. While such politicians may push back at Republican efforts to enact policies that increase inequality, they are unlikely to push for the boldest reforms.

It is worth pointing out that there are a few common misunderstandings about campaign finance that bear on this discussion. The first is that the Supreme Court decision in Citizens United is a major source of the problem.[4] The first problem with the emphasis on Citizens United is that the trend toward greater concentration of contributions was under way well before the case was decided in 2010. Second, Citizens United is primarily about the use of corporate and labor union treasury money to make independent campaign expenditures. Figure 8.2 contains information only about individual donors. So the problem is not Citizens United but rather the long-term trend that basically is related to wealth inequality, not to specific campaign finance policies. A second misunderstanding is that the surging number of small donors in recent elections has mitigated the influence of large donors. While claims about "influence" are not easy to evaluate, it is clear from the data that the increase in small donations has been swamped many times over by the contributions of the wealthy.

In conclusion, there are fundamental political impediments to dealing with income and inequality. The first is the polarized political system, in which many of the policies that might address economic inequality and wealth inequality are the source of that polarization. Thus, we are unlikely to see the necessary bipartisan consensus needed to make progress on inequality. The second is the increased reliance of our political system on the wealthiest of wealthy donors, which is likely to be a very limiting factor on our ability to pursue policies designed to ameliorate income and inequality.

Notes

1. We first noted this association in the mid-1990s, and it continued over the subsequent 25 years. See McCarty, Poole, and Rosenthal (1997).

2. See McCarty (2019, appendix A) for a nontechnical discussion of how the polarization measure is constructed.

3. The figure includes individual contributions to Super PACs and 527 organizations but excludes contributions to nondisclosing 501c(4) organizations. Were it possible to include contributions to nondisclosing 501c(4) organizations, the trend line would likely have been 1%–2% higher in recent elections.

4. Citizens United v. Federal Election Commission, 558 U.S. 310 (2010).

References

Bonica, Adam, Nolan McCarty, Keith T. Poole, and Howard Rosenthal. 2013. "Why Hasn't Democracy Slowed Rising Inequality?" *Journal of Economic Perspectives* 27(3): 103–124.

Bonica, Adam, and Howard Rosenthal. 2015. "The Wealth Elasticity of Political Contributions by the Forbes 400." SSRN 2668780.

McCarty, Nolan. 2019. *Polarization: What Everyone Needs to Know*. Oxford: Oxford University Press.

McCarty, Nolan, Keith T. Poole, and Howard Rosenthal. 1997. *Income Redistribution and the Realignment of American Politics*. Washington, DC: AEI Press.

McCarty, Nolan, Keith T. Poole, and Howard Rosenthal. 2016. *Polarized America: The Dance of Ideology and Unequal Riches*. 2nd ed. Cambridge, MA: MIT Press.

Piketty, Thomas, and Emmanuel Saez. 2003. "Income Inequality in the United States, 1913–1998." *Quarterly Journal of Economics* 118(1): 1–41.

IV
The Distribution of Human Capital

9

A Modern Safety Net

Jesse Rothstein, Lawrence F. Katz, and Michael Stynes

Earnings growth for typical workers slowed starting in the mid-1970s, and for two generations the living standards of most American households have consistently failed to keep pace with the rest of the economy (Economic Policy Institute 2019).

The slow growth of living standards and rising inequality are pressing national problems that affect all parts of American life. They call for rethinking our policies regarding the labor market and the public safety net. In recent discussions with colleagues in academia and the policy world, we've discovered that there's a surprising amount of consensus about policy responses to the problems of earnings stagnation, inequality, and poverty.[1]

Poverty is a major and persistent problem in the United States, and our current safety net system is inadequate. We believe a better-designed system needs to reflect four basic principles: (1) that all children deserve the resources they need to succeed; (2) that work will remain a core part of American society and needs to be better supported; (3) that job losses should not be devastating to families' economic circumstances; and (4) that those who are unable to gain employment deserve a stronger baseline of security.

These four premises call for distinct programs that we discuss in turn. First, however, it is important to recognize that tax and transfer programs can work around the edges to make our increasingly unequal labor market more humane, but they cannot make up for a labor market that fails to deliver for most workers. An economy that delivers broadly shared prosperity will also require an ambitious policy agenda to restore broadly shared wage growth. We turn to labor market policies at the end.

A Child Allowance

Stagnating wages and rising costs make raising children increasingly difficult for low- and middle-income families. Families need help with the costs of raising children. Accumulating evidence indicates that many of these costs are actually investments with high returns. Prenatal care, health care, nutritious food, high-quality child care, and housing in safe neighborhoods pay long-term dividends in children's development and repay taxpayers via increased future tax receipts and lower future transfer payments and criminal justice costs.[2] A society that fails to provide for all children is sacrificing its long-run prosperity.

Such a society is also unjust. Wealthy families are able to invest more in their children than poorer families, and this is a major contributor to intergenerational inequality (Rothstein 2019). You can't have equality of opportunity without broad access to childhood supports.

Other advanced countries—including Canada, the United Kingdom, and Australia—have universal programs to provide income supports to all families with children. In the United States, however, we provide them primarily through the Earned Income Tax Credit and the Child Tax Credit, each available only to families with working parents. The children left out are often the ones who need support the most.

We propose a single unified child allowance, available to all families with children regardless of parental work. This should be at least as generous as the $2,000 per year provided by the current Child Tax Credit (CTC), and it should scale with the number of children, perhaps with a supplement for younger children. Much research shows that extra income in early childhood and increased investments throughout childhood have large long-term benefits (Hoynes 2016; Hendren and Sprung-Keyser 2020). The allowance should be fully refundable so even low-income families who now miss out on the full CTC can benefit. At higher incomes, we would favor phasing it out sooner than the current CTC (say, at around $100,000 per year, close to the ninetieth percentile of the family income distribution).

The child allowance is only one part of a system of family supports. We also need to commit to high-quality supports for education (starting well before kindergarten), health care, parenting support, and decent housing in well-functioning neighborhoods for all children.

In-Work Supports

Our second premise is that work should pay enough to live on. Work is core to most people's lives and will remain so for the foreseeable future, but too many people can only find low-wage work. The Earned Income Tax Credit (EITC), our second-largest antipoverty program after Social Security (Fox 2018), is designed to supplement earnings from work. It has been highly successful. Extensive evidence shows that it has played an important role in drawing single mothers into the workforce, with benefits for both them and their children (Nichols and Rothstein 2015; Hoynes and Rothstein 2017). Moreover, the income support from the EITC not only helps families to meet their basic needs but also helps their kids achieve better long-run outcomes (Dahl and Lochner 2012).

But the EITC for adults without dependent children remains quite small. The principle that work should pay applies to them as well, and we should expand eligibility to ensure all adults can benefit from a sufficient EITC. We should also expand the EITC benefit, which has been stable in real terms even as our economy has grown and inequality has worsened.

Protection against Job Loss

Our dynamic labor market has been a source of prosperity, but dynamism imposes costs for workers and their families. The threat of job loss resulting from circumstances outside one's control is an enormous risk to family well-being. Evidence indicates that job loss leads to declines in earnings for many years thereafter (Davis and von Wachter 2011). Job-loss risk is nearly impossible to insure at an individual level. Unemployment insurance is thus a key part of the public safety net. The Unemployment Insurance program has had essentially the same form since 1935 and makes job loss much less devastating than it would otherwise be. There are no dramatic changes needed here, but reforms should ensure that the program's funding is adequate even for sharp downturns and should recognize that job searches may take longer, often dramatically so, in a deep recession.

A Safety Net for Those Who Don't Work

A humane society should not leave people without basic necessities. We can and should provide baseline support to those without work, beyond the limited duration of unemployment insurance benefits.

The welfare reform of the 1990s effectively eliminated support for nonworkers by making welfare contingent on employment, but work requirements without adequate employment supports have not worked and may have done more to keep eligible needy families from receiving benefits than prevent those who don't need them from participating. Caseloads have fallen dramatically, more than can be justified by the removal of the admittedly perverse incentives of the prereform system (Bitler and

Hoynes 2016). There will always be those who are unable to work or who are unable to find jobs. Supports for nonworkers are needed, especially in times and places with slack labor markets but even when markets are tight.

A general assistance program should provide a baseline floor of consumption for those in difficult circumstances. It should be free of cumbersome work and reporting requirements that serve to lock people out of the benefits they need to get by. It would function as a necessary complement to unconditional support for children and would phase out as the in-work supports phase in, to ensure a smooth transition into the labor market.

Strengthening Worker Bargaining Power

This four-part program we recommend—a universal child allowance, in-work support for all low-wage workers, robust unemployment insurance, and a last-resort safety net for those out of work—would represent a dramatic improvement over our current patchwork system but would not be enough. The median American worker earns less than $40,000 per year on a full-time, full-year basis. This is just 12% higher in real terms than in 1978 (Economic Policy Institute 2019), over a period in which the incomes of the top 1% have tripled (Piketty and Saez 2003, updated). If this median worker does not have children in the house, our transfer package will be of little help. It is simply not feasible to design a transfer program that reaches middle-income workers without shortchanging the truly poor. The only way to help these workers is by redressing the various ways that the labor market has stopped working for middle-class workers in the last two generations.

A range of policies are called for here. First and foremost, we need to maintain tight labor markets, which give workers the ability to say "no" to bad jobs and provide employers the incentive to upgrade job quality to recruit and retain workers. We also need to restore worker bargaining power through other mechanisms.

Bargaining between solitary workers and large employers is typically unbalanced, and the solution requires some form of collective bargaining and a meaningful role for worker voice. The downward wage trends we have seen since the 1970s are closely correlated with the decline of the labor movement. We need to better protect the right to join and form a union. We also need to explore new forms of bargaining that can work in today's low-unionization economy. Recent proposals for expanding the use of wage boards would establish minimum pay standards across states, sectors, and occupations—with worker and employer representatives included in the process—and should be further explored and piloted. Efforts to create bargaining processes should be paired with policies to balance the two sides' bargaining power, such as revamped antitrust measures to address excessive employer market power in the labor market.

Conclusion

Four decades of stagnating living standards and rising inequality have created enormous gaps between productivity and the compensation of typical workers that will not be filled overnight. It will take time to shift our labor market to one in which the benefits of growing productivity are more broadly shared. The policy changes we recommend may not be enough; technology, globalization, and unequal access to education and training opportunities have also contributed to increased labor market inequality.

Labor market policies that push back on the forces of inequality and immobility can help level the playing field, but even at its best, we cannot rely on the labor market to meet all income distribution needs. A redesigned safety net, addressing the four distinct needs we outlined, can complement better labor market policies, ensuring that growing prosperity benefits all Americans.

Notes

1. Our proposals here grew out of a discussion among a group of leading academic experts and former federal policymakers convened by the Jain Family Institute, the University of California Berkeley Opportunity Lab, and the Russell Sage Foundation in summer 2019.

2. We do not fully review this burgeoning literature. Example studies include Chetty, Hendren, and Katz (2016), Hoynes et al. (2019), Hoynes (2016), Elango et al. (2016), and Deming (2009). Broader reviews include Hoynes and Schanzenbach (2018) and Hendren and Sprung-Keyser (2019).

References

Bitler, M., and H. Hoynes. 2016. "Strengthening Temporary Assistance for Needy Families." Policy Proposal 4, The Hamilton Project, Brookings Institution, Washington, DC.

Chetty, R., N. Hendren, and L. F. Katz. 2016. "The Effects of Exposure to Better Neighborhoods on Children: New Evidence from the Moving to Opportunity Experiment." *American Economic Review* 106(4): 855–902.

Dahl, G., and L. Lochner. 2012. "The Impact of Family Income on Child Achievement: Evidence from the Earned Income Tax Credit." *American Economic Review* 102(5): 1927–1956.

Davis, S. J., and T. von Wachter. 2011. "Recessions and the Costs of Job Loss." *Brookings Papers on Economic Activity* 42(2): 1–72.

Deming, D. 2009. "Early Childhood Intervention and Life-Cycle Skill Development: Evidence from Head Start." *American Economic Journal: Applied Economics* 1(3): 111–134.

Economic Policy Institute. 2019. *State of Working America Data Library*. Washington, DC: Economic Policy Institute. https://www.epi.org/data/.

Elango, S., A. Hojman, J.-L. García, and J. J. Heckman. 2016. "Early Childhood Education." In *Economics of Means-Tested Transfer Programs in the United States*, Vol. 2, edited by R. Moffitt, 235–298. Chicago: University of Chicago Press.

Fox, L. 2018. *The Supplemental Poverty Measure: 2017*. Current Population Report P60–265, US Census Bureau, Washington, DC.

Hendren, N., and B. Sprung-Keyser. 2020. "A Unified Welfare Analysis of Government Policies." *Quarterly Journal of Economics* (forthcoming).

Hoynes, H. 2016. "Long-Run Impacts of Childhood Access to the Safety Net." *American Economic Review* 106(4): 903–934.

Hoynes, H., M. Bailey, M. Rossin-Slater, and R. Walker. 2019. "Is the Social Safety Net a Long Term Investment? Large-Scale Evidence from the Food Stamps Program." Working paper. https://gspp.berkeley.edu/assets/uploads/research/pdf/LR_SNAP_BHRSW_042919.pdf.

Hoynes, H., and J. Rothstein. 2017. "Tax Policy toward Low-Income Families." In *The Economics of Tax Policy*, edited by A. Auerbach and K. Smetters, 183–225. Oxford: Oxford University Press.

Hoynes, H., and D. Schanzenbach. 2018. "Safety Net Investments in Children." *Brookings Papers on Economic Activity*.

Nichols, A., and J. Rothstein. 2015. "The Earned Income Tax Credit." In *Economics of Means-Tested Transfer Programs in the United States*, Vol. 1, edited by R. Moffitt, 137–218. Chicago: University of Chicago Press.

Piketty T., and E. Saez. 2003. "Income Inequality in the United States, 1913–1998." *Quarterly Journal of Economics* 118(1): 1–41; for updated data (1917–2017), see https://eml.berkeley.edu/~saez/TabFig2018prel.xls.

Rothstein, J. 2019. "Inequality of Educational Opportunity? Schools as Mediators of the Intergenerational Transmission of Income." *Journal of Labor Economics* 37(S1): S85–S123.

10

Education's Untapped Potential

Tharman Shanmugaratnam

Let me start with what I believe to be the two big questions around education and its potential to act as a leveler and shape a better society.

First, we can no longer be confident that *meritocratic systems* will blunt the advantages and disadvantages that children bring with them from their homes and social backgrounds, at least not in the way that they did in a past era. In many countries, we see increasing polarization rather than leveling of achievements according to social backgrounds—in education, jobs, and lifetime incomes.

Second, and critically important, we have to ask how current education systems, already poorly fitted to the needs of today's labor markets, can prepare young people for a new era of work and help them meet their aspirations. It's not the first time we are experiencing technological change, but we know that the nature and spread of technology's impact on jobs will be different as artificial intelligence (AI) becomes increasingly potent. It is too early to have a confident read on which jobs and human tasks it will displace and which complementary or new jobs will emerge, but we must expect it to *impact a broader swathe of middle-class jobs*, including many more white-collar jobs, than previous waves of automation did. Those are the jobs that much of today's postsecondary education seeks to prepare people for.

We have to address these phase shifts—one in the way social backgrounds are increasingly shaping outcomes in life and the other in the way a more powerful form of digital automation will impact jobs and possibly usher in broader insecurity in the years to come. The combination of the two will be toxic. It will undermine faith in meritocracy itself and in the ability of both the state and markets to give everyone a fair chance of success. *It's a future that we have to avoid.*

How we invest in and organize education has to be at the core of how we tackle these challenges. Indeed, what ails education, particularly in highly decentralized systems like that in the United States, is that we have left it too much to the social and economic marketplace.

The market is not socially neutral. It practices its own forms of "social engineering." It starts with assortative mating, with better-educated individuals marrying each other—that's been on the rise almost everywhere. It continues with the much larger investments that well-off parents make in their children, beginning in the critical early years. That shift has been well documented in the United States—the way higher-educated and better-off parents are doing more to prepare their kids to get into the best preschools, spending much more on enrichment activities, and just spending more time with them.

It continues also in the tendency toward socially segregated neighborhoods. Studies of the US experience have thrown light on how neighborhoods matter, in tangible and intangible ways (Chetty, Hendren, and Katz 2016; Chetty and Hendren 2018). Importantly, too, as neighborhoods become increasingly different, so do schools, and the way teachers are sorted between schools in decentralized systems tends to reinforce the effects of social sorting of students. Finally, these differences in how children grow up is compounded in employment markets, with top-tier employers hiring excessively from the most prestigious universities or based on social pedigree.

Why Education Still Has Significant Potential as a Leveler

Nevertheless, there are several reasons for believing that education has significant untapped potential as a leveler. The first is that we have yet to *achieve scale in quality early interventions*, beginning with maternal health and continuing for children up to age three. This requires public resources, better-trained professionals, and active community involvement. While the evidence is not water-tight, the weight of expert opinion points to quality interventions at this very early stage as being the most effective way to uplift life chances among children born into disadvantage and yielding a significant social return (Heckman 2015; Elango et al. 2016; Ferrarello 2017; Felfe and Lalive 2018). Scaling them up is an opportunity.

The second reason for optimism lies precisely in the *divergent outcomes* we see across geographies, systems, and social backgrounds. It means there is *scope for leveling up*. We see that school systems in different countries have diverse achievement levels and degrees of social mobility. There must surely be scope to adapt and assimilate some of the best practices of systems internationally and achieve some convergence. In the same vein, for the same socioeconomic profile, the significant differences in educational achievement and social mobility outcomes within countries depending on where you grew up illustrate the scope for policies and institutions to close the gaps. Even the fact that children from well-off families are doing much better than before and that the gap between them and poorer children has widened shows what is possible. The relationship between income and achievement is not immutable.

A third reason stems from the *massive inefficiencies in tertiary education*, in a wide range of countries. There is a large mismatch between the demand and supply of skills, particularly for jobs in the broad middle. There is also some mismatch between the types of abilities of students and the pathways they're taking in tertiary education. If we can reduce these mismatches, we unlock significant human capital.

Fourth, there's still a large opportunity to invest in systems of lifelong learning. We are still far from making it the norm for people from *all segments of the workforce*—not just knowledge professionals—to get regular injects of knowhow and skills so they can keep growing over the course of their careers. We have to achieve that in order to arrest the common pattern of blue-collar and average white-collar wages stagnating once people hit middle age, while the upper end of the wage scale continues to grow.

So there's a lot more to be done, and reasons to avoid being pessimistic about education's potential. However, they require fundamental policy rethinking in a number of regards.

How Public Schools Can Underpin High-Performing Systems

One of the common features of the top-performing school systems internationally is that they rest on well-functioning public school systems. The countries at or near the top of the Organization for Economic Cooperation and Development's (OECD) Programme for International Student Assessment (PISA) rankings each achieve their high averages through public schools. In some cases, such as Singapore, the public schools also raise the peaks.

The most well-regarded education systems also have a strong element of government coordination aimed at achieving teacher quality and appropriate curriculum standards throughout the system, even with schools having autonomy in many other regards. There is no country with a decentralized school system in the upper band of the PISA rankings. They may have very strong individual schools, but they do not have high averages.

Sweden is an interesting case study. It decided to decentralize its system and hand schools to the private sector to run in 1992 (OECD 2015). Competition and parental choice—made possible through a universal voucher system—were expected to raise standards. The outcome was instead the sharpest decline in performance of any participating country in PISA between 2000 and 2012, to well below the OECD average. Sweden has sought to improve school accountability since then, but the basic lesson from moving to a decentralized, privately run system is clear. It resulted in greater social sorting and did not level up quality.

We have to take very seriously the idea of running public schools as a system rather than as a collection of individual parts, because that is how we can raise quality across the board. Centralized public school systems can of course be a disaster if they are badly governed or badly funded. But well-governed, well-funded public school systems bring critical advantages. First and foremost, they can do this through the way they develop and deploy their human capital—the teachers and professionals in the school system—through high standards of recruitment, rigorous training, competitive remuneration, and continuous career development through postings across the system. If you leave it to individual schools or even school districts to set standards or compete for teachers, you get extreme unevenness, and weaker districts and schools typically get less experienced teachers.

A second important reason for running schools as a system is to help spread best practices and innovations that crop up in one school to other schools. You do not get that easily in private school systems because the whole idea there is for individual schools to do well for themselves. Singapore also spreads best practices by moving school leaders around in the system every six years or so.

However, a generally neglected issue in public school systems is the need to move away from being egalitarian in form—where every student takes the same standardized curriculum and sits for the same final tests. That uniformity is still the norm in many countries, both advanced and developing, and it serves paradoxically to put down rather than pull up weaker students. The French school system, for example, has been egalitarian in form, but it leads to rather inegalitarian outcomes. A large number of children from blue-collar families end up leaving without a high school diploma (Aghion and Berner 2018). For those who do proceed to university (they can do so as long as they pass any subject in high school), a large number drop out after their first year, and some 70% do not complete their studies within three years (Lichfield 2015). French president

Emmanuel Macron's education reforms are changing this—including stronger technical and vocational education pathways and the introduction of selective university admission. They are bold because they are changing what it means to be egalitarian.

Rethinking Higher Education

We have to rethink higher education if we are to reduce the large mismatch of skills in labor markets and better develop the potential of a whole spectrum of young people.

We have taken the college premium too simplistically and shaped too much policy and politics around it. Encouraging more high school graduates to go to college is not going to earn them the college premium. The premium commonly cited is an average, but the distribution around the average deserves greater light of day. It has long been the case that those in the bottom quintile of college graduates in the United States earn a very small premium over high school graduates (Abel and Deitz 2014). That's among those who graduate; in fact, 40% of those who enroll in universities in the United States don't complete a degree within six years (National Center for Education Statistics 2019). Of those who do, a substantial proportion—some 40%—do not end up working at jobs that require a college degree (Abel, Deitz, and Su 2014). Graduate underemployment is likewise widespread in parts of Asia, such as India.

The real question for young people, and for public policy, is not whether they should stop after high school or go on to college. It must be about the form of tertiary education—academic or applied, traditional or dual/cooperative, two-year or four-year—that will best secure a skills premium and help them climb a ladder of skills in their careers.

We have overexpanded the traditional, academically oriented model of tertiary education in too many countries and need to *rebalance in favor of applied learning*. The theory of change is that people discover their abilities and interests when they do something applied. This does not mean we should focus their learning on specific or hard skills. We have to develop in them the broader set of soft and hard skills that will enable them to keep adapting throughout their lives. But neither can it be said that a traditional or liberal arts education is the only way, or even the best way, to develop soft skills such as creativity, teamwork, and cross-cultural skills. We can and must pay attention to developing these skills through the applied route as well.

Lifelong Learning: Beyond the Mantra

Lifelong learning has become a mantra everywhere, but we have a long way to go. It requires strong tripartite and other social partnerships to work well.

We have to recognize, however, that there is a difference in the motivations and incentives of firms and workers. The firm would typically want to focus training on the skills specific to its needs. Workers have the incentive to pick up skills that help them develop their careers—which will inevitably take them to other employers or even other sectors.

In Denmark, most training is supported by employers but conducted by public institutions. People are able to attend a course they desire, even if it does not match their employer's immediate needs. In some other Northern European countries, however, firm-specific training dominates. We need a balance between the two approaches, even as we step up both.

Above all, we need greater strategic focus in public policy on reskilling and upskilling workers. Past eras of technological progress led to a movement of labor from low-productivity to higher-productivity activities, such as from initially low-productivity agricultural work to manufacturing and later to modern services. That followed Arthur Lewis's description of economic development. Now, we see *a reverse Lewisian movement in several advanced economies*, with a new wave of digital automation pushing people from relatively higher-productivity manufacturing jobs into lower-productivity and lower-wage services jobs. It's a trend we have to avert.

The most careful studies point to the potential for future tasks and jobs that complement the new technologies, including AI, and for new areas of work to emerge. But *whether we get there depends on what we do now*—to develop coalitions of industry, government bodies, unions, and educational institutions that anticipate these new job demands in each sector and curate programs that enable people to develop new skills and stay in a high-productivity sphere of activity. We've got to get on with it.

References

Abel, R. Jaison, and Richard Deitz. 2014. "College May Not Pay Off for Everyone." *Federal Reserve Bank of New York Liberty Street Economics (*blog), September 4, 2014.

Abel, R. Jaison, Richard Deitz, and Yaqin Su. 2014. "Are Recent College Graduates Finding Good Jobs?" *Current Issues in Economics and Finance.* New York: Federal Reserve Bank of New York.

Aghion, Philippe, and Benedicte Berner. 2018. "Macron's Education Revolution." *Project Syndicate*, March 7, 2018.

Chetty, Raj, and Nathaniel Hendren. 2018. "The Effects of Neighborhoods on Intergenerational Mobility I: Childhood Exposure Effects." *Quarterly Journal of Economics* 133(3): 1107–1162.

Chetty, Raj, and Nathaniel Hendren. 2018. "The Effects of Neighborhoods on Intergenerational Mobility II: County Level Estimates." *Quarterly Journal of Economics* 133(3): 1163–1228.

Chetty, Raj, Nathaniel Hendren, and Lawrence F. Katz. 2016. "The Effects of Exposure to Better Neighborhoods on Children: New Evidence from the Moving to Opportunity Experiment." *American Economic Review* 106(4): 855–902.

Elango, Sneha, Jorge Luis García, James J. Heckman, and Andrés Hojman. 2016. "Early Childhood Education." In *Economics of Means-Tested Transfer Programs in the United States II*, edited by R. Moffitt, R, 235–298. Chicago: University of Chicago Press.

Felfe, Christina, and Rafael Lalive. 2018. "Does Early Child Care Affect Children's Development?" *Journal of Public Economics* 159: 33–53.

Ferrarello, Molli. 2017. "Does Pre-K Work? Brookings Experts Weigh In on America's Early Childhood Education Debate." *Brookings Now* (blog), May 26, 2017.

Heckman, James. 2015. "Pre-K Researchers Can't Get Past the Third Grade." *The Hechinger Report*, October 15, 2015. https://hechingerreport.org/pre-k -researchers-cant-get-past-the-third-grade/.

Lichfield, John. 2015. "French Universities Crisis: Low Fees and Selection Lotteries Create Headaches in Higher Education." *The Independent*, September 25, 2015. www.independent.co.uk/news/world/europe/french-universities-crisis-low -fees-and-selection-lotteries-create-headaches-in-higher-education-10517241 .html.

Organization for Economic Cooperation and Development (OECD). 2015. *Improving Schools in Sweden: An OECD Perspective*. OECD Publishing, Paris.

U.S. Department of Education, National Center for Education Statistics (NCES). 2019. *The Condition of Education 2019* (2019-144), Undergraduate Retention and Graduation Rates. Washington, DC: National Center for Education Statistics.

V

Policies toward Trade, Outsourcing, and Foreign Investment

11

Why Was the "China Shock" So Shocking–and What Does This Mean for Policy?

David Autor

China's meteoric rise as a world manufacturing power commenced in the early 1990s and was heralded and amplified by its elevation to Permanent Normal Trading Status with the United States and accession to the World Trade Organization at the start of the new millennium. A rapidly growing body of literature finds that China's subsequent export surge, which drove the US merchandise trade deficit from 2.7% to 5.7% of GDP between 1998 and 2007, left large and enduring scars on aggregate US manufacturing employment, on workers initially employed in manufacturing establishments competing with China, and on local labor markets specializing in labor-intensive manufacturing, in which China gained comparative advantage (Bernard, Jensen, and Schott 2006; Autor, Dorn, and Hanson 2013; Autor et al. 2014; Ebenstein et al. 2014; Acemoglu et al. 2016; Autor, Dorn, and Hanson 2016; Caliendo, Dvorkin, and Parro 2019).

The scale and duration of these impacts, known collectively as the "China shock," took economists and policymakers by surprise and initially faced some skepticism from trade scholars.[1] One does not have to be a trade theorist or an industrial engineer, however, to notice that the precipitous fall in US manufacturing that began in the late 1990s and continued for almost fifteen years was without parallel in the post-Depression era and that it had no plausible technological origin.[2]

Was there something especially severe about the China shock? Or was there something especially vulnerable about China-shocked places within the United States?[3] And how do the answers to these questions inform our thinking about adjustments to labor market shocks going forward?[4]

Context: Declining Labor Market Fluidity

Since the early 1980s, three fundamental dynamics of the US labor market have been shifting in a direction that increased the vulnerability of less-educated workers to adverse labor demand shocks.

The first is that the real and relative earnings of US workers who hadn't attended college—meaning those with high school or lower education—have either stagnated or fallen since 1980. This development was particularly adverse for non-college-educated men. Importantly, these men were at that time (and are to this day) heavily overrepresented in US manufacturing. In 1980, 22.9% of all US workers, 27.2% of all male workers, 27.4% of all non-college-educated workers, and 31.2% of all non-college-educated male workers were employed in manufacturing.[5] Labor demand was shifting sharply against non-college-educated workers even prior to the China shock, and non-college men were doubly exposed, because of both prevailing wage trends and their overrepresentation in manufacturing.

A second fundamental shift occurring simultaneously was the slowing or reversal of the strong force of regional income convergence that had prevailed in the United States during the first three decades after World War II (Barro 1992; Berry and Glaeser 2005; Moretti 2011; Austin, Glaeser, and Summers 2018). For reasons that remain poorly understood, income levels across states and Metropolitan Statistical Areas essentially stopped converging after 1980 (Berry and Glaeser 2005; Ganong and Shoag 2017; Austin, Glaeser, and Summers 2018). Whereas high local unemployment rates did not tend to persist for more than a few years in the first four postwar decades (Blanchard and Katz 1992), they became substantially more persistent from the mid-1980s onward (Russ and Shambaugh 2019). Simultaneously, the frequency of US household moves at every distance (between addresses, across counties, and across states) fell by roughly half between 1980 and 2019 (Molloy et al. 2016). These attenuating forces of arbitrage imply that local labor markets likely became *more local* in recent decades.

A final fundamental shift is that the robust urban wage premium that prevailed among workers with and without a college education in the postwar era *flattened* after 1990 among non-college-educated workers. In the years between (at least) 1950 and 1990, both groups earned substantially more in dense urban locations (Autor 2019). After 1990, however, the urban wage premium for workers with and without college diverged, becoming slightly steeper for the former group and *substantially* shallower for the latter group—losing approximately two-thirds of its slope between 1990 and 2015 (Baum-Snow, Freedman, and Pavan 2018; Autor 2019). While this pattern is less well known than the changing patterns of regional nonconvergence (and even more poorly understood), it is plausibly related—suggesting that even as wages for those without college were weakening, the urban wage premium available to these workers was rapidly eroding. Accordingly, urban labor markets likely offered less of an escape route for less-educated workers facing weak local labor markets, and this may in turn (partly) explain the slowing mobility of workers with no college to highly educated, high-wage regions (Ganong and Shoag 2017).

Putting these pieces together, the US labor market after 1980 was becoming less fluid and more brittle than in prior decades. These tectonic shifts created great vulnerability to the China shock.

Reversal of Fortune: The Geography of the China Shock

Although it is conventional wisdom that US manufacturing employment has been on the wane since the end of World War II, this view conflates the *share* of employment in manufacturing with the number of workers in manufacturing. Apart from cyclical fluctuations, the number of workers employed in US manufacturing grew more or less steadily from 1945 to 1979, increasing from 12.5 million workers in late 1945 to 19.3 million workers in late 1979. The numerical erosion of US manufacturing employment commenced with the deep early 1980s recession, which was particularly damaging to heavy industry in the upper Midwest. Net US manufacturing employment gradually contracted by two million workers over the 20 years between 1979 and 1999 (i.e., prior to China's WTO accession).

Despite this aggregate decline, employment in labor-intensive manufacturing was either steady or *rising* (until 2000) in the South Atlantic, East South Central, and West South Central regions of the United States. These regions, where labor unions were largely absent and wage and education levels were low, held a comparative advantage in labor-intensive manufacturing.[6] These regions would soon face stiff competition from another low-wage, nonunion, labor-intensive manufacturing location, however: China.

While it is widely understood that commuting zones (CZs) exposed to China's rise saw steep manufacturing employment losses since 2000, figure 11.1 shows that the precursor to these recent losses was a pronounced increase in manufacturing employment in the 1970s. Reflecting the southern migration of US manufacturing during this decade (Fort, Pierce, and Schott 2018; Russ and Shambaugh 2019), the fraction of adults without a college degree employed in manufacturing in *future* China-exposed CZs rose steeply in both relative and absolute terms in the 1970s. This rise was fleeting, however. The fraction of these adults employed in manufacturing fell differentially in China-exposed CZs in

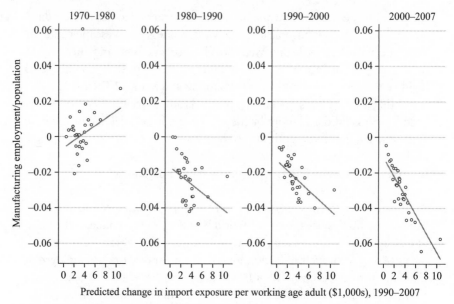

Figure 11.1
Commuting zone level bin scatters of decadal change in manufacturing employment to population rate among workers without college versus China shock exposure during 1990–2007. This figure plots the estimated decadal change in the fraction of non-college-educated adult CZ residents ages 16 to 64 who are employed in manufacturing against the predicted change in import exposure per worker between 1990 and 2007. Each point in the bin scatter represents one-thirtieth of non-college-educated adults at the start of the decade. Regression line is fit to 722 CZ level observations weighted by the number of adult CZ residents at the start of the decade.

both the 1980s and 1990s—before plummeting between 2000 and 2007 as Chinese imports surged.

Though not depicted in this figure, real wages were simultaneously rising rapidly in the 1980s among non-college-educated workers in future China-exposed CZs, even as wages for non-college-educated men were falling sharply nationwide. But this positive wage trend moderated in the 1990s as import competition from China rose. It then reversed dramatically between 2000 and 2007 as China-exposed CZs bore the brunt of rising import competition.

As manufacturing employment dropped in China-exposed CZs, the rate of *overall* employment to population among workers without college degrees fell along with it. Why were these workers not quickly reabsorbed by other employers? One critical piece of the explanation is the surge in the merchandise trade deficit during these same years (Autor,

Dorn, and Hanson 2013). When the United States began importing manufactured goods far in excess of its exports, this almost necessarily meant that US manufacturing employment would have to contract. For China-exposed local labor markets to maintain constant employment, displaced manufacturing workers would have had to rapidly find employment in entirely new lines of work outside manufacturing. That was unlikely to happen quickly, particularly among less-educated adults.

In sum, China's rise heralded a swift reversal of fortune for labor-intensive Southern US manufacturing. The local labor markets most exposed to China's rise in the 1990s and the next decade were those that most benefited from US manufacturing's southern migration during the two preceding decades.

Some Nonshocking Conclusions

The labor market adjustment challenges facing the United States precede and supersede its trade adjustment problems. The China shock laid these issues bare but did not cause them. It did, however, afflict places that arguably had the fewest outside options. Had China's rise never occurred, these regions would surely have eventually ceded their labor-intensive manufacturing activities to other low-wage countries. But this process would have been more gradual and less "shocking."

Given what we now know about the speed and magnitude of the China shock and the unpreparedness of the US labor market to absorb this shock, it's no longer heretical to say that *gradualism* rather than shock therapy would have made for better trade policy toward China's rise in the early twenty-first century. But the United States is unlikely to see another China trade shock in the coming decades—neither from China nor from another country. Focusing our policy on adapting to future China shocks would be a case of fighting the last war.

The labor market challenges ahead appear more likely to stem from new technologies that may accelerate the pace of automation, such as robotics and artificial intelligence (see Acemoglu and Restrepo 2019, 2020). These automation impacts, and accompanying labor market changes, will likely be *less* regionally concentrated and *slower moving* than the China shock but they will require substantial labor market adjustments nevertheless. The China shock offers overwhelming evidence that the US labor market is ill-prepared to make such adjustments.

How can we facilitate those adjustments? The United States already has one large-scale public program aimed at facilitating worker adjustment to involuntary job loss: the Trade Adjustment Assistance (TAA) program, which couples retraining incentives with extended unemployment insurance for displaced workers. As its name implies, TAA is aimed exclusively at assisting trade-displaced workers and hence cannot (as currently configured) assist workers facing technological disruptions. This constraint would matter little if TAA was ineffective, but recent quasi-experimental analysis suggests otherwise. Workers quasi-randomly assigned to receive TAA support experience a substantial boost in employment and earnings for a full decade after treatment (Hyman 2018). This evidence does not imply that TAA is a model program, but it demonstrates that we have tools in the toolbox.[7] We should deploy those tools more broadly while simultaneously investing in innovation and evaluation to make them more effective. And as is by now self-evident, we should *not* condition workers' access to adjustment assistance on whether the proximate cause of job displacement is trade, technology, or some other unanticipated shock.

Even if TAA had been massively reinforced during the China shock, however, it could not possibly have redressed the damage done by a major manufacturing upheaval—or by decades of earnings and employment stagnation faced by workers without a college degree. Such after-the-fact reskilling and redistribution programs cannot undo these concentrated harms or the adverse trends that preceded them. As a profession, we economists should think broadly and analytically about how to fortify institutions and shape labor markets, as Blanchard and Rodrik urge in their introduction to this volume, to restore opportunity to the majority of workers who lack a four-year college degree.[8] Perhaps the most consequential lesson of the China shock is that this long-festering problem will not take care of itself.

Notes

1. Houseman (2018) provides a lucid analysis of why the conventional wisdom attributing falling US manufacturing to rising productivity does not apply to the 1990s and the next decade.

2. US manufacturing employment fell by 20.4%, from 17.3 million to 13.8 million workers, between November 1999 and November 2007 (US Bureau of Labor Statistics, series CES3000000001), prior to the start of the Great Recession. It dropped by a further two million workers during the Great Recession period from December 2007 to June 2009 (see https://www.nber.org/cycles.html), for a cumulative fall of 32.1%. Given that trade volumes fell precipitously during the recession, this latter fall was probably not caused by import competition.

3. A separate question deserving study, though not here, is why these effects were so shocking to economists.

4. My substantive arguments here parallel those in the excellent recent working papers by Eriksson et al. (2019) and Russ and Shambaugh (2019). The (modest) data analysis presented here is original to my presentation at the Peterson Institute for International Economics, as are many of the specifics of the argument.

5. Author's calculations based on 1980 Census IPUMS for adults age 16–64, weighting by annual hours worked. In the same year, 17.1% of all working women and 22.4% of all working non-college-educated women were employed in manufacturing.

6. These groupings are as follows. New England: CT, ME, MA, NH, RI, VT; East North Central: IN, IL, MI, OH, WI; Middle Atlantic: NJ, NY, PA; South Atlantic: DE, DC, FL, GA, MD, NC, SC, VA, WV; East South Central: AL, KY, MS, TN; West South Central: AR, LA, OK, TX.

7. For further details on training programs for non-college-educated adults that have shown good results under experimental evaluation, see the discussion of sectoral training programs in Autor, Li, and Notowidigdo (2019).

8. See Autor, Mindell, and Reynolds (2019) for policy ideas on shaping innovation and institutions to improve the future of work.

References

Acemoglu, Daron, and Pascual Restrepo. 2019. "The Wrong Kind of AI? Artificial Intelligence and the Future of Labor Demand." Working Paper 25682, National Bureau of Economic Research, Cambridge, MA.

Acemoglu, Daron, and Pascual Restrepo. 2020. "Robots and Jobs: Evidence from US Labor Markets." *Journal of Political Economy* 128(6): 2188–2244.

Acemoglu, Daron, David Autor, David Dorn, Gordon H. Hanson, and Brendan Price. 2016. "Import Competition and the Great US Employment Sag of the 2000s." *Journal of Labor Economics* 34(S1): S141–S198.

Austin, Benjamin, Edward Glaeser, and Lawrence Summers. 2018. "Jobs for the Heart-land: Place-Based Policies in 21st Century America." *Brookings Papers on Economic Activity* Spring: 151–240.

Autor, David, David Dorn, and Gordon H. Hanson. 2013. "The China Syndrome: Local Labor Market Effects of Import Competition in the United States." *American Economic Review* 103(6): 2121–2168.

Autor, David, Anran Li, and Matthew Notowidigdo. 2019. "Preparing for the Work of the Future: A Research Agenda." Technical Report, J-PAL: North America.

Autor, David, David A. Mindell, and Elizabeth B. Reynolds. 2019. "The Work of the Future: Shaping Technology and Institutions." MIT Work of the Future Task Force Report, Massachusetts Institute of Technology, Cambridge, MA.

Autor, David H. 2019. "Work of the Past, Work of the Future." *AEA Papers and Proceedings* 109: 1–32.

Autor, David H., David Dorn, and Gordon H. Hanson. 2016. "The China Shock: Learning from Labor Market Adjustment to Large Changes in Trade." *Annual Review of Economics* 8(1): 205–240.

Autor, David H., David Dorn, Gordon H. Hanson, and Jae Song. 2014. "Trade Adjustment: Worker-Level Evidence." *Quarterly Journal of Economics* 129(4): 1799–1860.

Barro, Robert J. 1992. "Convergence." *Journal of Political Economy* 100(2): 223–251.

Baum-Snow, Nathaniel, Matthew Freedman, and Ronni Pavan. 2018. "Why Has Urban Inequality Increased?" *AEA: Applied Economics* 10(4): 1–42.

Bernard, Andrew B., J. Bradford Jensen, and Peter K. Schott. 2006. "Survival of the Best Fit: Exposure to Low-Wage Countries and the (Uneven) Growth of U.S. Manufacturing Plants." *Journal of International Economics* 68(1): 219–237.

Berry, Christopher R., and Edward L. Glaeser. 2005. "The Divergence of Human Capital Levels across Cities." *Papers in Regional Science* 84(3): 407–444.

Blanchard, Olivier Jean, and Lawrence F. Katz. 1992. "Regional Evolutions." *Brookings Papers on Economic Activity* 1: 1–75.

Caliendo, Lorenzo, Maximiliano Dvorkin, and Fernando Parro. 2019. "Trade and Labor Market Dynamics: General Equilibrium Analysis of the China Trade Shock." *Econometrica* 87(3): 741–835.

Ebenstein, Avraham, Ann Harrison, Margaret McMillan, and Shannon Phillips. 2014. "Estimating the Impact of Trade and Offshoring on American Workers Using the Current Population Surveys." *Review of Economics and Statistics* 96(4): 581–595.

Eriksson, Katherine, Katheryn Russ, Jay C. Shambaugh, and Minfei Xu. 2019. "Trade Shocks and the Shifting Landscape of U.S. Manufacturing." Working Paper 25646, National Bureau of Economic Research, Cambridge, MA.

Fort, Teresa C., Justin R. Pierce, and Peter K. Schott. 2018. "New Perspectives on the Decline of US Manufacturing Employment." *Journal of Economic Perspectives* 32(2): 47–72.

Ganong, Peter, and Daniel Shoag. 2017. "Why Has Regional Income Convergence in the U.S. Declined?" *Journal of Urban Economics* 102:76–90.

Houseman, Susan N. 2018. "Understanding the Decline of U.S. Manufacturing Employment." Technical Report 18–287, Kalamazoo, MI: W. E. Upjohn Institute.

Hyman, Benjamin. 2018. "Can Displaced Labor Be Retrained? Evidence from Quasi-random Assignment to Trade Adjustment Assistance." Working paper, University of Chicago.

Molloy, Raven, Christopher L. Smith, Ricardo Trezzi, and Abigail Wozniak. 2016. "Un-derstanding Declining Fluidity in the U.S. Labor Market." *Brookings Papers on Economic Activity* 47(1): 183–259.

Moretti, Enrico. 2011. "Local Labor Markets." In *Handbook of Labor Economics*, Vol. 4, 1237–1313. Amsterdam: Elsevier.

Russ, Katheryn, and Jay Shambaugh. 2019. "Education and Unequal Regional Labor Market Outcomes: The Persistence of Regional Shocks and Employment Responses to Trade Shocks." Working paper, Federal Reserve Bank of Boston.

US Bureau of Labor Statistics. 2019. "Employment, Hours, and Earnings from the Current Employment Statistics Survey (National)." Series CES3000000001. https://data.bls.gov/timeseries/CES3000000001.

12

Trade, Labor Markets, and the China Shock: What Can Be Learned from the German Experience?

Christian Dustmann

Introduction

Trade creates net benefits for consumers and producers alike and raises GDP (see, among many others, Romer and Frankel 1999; Alcala and Ciccone 2004; Samuelson 1962). However, it also has distributional effects. Evidence from the integration of China into the global economy indicates that detrimental effects of trade were concentrated among specific groups of workers, predominantly those who worked in industries that compete with imported goods (for the United States, see Autor, Dorn, and Hanson 2013; Pierce and Schott 2016; for Germany, see Dauth, Findeisen, and Südekum 2014).

One way to limit the distributional effects of trade on workers would be simply to tax it out of existence via high tariffs on imports. This "solution" is sometimes propagated by politicians,[1] but it is certainly not a policy many economists would agree with. Another approach is to continue reaping the benefits from trade but ensure that those in danger of losing out are appropriately prepared to fend off any negative consequences and/or are appropriately compensated.

I want to focus here on the second point. To do that, I would like to propose some insights based on the German experience, which was different from that of the United States in many respects, and address the issue from the perspective of a labor economist.

Trade with China and the German Experience

A number of recent works have shown that the substantial increase in imports to the United States from China in recent decades led to large but highly concentrated negative labor market outcomes for those workers most exposed to these imports (Autor, Dorn, and Hanson 2013; Pierce and

Schott 2016). While US exports grew as well during this period, the change in export flows was much smaller and thus not able to offset the negative import effects for the workers most harmed.[2] A key question that arises is whether this experience has been repeated in other industrialized countries.

Germany, the world's fourth-largest economy, is an interesting case. While the United States had a large and growing trade deficit, Germany had an account surplus and relatively balanced trade with China (Dauth, Findeisen, and Südekum 2017). Its annual trade balance with China increased by about $36 billion from 2000 to 2014, while the US trade balance decreased by $196 billion during the same period, according to data from the World Input Output Database (Timmer et al. 2014). That happened despite the fact that Germany was not only affected by the "China shock" but experienced a twin shock, with large increases in imports from emerging economies in Eastern Europe and threats in manufacturing industries of outsourcing to these economies from the early 1990s onward. The value of German goods imports from China grew from $8.34 billion in 1993 to $103.33 billion in 2015, while imports from Eastern European countries grew from $23.42 billion in 1993 to $188.54 billion in 2015, according to UN Comtrade data (see United Nations International Labour Organization 2019; United Nations Statistics Division 2019).

Despite these large import shocks, it is fair to say that Germany largely benefited from trade with China and Eastern Europe, with little evidence of overall negative effects on its labor market (Dauth, Findeisen, and Südekum 2014). That does not mean that there were no losers, as illustrated, for example, by Klein, Moser, and Urban (2010), Dauth, Findeisen, and Südekum (forthcoming), and others. However, the large negative effects that certain workers in more import-exposed US labor markets experienced because of the China shock were largely absent from the German experience. Moreover, some workers saw significant gains as a result of rising export exposure not only to China but also to Eastern Europe. Dauth, Findeisen, and Südekum (forthcoming) find that workers in highly export-exposed industries saw gains both at their original job and through switching to other firms within the same industry, the latter channel being especially important for high-skilled workers. We find corroborating evidence in preliminary work illustrating that the positive effects of these export shocks extended up the production chain to intermediate industries (de Ruijter and Dustmann 2019). This amplification of positive export shocks came through both Germany's and other countries' increased exports to China and Eastern Europe. Manufacturing employment, the big loser from increased trade with China in the

United States, was a net beneficiary in Germany. While manufacturing employment declined by about 10% from 2000 to 2018 in Germany, much in line with an ongoing shift toward service industries throughout developed countries and labor-saving technological change, manufacturing employment dropped by over 23% in the United States during the same period, according to data from the United Nations International Labor Organization (2019). Also, trade with China has not been identified as a negative factor for Germany in public debate, again unlike in the United States.[3] Understanding the reasons for these differences may be a key ingredient in preparing for future challenges to the labor market, be they from future trade shocks, technology shocks, or immigration.

What Makes Germany Different?

Thus, the same trade shock had apparently opposite effects on two highly industrialized open economies, Germany and the United States, with Germany sustaining balanced trade accounts with China while the United States experienced a large and increasing trade deficit.

There are potentially four aspects that contribute to explaining these differences. First, one important factor is Germany's industry structure, being highly competitive in the production of goods demanded by China's expanding industrial sector as well as in high-end automobiles for China's increasingly wealthy consumers, while benefiting from imports of upstream Chinese goods that reduce costs of production and enhance German competitiveness. Hardly any research has looked into changes in labor market outcomes for countries outside the United States resulting from the production chain effects of China's growth. De Ruijter and Dustmann (2019) find that the effects of growth in Chinese (and Eastern European) demand and productive capacity led to significantly increased labor demand for German workers in both the manufacturing and services sectors. While direct changes in trade flows significantly increased demand for workers in the manufacturing sector, upstream effects were nearly as large. Changes in labor demand for service workers were nearly as large (in absolute terms) as those for manufacturing workers, but the effect came nearly entirely via upstream effects. Moreover, and in contrast to the United States, which has long been a more insular country economically, we find that Germany greatly benefits from greater economic integration with its neighbors and those farther afield. Exports from third countries to China drove increased demand for German workers via increased demand for German intermediate inputs.

Second, the trade shock with China was also felt differently in Germany than in its industrialized continental European neighbors, such as France (Malgouyres 2017) and Italy (Federico 2014), which were more negatively affected. One important contributor to these differences lies in more flexible industrial relations in Germany, which are set outside the policy domain. Other European countries with more rigid labor market regulations saw firms struggle in the face of import competition (for an excellent example in Portugal, see Branstetter et al. 2019). In the late 1990s and early the next decade, German industry responded more flexibly to trade challenges first from Eastern Europe and then from China through downward adjustment of wages, in particular at the lower end of the wage distribution. This became possible partly through the opening up of region- and industry-wide wage agreements for firms that were under particular pressure, where new agreements were then negotiated at the firm level between employers, unions, and work councils. While this led to a widening of the wage gap at the low end of the wage distribution from the mid-1990s onward (see Dustmann, Ludsteck, and Schoenberg 2009), it also helped the competitiveness of German industry and kept production and jobs in the country (see Dustmann et al. 2014; see also Baumgarten and Lehwald 2019, who demonstrate that flexibility).

Third, Germany's industrial relations and vocational education system are likely to have helped it respond to the trade shock differently than the United States. This different response may have had two main sources: better preparedness and willingness of firms to retrain workers, and better preparedness of the workforce to reskill and upskill. This is illustrated in a slightly different context in a recent paper by Battisti, Dustmann, and Schönberg (2019) on the effects of technological and organizational change (T&O) on workers. They show that although T&O reduces firm demand and eliminates routine-task jobs relative to abstract-task jobs, affected *workers* who held these jobs faced no higher probability of non-employment or lower wage growth than unaffected workers. Rather, firms that adopt T&O play an important and active role in curtailing its potentially harmful effects by offering affected workers retraining opportunities to upgrade to jobs that are more abstract. Firms thus seem to play an active role in ameliorating the possibly harmful effects of T&O. Negative employment effects appear only for workers older than 55, regardless of educational background. A very interesting aspect is that retraining effects are largest for workers in firms that run large apprenticeship training programs and have strong union representation. Thus, what seems essential here is that firms already have the "technology" in place to retrain and upskill workers—which is the case for firms that have training programs in place to train apprentices. Moreover, unions in Germany strongly insist on retraining activities, and firing workers in firms with high levels of union representation is generally more costly. This reinforces an important point: it is worthwhile for firms to retrain workers if the alternative of firing them and hiring better-skilled workers induces higher costs.

Fourth, another key aspect is how prepared workers are to absorb shocks induced by trade or technology. If occupational skills are highly specific and tailored only to very particular production processes (particularly if acquired in a learning-by-doing way), it may be difficult for workers to be reskilled, as the complementary understanding that supports such skill transformation can be lacking. For instance, for workers employed in the toolmaking industry, knowledge about supportive IT technology, physical properties of materials, and more general insight into production chains will help when reskilling and upskilling. Thus, occupational training that combines on the job training with more fundamental occupation-specific and academic knowledge will add considerable flexibility to retraining possibilities, in contrast to forms of on the job learning where workers acquire skills for only a very specific set of occupational tasks. This increased aptitude for retraining can facilitate and ease workers' switches from import-affected industries to export-oriented industries within the same or a similar occupation group.

The German apprenticeship system provides occupation-specific knowledge acquisition that may help workers respond flexibly to shocks in the future by preparing them for particular occupations through a combination of workplace-based occupation-specific general knowledge and school-based abstract and academic skills (see Dustmann and Schönberg 2012). A broader understanding of occupation-specific production processes therefore helps support the upgrade of skills that involve new technologies. Thus, while for instance the trade shocks of the 1990s and the next decade may have led to the manufacturing of simple tools being delegated to Chinese or Eastern European producers, manufacturing of precision tools may have experienced new export opportunities. Cheaper upstream imports and new export markets support production, while workers' broader skill base facilitated switching from the production of standard tools to the production of precision tools.

A further important aspect of the German apprenticeship training system is that it develops a wide range of inherent abilities, such as creative skills and manual abilities, talents that may go wasted in an education system focused solely on the development of academic talent. Consequently, it raises the productivity of a far larger pool of workers and provides career opportunities for workers whose poor academic abilities would otherwise restrict them to poorly paid and volatile employment opportunities. Moreover, at the level of the economy, the development of nonacademic skills creates comparative advantage in the production of goods that require such inputs. Thus, broad occupation-related training programs, combined with opportunities for lifelong skill development and possibilities for upskilling and reskilling, seem like crucial ingredients for preparing workers for labor market shocks from trade, technology, or migration.

Discussion and Conclusions

The China shock is in large part over: trade balances have leveled off since around 2014, and there are signs that China's economic growth is weakening and that its economy is increasingly oriented domestically. Any future shocks will most likely look quite different from the recent China shock and may emanate from a different region. India and Southeast Asia are already exporting significantly more than in the past, while Africa's population of over 1.2 billion, projected by the United Nations to more than double to 2.5 billion by 2050, means that it will eventually be a significant economic force as well. Future shocks may also be of an entirely different character: cheaper transportation and global communication means that large-scale migration is more feasible than ever before; automation of production, including artificial intelligence (AI), has significant economic promise but also presents significant peril; and the full nature of the coming climate change shocks is not yet apparent. It is unlikely that the economic shocks of the future will affect the same workers, in the same ways, as the China shock did. For that reason, by focusing the policy discussion on trade policy exclusively, we may overlook other looming challenges. Instead, it may be more fruitful to discuss how to design industrial policies, labor market policies, and education and training policies so that modern economies can adapt flexibly to a range of possible shocks. These policies should emphasize improved worker-firm relationships and firm-based training, so that countries have flexible workforces that can reskill and upskill in response to changing economic landscapes. In this way, countries can ensure that labor markets are resilient while still remaining competitive.

Notes

I would like to thank Stan de Ruijter for research assistance and many constructive comments.

1. The Trump administration's trade war with China is the most prominent recent example of a politician advocating protectionist measures in an effort to protect jobs, but it has many corollaries both in the United States (e.g., the infamous Depression-exacerbating Smoot-Hawley Tariff Act of 1930) and internationally (e.g., UKIP and other Euroskeptic parties).

2. Some recent work by trade economists shows that nevertheless the United States did benefit from the export opportunities trade with China created, and that any overall net negative employment effects of trade with China may have been almost entirely offset by increased exports alone (Feenstra, Ma, and Xu 2019). However, note that this does not contradict earlier findings: workers benefiting from export growth are not necessarily those harmed by import competition; negative distributional effects are thus still very possible because of the concentrated nature of the effects of Chinese import growth.

3. While President Trump has consistently characterized China as stealing from ("ripping off") the United States, no similar rhetoric has emerged in any significant way in Germany. The most prominent populist movement, the far right AfD, has not come out in favor of increased protectionism beyond general Euroskepticism. Meanwhile, prominent politicians have generally not been shy about publicizing efforts to strengthen ties with China (see, e.g., www.reuters.com/article/us-germany-china/germany-and-china-vow-to-deepen -ties-amid-trump-concerns-idUSKBN18S4CC and www.cnbc.com/2019/01 /18/germany-and-china-pledge-to-open-markets-deepen-financial-cooperation .html).

References

Alcala, Francisco, and Antonio Ciccone. 2004. "Trade and Productivity." *Quarterly Journal of Economics* 119(2): 613–646.

Autor, David H., David Dorn, and Gordon H. Hanson. 2013. "The China Syndrome: Local Labor Market Effects of Import Competition in the United States." *American Economic Review* 103(6): 2121–2168.

Battisti, Michele, Christian Dustmann, and Uta Schönberg. 2019. "Technological and Organizational Change and the Careers of Workers." University College London, mimeo.

Baumgarten, Daniel and Sybille Lehwald. 2019. "Trade Exposure and the Decline in Collective Bargaining: Evidence from Germany," CESifo Working Paper Series 7754, CESifo Group Munich.

Branstetter, Lee G., Brian K. Kovak, Jacqueline Mauro, and Ana Venancio. 2019. "The China Shock and Employment in Portuguese Firms." NBER Working Paper 26252, National Bureau of Economic Research, Cambridge, MA.

Dauth, Wolfgang, Sebastian Findeisen, and Jens Südekum. 2014. "The Rise of the East and the Far East: German Labor Markets and Trade Integration." *Journal of the European Economic Association* 12(6): 1643–1675.

Dauth, Wolfgang, Sebastian Findeisen, and Jens Südekum. 2017. "Trade and Manufacturing Jobs in Germany." *AEA Papers and Proceedings* 107(5): 337–342.

Dauth, Wolfgang, Sebastian Findeisen, and Jens Südekum. "Adjusting to Globalization in Germany." *Journal of Labor Economics* (forthcoming).

de Ruijter, Stan, and Christian Dustmann. "Imports and Exports: Effects on Labor Markets throughout the Production Chain." University College London, mimeo (forthcoming).

Dustmann, Christian, Bernd Fitzenberger, Uta Schönberg, and Alexandra Spitz-Oener. 2014. "From Sick Man of Europe to Economic Superstar: Germany's Resurgent Economy." *Journal of Economic Perspectives* 28(1): 167–188.

Dustmann, Christian, Johannes Ludsteck, and Uta Schönberg. 2009. "Revisiting the German Wage Structure." *Quarterly Journal of Economics* 124(2): 843–881.

Dustmann, Christian, and Uta Schönberg. 2012. "What Makes Firm-Based Vocational Training Schemes Successful? The Role of Commitment." *American Economic Journal: Applied Economics* 4(3): 36–61.

Federico, Stefano. 2014. "Industry Dynamics and Competition from Low-Wage Countries: Evidence on Italy." *Oxford Bulletin of Economics and Statistics* 76(3): 389–410.

Feenstra, Robert C., Hong Ma, and Yuan Xu. 2019. "US Exports and Employment." *Journal of International Economics* 120: 46–58.

Feigenbaum, J., and A. Hall. 2015. "How Legislators Respond to Localized Economic Shocks: Evidence from Chinese Import Competition." *Journal of Politics* 77(4): 1012–1030.

Klein, Michael W., Christoph Moser, and Dieter M. Urban. 2010. "The Contribution of Trade to Wage Inequality: The Role of Skill, Gender, and Nationality." NBER Working Paper 15985, National Bureau of Economic Research, Cambridge, MA.

Malgouyres, Clément. 2017. "The Impact of Chinese Import Competition on the Local Structure of Employment and Wages: Evidence from France." *Journal of Regional Science* 57(3): 411–441.

Pierce, Justin R., and Peter K. Schott. 2016. "The Surprisingly Swift Decline of US Manufacturing Employment." *American Economic Review* 106(7): 1632–1662.

Romer, David, and Jeffrey Frankel. 1999. "Does Trade Cause Growth?" *American Economic Review* 89(3): 379–399.

Samuelson, Paul A. 1962. "The Gains from International Trade Once Again." *Economic Journal* 72(288): 820–829.

Timmer, Marcel P., Abdul Azeez Erumban, Bart Los, Robert Stehrer, and de Vries J. Gaaitzen. 2014. "Slicing Up Global Value Chains." *Journal of Economic Perspectives* 28(2): 99–118.

United Nations International Labour Organization. 2019. ILOSTAT Manufacturing Employment. https://ilostat.ilo.org/data/.

United Nations Statistics Division. 2019. United Nations Commodity Trade Statistics Database (comtrade). New York: United Nations. http://comtrade.un.org/.

13

Combating Inequality: Rethinking Policies to Reduce Inequality in Advanced Economies

Caroline Freund

The effect of international trade on income inequality is not clear-cut. At the global level, trade-led growth has been a strong force for equality, as incomes in poor countries began to catch up with those in rich countries after a long period of divergence. That same force, however, has put pressure on production workers in advanced countries that are finding it harder to compete in the global economy. As a result, within-country inequality can be exacerbated by trade.

The United States and the United Kingdom, in particular, experienced regionally concentrated job losses as a result of rapidly expanding imports from poor countries. Many workers in manufacturing industries competing with cheaper imported goods lost their jobs. Because firms tend to locate near other firms in the same industry, job losses were highly concentrated in some regions, making it difficult for workers to find new jobs. Regional disparities grew, with some people feeling left behind.

But such job losses did not occur in all advanced countries. Growing trade with low-income countries was not associated with major manufacturing losses and widening regional disparities in all advanced countries. There is variation in employment, wage, and inequality outcomes, implying that circumstances and policies matter. The advanced countries that adjusted most easily to rapidly expanding trade with low-income countries, Japan and Germany, are different from the countries that were most negatively affected, the United States and United Kingdom.

There are three distinguishing features of the countries that adjusted more easily: (1) they maintained trade surpluses as trade expanded; (2) secondary education, especially in math and science, was of relatively high quality; and (3) they had release valves in place, either labor adjustments or place based, that helped workers adjust to structural changes.

In contrast, trade policies among all the advanced countries were almost identical, implying that adjusting to the changing global economy had little to do with tariffs and other barriers to trade.

Rapidly Rising Trade Disrupted the Global Economy

The 1990s and the early years of the following decade were an extraordinary period for trade. There were unprecedented changes in trade policy that are unlikely to be repeated. The Uruguay Round of trade negotiations under the General Agreement on Tariffs and Trade (GATT) and the formation of the World Trade Organization (WTO) increased market access among members and created a more predictable trade system; China liberalized trade and joined the WTO in 2001; Eastern Europe opened to multilateral trade, with 12 countries eventually joining the European Union (EU); and the North American Free Trade Agreement (NAFTA) went into force, liberalizing trade between the United States, Canada, and Mexico. Meanwhile, the average tariff in developing countries fell from about 35% to about 10% now.

What happened? Trade grew twice as fast as income, supported largely by rapid growth in developing countries. Developing countries' share of world exports doubled from 15% in 1990 to almost 30% in 2018. Growth (at purchasing power parity) in the developing world averaged 4.6%, compared to 3.4% in advanced countries. Over one billion people escaped poverty, in large part because of the rapid growth that trade engendered. This period of convergence led to a dramatic decline in global inequality, because the world's poor were finally catching up with the world's rich.

But greater competition in global markets did not benefit everyone. Some manufacturing communities in the United States suffered as jobs shifted to China (Autor, Dorn, and Hanson 2013). Evidence shows that low-skilled production workers in the United Kingdom were also negatively affected by the import shock (Adem 2018). Both countries experienced relatively sharp job losses in manufacturing, stagnating real wages, growing regional disparities, and an increase in income share accruing to the top 1% of earners.

These extreme experiences, however, were not common to all advanced countries. The share of manufacturing in total value added has fallen by about 5% since the early 1990s in the United States and United Kingdom. In contrast, it remained roughly constant in Japan and Germany. While all four countries have seen declines in manufacturing employment as productivity improved with automation, production workers in Japan and Germany have fared relatively better (figure 13.1).

Similarly, the rise in extreme incomes has not occurred in all rich countries. The share of income going to the top 1% rose sharply in the United States and United Kingdom (6% and 4%, respectively), but in Germany

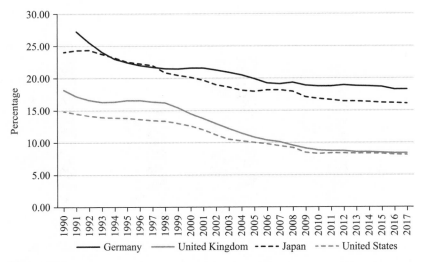

Figure 13.1
Manufacturing share of employment, 1990–2017. *Source*: Haver Analytics (2019).

their share remained fairly flat, and in Japan it has contracted since 1990. Whereas the United States and United Kingdom saw rising regional disparities, in Germany regional incomes converged, while in Japan disparities were low and flat over the period (figure 13.2).

The variation in outcomes cannot be attributed to trade policies, as tariffs in the United States and United Kingdom were similar to those in other advanced countries (figure 13.3). In fact, the United Kingdom had the same trade policy as Germany and other EU members. Such relatively open trade policies support competition, pushing resources into their most productive uses and allowing manufacturers to take advantage of cheaper imported inputs.

Similarly, changes resulting from technological progress and automation also likely affected all countries in comparable ways. Thus, the differences in outcomes for manufacturing and incomes are more closely related to endowments and other macro and labor policies than to trade policies.

A defining feature of the United States and United Kingdom during this period of rapid trade growth was a large and growing trade deficit. In contrast, Germany and Japan maintained sizable surpluses (figure 13.4). Investment was flowing into the Anglo countries, financing a boom in consumption and construction. Before 2008, while the global economy was booming, the construction and consumption bubble largely offset the shock from growing imports. The financial crisis, however, eventually reduced

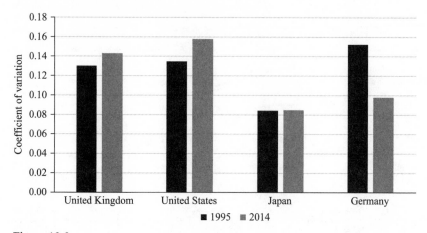

Figure 13.2
Coefficient of variation of regional disposable income, 1995 and 2014. *Source*: OECD (2016a).

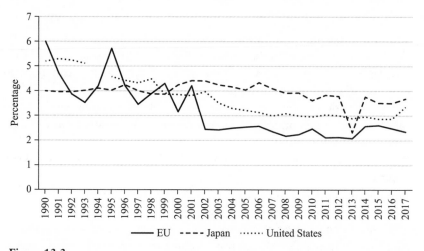

Figure 13.3
Average tariffs. Simple average, applied rate, 1990–2017. *Source*: World Bank, *World Development Indicators* (2019a).

demand for construction materials and consumer goods. Manufacturing firms that could not compete in an environment of more intense global competition were pushed out of business.

Foreign capital inflows also supported extraordinary incomes in the financial sector. In both the United Kingdom and United States, extreme wealth became increasingly concentrated in these sectors, a feature that was unique compared to other advanced countries. In both countries,

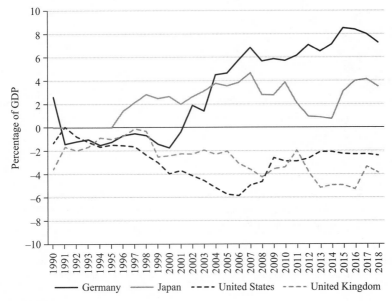

Figure 13.4
Current account balance, percent of GDP, 1990–2018. *Source*: World Bank, *World Development Indicators* (2019a).

more than 20% of billionaire wealth was made in finance and real estate, compared to only 1% in Germany, 3% in other advanced European countries, and 4% in Japan, and more than double the levels in 1996 (Freund and Oliver 2016). The effect of globalization on the right tail of the income and wealth distributions was closely tied to surging financial inflows.

Preparation for Work and Policies to Support Workers

The same countries that experienced the biggest shock from the financial crisis, trade, and technology were the least equipped to handle it. Employment increasingly requires skilled workers, especially those trained in science, technology, engineering, and mathematics (STEM) (Altonji, Kahn, and Speer 2016; Deming and Kahn 2018), but the quality of education in the United States and United Kingdom was low and had been deteriorating. These two countries also did not have strong labor-adjustment policies in place to support the workers whose livelihoods were at risk.

The workers most at risk from trade and technology are low-skilled workers with high school or less education. The quality of secondary education in the United States and United Kingdom is relatively poor. Figure 13.5 illustrates the performance of students on the Programme for

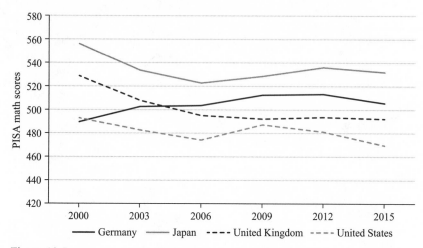

Figure 13.5
Average scores of 15-year-old students on the PISA mathematics literacy scale, by education system, scores range from 0 to 1000, 2000–2015. *Source*: OECD (2016b).

International Student Assessment (PISA), a triennial international survey of cohorts of 15-year-olds given around the world in math. Students in Germany and Japan perform much better than those in the United States and United Kingdom in all categories, especially math.

The United States is also an outlier in terms of labor policies (Bown and Freund 2019). As shown in figure 13.6, passive programs, such as unemployment insurance, that provide a cushion for laid-off workers are relatively small. Active programs, such as retraining, wage subsidies, and job placement services, are also largely absent. The United Kingdom performs slightly better but also lags behind other OECD countries.

The most effective model for business and workers couples simple business and labor regulations with worker protections, such as in Denmark. Denmark ranks fourth on the World Bank's Ease of Doing Business list (World Bank 2019b). The regulatory environment is designed to promote an efficient private sector, encouraging business formation and the expansion of productive firms, and forcing unproductive firms to exit. Worker protections, the most generous in the OECD, provide people with stable incomes and adequate opportunities.

In contrast, in the United States, the one credible jobs program—Trade Adjustment Assistance (TAA)—has been too small to have a major impact. New research shows that TAA can be effective and have long-term positive consequences for workers who receive training (Hyman 2018), but providing assistance only to workers who lose jobs because of

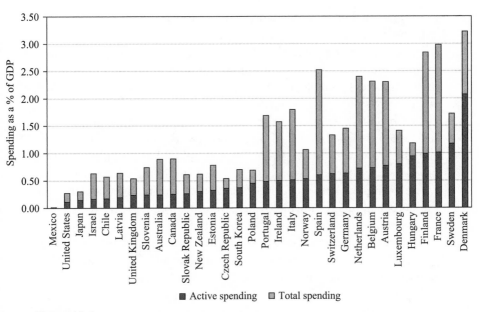

Figure 13.6
Labor-adjustment policies, percent of GDP. *Sources*: OECD (2016b) and Bown and
Freund (2019).

trade competition and offshoring is cumbersome to administer, resulting
in few workers actually receiving support. Assigning a cause for job loss
is not straightforward, as technology, trade, and demand are interlinked.
Moreover, in small towns, the employment effects of manufacturing
plant closures spread well beyond the firms' walls. In 2010, two million
manufacturing workers lost their jobs in the aftermath of the financial
crisis, but only 280,000 workers were certified for TAA and only 90,000
received training.

Moreover, TAA is the wrong way to help workers. As long as workers
lose their job through no fault of their own, all workers should receive the
same kind of assistance. Textile and furniture workers who have lost their
jobs because of cheaper imports are not alone. Travel agents, coal min-
ers, and retail workers have all experienced extensive job losses because
of changing technologies or demand shifts. Labor-adjustment policies are
essential for all these workers. Finally, focusing on TAA perpetuates the
narrative that trade and offshoring are largely responsible for job loss.

Economists have typically preferred to focus spending on people
rather than places, but there are examples of place-based policies working, especially during downturns. In Japan, worker support from active

labor market policies is limited (figure 13.6). Instead, Japan has relied more on place-based policies, supporting areas where dislocations happen. Local authorities are charged with designing a job creation plan and then compete for supportive government subsidies. Evidence suggests that the program increases employment, especially in the agricultural, retail trade, and services sectors (Kazekami 2017).

In the United States, the relatively successful $80 billion auto bailout functioned like a place-based policy because the industry was agglomerated in towns in the Midwest. For example, Elkhart, Indiana, which produces one of every two recreational vehicles in the United States and where unemployment reached 20% in 2009, benefited significantly from the auto bailout. Its unemployment rate has been relatively low and falling—now hovering below 3%.

To conclude, the trade shock at the turn of the millennium was exceptional. There were confounding factors in the United States and United Kingdom that exacerbated the effect on workers. In particular, their large and growing trade deficits, expanding financial sectors, weak secondary education, and the absence of robust labor adjustment (or place-based) policies left many workers behind.

Going forward, policies to prevent large and growing imbalances, improve STEM education for a more demanding labor market, and make greater use of adjustments will be essential to protect and prepare workers for the changing nature of work.

Trade protection, however, is not the answer. Rather, policies to prevent excessive current account deficits, through fiscal restraint, promoting saving, and avoiding exchange rate overvaluation, remain central.

References

Adem, Anwar. 2018. "Distributional Effect of Import Shocks on the British Local Labour Markets." Lancaster University, mimeo.

Altonji, Joseph G., Lisa B. Kahn, and Jamin D. Speer. 2016. "Cashier or Consultant? Entry Labor Market Conditions, Field of Study, and Career Success." *Journal of Labor Economics* 34(S1): S361–S401.

Autor, David H., David Dorn, and Gordon H. Hanson. 2013. "The China Syndrome: Local Labor Market Effects of Import Competition in the United States." *American Economic Review* 103(6): 2121–2168.

Bown, Chad, and Caroline Freund. 2019. "Active Labor Market Policies: Lessons from Other Countries for the United States." PIIE Working Paper 19-2, Peterson Institute for International Economics, Washington, DC.

Deming, David, and Lisa B. Kahn. 2018. "Skill Requirements across Firms and Labor Markets: Evidence from Job Postings for Professionals." *Journal of Labor Economics* 36(S1): S337–S369.

Freund, Caroline, and Sarah Oliver. 2016. "The Origins of the Superrich: The Billionaires Characteristics Database." PIIE Working Paper 16-1, Peterson Institute for International Economics, Washington, DC.

Haver Analytics. 2019. Advanced Economy Database.

Hyman, Benjamin G. 2018. "Can Displaced Labor Be Retrained? Evidence from Quasi-random Assignment to Trade Adjustment Assistance." Working paper, University of Chicago.

Kazekami, Sachiko. 2017. "Evaluating Place-Based Job Creation Programs in Japan." *IZA Journal of Labor Policy* 6(1).

Organization for Economic Cooperation and Development (OECD). 2016a. *Regions at a Glance*. Paris: OECD.

Organization for Economic Cooperation and Development (OECD). 2016b. Programme for International Student Assessment (PISA). Paris: OECD. www.oecd.org/pisa/data/.

World Bank. 2019a. *World Development Indicators*. Washington, DC: World Bank.

World Bank. 2019b. *Ease of Doing Business*. Washington, DC: World Bank.

VI

The (Re)distribution of Financial Capital

14

How to Increase Taxes on the Rich (If You Must)

N. Gregory Mankiw

I would like to begin with what I hope is a noncontroversial proposition: rich people are not all the same.

I bring up this fact because we live in a time when inequality is high, when demonizing the rich is popular in some political circles, and when various policies are being proposed to increase the redistribution of economic resources. In this brief chapter, I won't comment on whether we should redistribute more. That question is hard, and it involves economics less than it involves political philosophy, which is not my comparative advantage. Rather, I will assume we are going to increase redistribution and discuss alternative ways to do so. As we evaluate the many proposals, it is worth keeping in mind some of the ways rich people differ from one another.

Consider two hypothetical CEOs of major corporations. Each of them earns, say, $10 million a year, putting them in the top 0.01% of the income distribution. But other than in their incomes, the two executives are very different.

One executive, whom I will call Sam Spendthrift, uses all his money living the high life. He drinks expensive wine, drives a Ferrari, and flies his private jet to lavish vacations. He gives large amounts to political parties and candidates, hoping these contributions will get him an ambassadorship someday. When that does not work, he spends large sums financing his own quixotic run for the presidency.

The other executive, whom I will call Fran Frugal, makes just as much money as Sam, but she takes a different approach to her good fortune. She lives modestly, saving most of her earnings and accumulating a sizable nest egg. She forgoes the opportunity to influence the political process. Instead, she invests her money in successful start-ups, which she is quite good at identifying. She plans to leave some of her wealth to her children, grandchildren, nephews, and nieces. Most of her wealth, however, she plans to bequeath to the endowment of her alma mater, where it will support financial aid for generations to come.

Ask yourself: Who should pay higher taxes, Sam Spendthrift or Fran Frugal?

I can see the case for taxing them the same. After all, they have the same earnings. One might argue that how they choose to spend their money is not an issue for the government to judge or influence.

I am more inclined, however, to think Ms. Frugal should be taxed less than Mr. Spendthrift. The argument is Pigovian. Ms. Frugal's behavior confers positive externalities, both on members of her extended family and on the beneficiaries of her charitable bequest. Moreover, by increasing the economy's capital stock, her saving reduces the return to capital and increases labor productivity and real wages. If one is concerned about the income distribution, this pecuniary externality can also be viewed as desirable.

What I find hard to believe is that Ms. Frugal should face higher taxes than Mr. Spendthrift. But that is what occurs under some of the policy proposals now being widely discussed. I am referring in particular to the wealth taxes advocated by Senators Elizabeth Warren and Bernie Sanders, both of whom ran for the Democratic nomination for president in 2020. These taxes, if successfully implemented, would hit Fran Frugal hard but would be much easier on Sam Spendthrift.

There are better ways to redistribute economic resources, ways that do not penalize frugality. In particular, I am attracted to the policy championed by Andrew Yang, the former tech executive and entrepreneur who also ran for the Democratic nomination. Mr. Yang proposed to enact a value-added tax and use the revenue to provide every American adult with a universal basic income of $1,000 per month, which he called a "freedom dividend."

It's easy to see how the Yang proposal would work. Value-added taxes are essentially sales taxes, and they have proven remarkably efficient in raising revenue in many European countries. And because the dividend is universal, it would be simple to administer.

The idea of a universal basic income is not new, but it is bold. Of course, the idea has its critics. But, from my perspective, the critics often rely on arguments that do not hold up under scrutiny. Let me use an example to explain why.

Consider two plans, plan A and plan B, aimed at providing a social safety net. (For our purposes here, let's keep things simple by assuming both are balanced-budget plans.)

- Plan A. A means-tested transfer of $1,000 per month aimed at the truly needy. The full amount goes to those with zero income. The transfer is phased out: recipients lose 20 cents of it for every dollar of income they earn. These transfers are financed by a progressive income tax: the government taxes at 20% all income above $60,000 per year.
- Plan B. A universal transfer of $1,000 per month for every person, financed by a 20% flat tax on all income.

Would you prefer to live in a society with safety net A or safety net B?

When I asked this question to a group of Harvard undergraduates, over 90% concluded that plan A is better. Their arguments were roughly as follows. Plan A targets transfer payments on those who need the money most. As a result, it requires a smaller tax increase, and the taxes are levied only on those with high incomes. Plan B is crazy. Why should rich people like Bill Gates and Jeff Bezos receive a government transfer? They don't need it, and we would need to raise taxes more to pay for it.

Superficially, those arguments might seem compelling, but here is the rub: the two policies are equivalent. Look at the net payment—that is, taxes less transfers. Everyone is exactly the same under the two plans. A person with zero income gets $12,000 per year in both cases. A person with annual income of $60,000 gets zero in both cases. A person with income of $160,000 pays $20,000 in both cases. And everyone always faces an effective marginal tax rate of 20%. In other words, everyone's welfare is identical under the two policies, and everyone faces the same incentive. The difference between plan A and plan B is only a matter of framing.

This example teaches two lessons. First, if you find something like plan A attractive and you recognize the equivalence of plan A and plan B, you should find something like plan B attractive. Many critics of universal basic income fail to make this leap because they do not notice the equivalence of these two approaches. Once you see the equivalence, plan B is easier to embrace. And it looks even better when you realize that universal benefits and flat taxes are easier to administer than means-tested benefits and progressive taxes.

The second lesson from this example is how misleading it can be to focus on taxes and transfers separately. It is accurate to say that plan A has lower taxes, more progressive taxes, and more progressive transfers. But so what? Those facts do not stop it from being precisely equivalent to plan B. The equivalence is clear only when taxes and transfers are considered together.

I stress this fact because it is all too common to see academic papers and media articles describe the distribution of taxes without considering the distribution of the transfers they finance. Such presentations of the data are incomplete to the point of being deceptive. With incomplete reporting, one might be led to conclude that a society using plan A is more progressive than a society using plan B. But that is not the case, because the policies are functionally the same.

Finally, I should note that the safety net described by either plan A or plan B is just a version of the negative income tax that Milton Friedman proposed in his book *Capitalism and Freedom* back in 1962. I remember reading about it as a student 40 years ago and thinking it was a good idea, and I was not alone in that judgment: in 1968, more than 1,000 economists signed a letter endorsing such a plan, including luminaries such as James Tobin, Paul Samuelson, Peter Diamond, and Martin Feldstein. Andrew Yang's version, which focuses on taxing consumption rather than income, is even better than Friedman's, because it wouldn't distort the incentive to save and invest.

Could 1,000 economists all be wrong? Well, yes, they could, but my judgment is that in this case they are not. A universal basic income, financed by an efficient tax such as a value-added tax (or perhaps a carbon tax), might be a social safety net well worth considering.

I am not predicting that this idea will have much success in the current political environment, but I find it reassuring that good ideas keep popping up in the political discourse. Maybe someday they might even influence actual policy.

Reference

Friedman, Milton. 1962. *Capitalism and Freedom*. Chicago: University of Chicago Press.

15

Would a Wealth Tax Help Combat Inequality?

Lawrence H. Summers

Emmanuel Saez and Gabriel Zucman have made an important contribution to public finance thinking and the policy debate more generally by placing wealth taxation on the US agenda. In a series of widely publicized studies, they have argued that American wealth inequality has increased very substantially to unacceptable levels, that wealth taxation is a desirable way to curb the influence of the very wealthy even if no revenue is raised, and that wealth taxation is politically and administratively feasible (Saez and Zucman 2019a, 2019b, 2019c). Their ideas are included in the platforms of several 2020 presidential candidates.

I share Saez and Zucman's enthusiasm for increasing tax progressivity and for curbing the influence of moneyed interests on American society. However, in this chapter I argue that Saez and Zucman make a variety of claims that are not supportable by serious professional economic research. Those concerned with progressivity and reducing the role of money in politics would be taking an enormous risk by committing themselves to Saez and Zucman's policy proposals rather than alternative approaches based on existing tax reform agendas that could raise more revenue more reliably while contributing more to economic efficiency and fairness.

In what follows, I make four points. First, Saez and Zucman substantially overstate the erosion of progressivity of the US tax system and the increase in wealth inequality. While there is much room for methodological debate on these matters, it is noteworthy that every choice Saez and Zucman make goes in the direction of their ideological preconceptions. Second, implementing wealth taxation would not address the major concerns about the role of money in American politics but instead would, by encouraging greater contributions to tax-deductible vehicles, likely increase the influence of the wealthy on American society. Third, the revenue estimates offered by Saez and Zucman are substantially exaggerated—likely by a factor of around two relative to any wealth tax that could plausibly be adopted in the United States. Fourth, there are alternative approaches to progressive revenue raising that are more feasible, more reliable, raise more revenue, and are more consistent with economic efficiency. I conclude that wealth taxation should be the subject of extensive academic research but that its serious political consideration is premature.[1]

The Facts on Wealth Inequality, Income Inequality, and Tax Progressivity

Saez and Zucman's estimates of levels and trends in wealth and income inequality and tax progressivity have been considered by a number of other scholars (Kopczuk 2019; Auten and Splinter 2019; Smith, Zidar, and Zwick 2019). While they deserve much credit for focusing attention on the estimation of trends in inequality, their estimates are more of a first word than a last one. It is revealing that they purport to estimate the taxes paid by Forbes 400 individuals in 2018, even though these people had not yet filed their tax returns at the time they wrote.

Auten and Splinter (2019a, 2019b) improve on Saez and Zucman's procedures for using tax-return data to measure the distribution of income by, for example, imputing profit income in a more realistic way. Their estimate is that the increase in the share of income going to the top 1% has increased by 1.7% rather than 11.3% since 1960. And while Saez and Zucman treat the period before 1964, when top marginal tax rates were 90% or more, as a golden age, the usual view of economists has been that these rates encouraged a wide variety of shelter activities that had the effect of reducing tax revenues and creating the appearance but not the reality of an egalitarian income distribution.[2]

With respect to wealth inequality, the procedures used by Saez and Zucman have been convincingly criticized by Smith, Zidar, and Zwick (2019), who raise questions in particular about the treatment of private business and about the dubious assumption that the wealthy accrue interest income at very low rates, leading to very high imputations of fixed-income wealth. Their work suggests that the Saez and Zucman estimates of wealth share of the top 0.1% should be revised downward by 25% and that the estimates of the total wealth held by those with more than $50 million should be revised downward by 44%. Relatedly, Kopczuk (2019) points out the significant differences between the Saez and Zucman series (Saez and Zucman 2019a, 2019b, 2019c, 2019d) and prior work, including their own (Piketty, Saez, and Zucman 2018), and cautions that the concentration of wealth is an unknown, so any estimate of a wealth tax's revenue potential is highly uncertain.[3]

As important as these statistical issues is a conceptual issue. Perhaps the most important progressive achievement of American society over the last 70 years has been the vast expansion of Social Security and the introduction of public funding of health care for the elderly and the poor through Medicare and Medicaid, respectively. How do these show up in Saez and Zucman's calculations?

Because the payroll tax has a ceiling and has risen very substantially, Social Security and health care show up as reducing tax progressivity! The value of the nest egg represented by Social Security is not recognized as wealth, and the value of the benefits provided by Medicare and Medicaid is not recognized as income. So, the major progressive achievements of the period Saez and Zucman consider show up in their analysis as antiegalitarian failures. (A better procedure would have been to net payroll taxes against benefits paid or to omit payroll taxes from the analysis.)

None of this is to deny that rising inequality is a serious problem in the United States or that more tax progressivity is desirable, but rather it is to call into question the specific claims of Saez and Zucman. Their new estimates of wealth concentration and tax progressivity were highly publicized, especially by the *New York Times* (Leonhardt 2019), before they were subjected to serious professional peer review. I expect that, as they are carefully scrutinized, their most dramatic claims will be substantially attenuated.[4]

Wealth and Political Influence

Saez and Zucman stress that, for them, the main point of increasing taxes on the wealthy is not raising revenue but instead scaling back the pernicious effects of wealth and power on society. They write, "But [revenue needs are] not the fundamental reason higher top marginal income tax rates are desirable. Their root justification is not about collecting revenue. It is about regulating inequality and the market economy. It is also about safeguarding democracy against oligarchy."

There is a scale problem here. I recall asking someone well informed how much of a contribution to a presidential campaign it would take to get substantial one-on-one access to the candidate or favorable consideration for an ambassadorship. The answers I received were below one million dollars. Similarly, to be one of the top ten individual supporters of one of our two major political parties would cost less than 10 million dollars per two-year election cycle.

No imaginable wealth tax is going to make it infeasible for billionaires or even those with several hundred million dollars to continue to purchase this level of access for as long as they wish. Even if there were some tax effect and contributions were attenuated, economic reasoning suggests that the primary impact would be a reduction in the price of influence, not the removal of influence.

Surely, the main problems with political money do not involve individual giving of the kind that might be diminished by a wealth tax. They involve corporate contributions to candidates or corporate lobbying activities, such as the five lobbyists per member of Congress representing the financial services industry as the Dodd-Frank bill was being debated. Also important are commercial interests that are shared by many people who do not stand out for their wealth. Think of the dairy producers, the life insurance agents, the auto dealers, the realtors, or community hospitals, all of whom are enormously effective in maintaining special interest provisions that few economists would defend. I can report from personal experience that the community banks were far more influential when financial regulation was being debated than any hedge fund mogul or big bank.

When I have asked advocates of wealth taxation concerned with curbing political influence for an example of the problem they hope to solve, the most common answer I receive is a derisive reference to the Koch brothers. This is absurd. They are billionaires. Even a 6% wealth tax would not meaningfully attenuate their ability to make political contributions.

Anand Giridharadas (2019) more convincingly argues along these lines: the wealthy shape society not just through their contributions to the political process but, for example, by funding charter schools or elite universities whose actions then reduce pressure for appropriate public solutions to social challenges that threaten the wealthy. This is to my mind a legitimate concern, but wealth taxation would exacerbate any problems here. By taxing wealth on an annual basis, wealth taxation would increase the incentive for the wealthy to make transfers to philanthropic vehicles earlier in life. This would accelerate the society-shaping spending of the wealthy, particularly in the presence of rules like the 5% annual payout rule for foundations. On balance, I think this may be socially desirable, as I think of the Gates Foundation's beneficial work on AIDS, but it would nonetheless increase the influence of the wealthy on society.

None of this is to deny in any way the excessive influence of money in contemporary American politics. It is rather to suggest that wealth taxation is not a productive policy avenue for mitigating the problem and that if the wealthy can no longer hoard their wealth on attractive terms, they are likely to spend it in ways that may increase their social influence.

Will Wealth Taxes Work?

Saez and Zucman estimated that a 2% wealth tax on fortunes of more than $50 million and 3% on fortunes above $1 billion would raise $2.75 trillion over the next decade. They subsequently estimated that raising the 3% tax to 6% would raise another $1 trillion. Strikingly, they base this calculation on their overstated estimates of top wealth and an assumed 15% avoidance rate, which they take to be independent of the tax rate. This last assumption is inconsistent with professional economic practice (which assumes that, as tax rates rise, avoidance efforts and disincentive effects increase) and therefore suggests the arbitrary character of their estimates.

Sarin and Summers (2019a, 2019b) suggest that Saez and Zucman substantially overestimate the revenue potential of the wealth tax for three reasons. First, they estimate the revenue that a fully implemented wealth tax could raise in 2019 and then assume this figure will grow by 5.5% per year, which they adopt as the forecasted growth rate of nominal GDP, citing the Congressional Budget Office (CBO).

In reality, it is inconceivable that a whole new federal tax requiring substantial new assessment procedures could be implemented without a phase-in of several years. Moreover, Saez and Zucman miscite the CBO, which in fact assumes a growth rate of 4%.

Second, as previously noted, Saez and Zucman substantially overstate the share of wealth attributable to those they propose to tax. The calculations of Smith, Zidar, and Zwick (2019) suggest that the wealth tax base is about half as large as Saez and Zucman estimate. If so, this would mean that their revenue estimate for this reason alone needs to be reduced by at least 40%. Part of Saez and Zucman's optimism regarding the administrability of a wealth tax is based on the mistaken belief that 80% of top wealth is invested in liquid assets with public market values; Smith, Zidar, and Zwick (2019) show that the correct share is only 50%, which will increase the difficulty of wealth tax administration and decrease its revenue potential relative to Saez and Zucman's assumptions.

Third, the 15% avoidance estimate made by Saez and Zucman is not grounded in evidence other than claims that their administration will be rigorous and that there will be no exemptions.[5] Natasha Sarin and

I make the point that estate tax collections are only about one-eighth of what one would calculate as expected revenue using Saez and Zucman's methods (Sarin and Summers 2019a). We explain that this is because of various avoidance devices such as the use of trusts, the division of assets among family members, gifts to charity, and unreasonably low valuations of illiquid assets, as well as various devices involving borrowing and lending. Even after adjusting the estate tax rate to account for the fact that much estate wealth is not subject to taxation—primarily because of spousal bequests and charitable contributions—estate tax collections are still only around 40% of what would be expected based on Saez and Zucman's approach.

Taking these three factors together, I think an optimistic 10-year revenue estimate for the Saez-Zucman proposal, even assuming no reduction at all in the incentive to accumulate fortunes, is 50% below the estimate they put forward. In thinking about incentive effects, it is worth emphasizing that, for billionaires investing in bonds, the wealth tax will be equivalent to an income tax levied at a rate of over 200%.

This estimate also takes no account of the substantial reductions in wealth or income as a result of the corporate tax increases, accrued capital gains taxes, higher individual marginal rates, and greatly increased regulation also proposed by wealth tax advocates, so it likely overstates wealth tax collections in a political climate where wealth taxes could be implemented.

It is easy to say, as Saez and Zucman do, that their plan is to enact a loophole-free wealth tax that cannot be gamed, but this is not what actual legislatures will do. It is noteworthy that, because of their impracticality, more than three-quarters of the wealth taxes that were in place in Europe two decades ago have been eliminated altogether. Nowhere else in the world do wealth taxes placed only on a small fraction of the population raise anything like the 1% of GDP projected by Saez and Zucman.

While the idea does not fit easily into academic models, in reality it is very difficult to tax people when they are not receiving cash. For example, there will be enormous resistance to taxing business owners on some appraised value of their business, especially since any appraisal is likely to be arbitrary. Examples of wealth taxes that will likely be difficult to administer or seem to Congress to be unfair include their incidence on those with substantial holdings in private businesses such as Airbnb, where corporate rules preclude borrowing against stock and there is no market in which it can be sold, or family-controlled public entities such as the New York Times Company, where a wealth tax would over time force the Sulzbergers to sell off their interests. More broadly, high wealth taxes would force founders such as the Waltons, Bill Gates, or Mark Zuckerberg to sell down their holdings in the companies they founded much faster than they do currently. There is also the issue of the classic family-owned business, such as a group of car dealerships, where a wealth tax might over time force divestiture.

These examples may not seem compelling, but considerations of this kind explain why the US estate tax raises so little revenue. The estate tax is a wealth tax. Because it is applied only once a generation it should be easier to administer than the Saez Zucman plan. Yet it is shot through with loopholes and raises limited revenue. This I think is highly predictive with respect to wealth tax proposals.

Issues of Political Strategy

Even if all the preceding arguments are correct, Saez and Zucman and the political figures they advise may have performed an important service. The fact that wealth taxes are under serious discussion widens the Overton window with respect to tax reform. Reform ideas that would have seemed radical even a few years ago seem mild compared to wealth taxes, and I believe a Democratic president who used the window of opportunity at the beginning of their administration to enact a wealth tax would be making a grave mistake. First, there is very little chance that such a proposal would pass through the Senate, especially if the Republicans maintain control. Second, even if a wealth tax passed, it would certainly be challenged on constitutional grounds, and the current Supreme Court would be more likely than not to reject it (Hemel and Kysar 2019). Why spend so much political capital on a proposal that is unlikely to ever be implemented?

While there is polling suggesting considerable public support for wealth taxes, I am not sure this support would hold up in the face of a range of stories about entrepreneurs and families being forced to relinquish controlling interests in businesses. At a broader philosophical level, as one contemplates taxes levied on less than 0.1% of the population, the question arises of where a measure stops being a tax and starts being a taking. My guess is that most Americans would find the idea that the federal government should confiscate one-quarter of the wealth of all billionaires to be unfair and unattractive. A 6% wealth tax simply spreads the confiscation over four or five years.

Academic progressives who are attracted to the idea of such takings should ponder the success of President Trump in attracting votes from those with low and moderate incomes despite all his flaunting of his wealth. They should also recall that George McGovern was booed off the stage when, at a UAW convention, he proposed massive increases in estate taxes on very large estates.

On a very optimistic reading, the wealth tax will raise $2 trillion in a highly progressive way. Natasha Sarin, Joe Kupferberg, and I (Sarin, Summers, and Kupferberg 2020) show that a tax reform agenda focused on improving compliance, closing loopholes and shelters, reforming capital gains taxation, and restoring tax rates cut under President Trump can raise nearly $4 trillion in a highly progressive way.

The tax reform approach we support has the virtue of raising far more revenue than the wealth tax approach. Whatever the wealth tax approach does to control the malign influence of money in politics, it does twice as much damage. Moreover, by focusing on closing loopholes and attacking shelters, it increases economic efficiency. For example, taxing capital gains at the same rate as other income discourages people from working to convert income into the form of capital gains, and taxing accrued gains when a taxpayer dies or contributes a stock to charity encourages the reallocation of capital when investors regard it as appropriate. Similarly, increased compliance efforts discourage the international diversion of income or efforts to earn income in unrecorded form. An additional virtue of the tax reform approach is that by broadening the tax, it makes it more feasible to raise tax rates should it prove necessary.

Conclusion

While I do not support Saez and Zucman's policy recommendation for the United States, at least for the foreseeable future, and I have considerable doubts about some of their calculations, I congratulate them on the way they have opened up new areas for inquiry and debate. Because of their efforts, concerns that American capitalism is entering another Gilded Age now occupy a central place in economists' discussions of tax policy. While wealth taxes seem to me not ready for prime time, I could certainly imagine that a moment would come when they would find a place in our tax system. That moment may come sooner because of Saez and Zucman's work.

Notes

1. These comments relate to my joint work in this area with Natasha Sarin.

2. Auten, Splinter, and Nelson (2016) provide an overview of the evidence. Okner (1975) estimated that millionaires paid an effective tax rate of just 19%

in 1966, despite top statutory rates of 70%. Plesko (1994), Slemrod (1996), and Carroll and Joulfaian (1997) discuss income shifting from C-corporations to S-corporations following the 1986 Tax Reform Act, while Feldstein (1995) and Auten and Carroll (1999) examine the behavioral response of individual taxable income to the 1986 changes in tax rates. Gordon and Slemrod (2000) and Clarke and Kopczuk (2017) document that high differentials in individual versus corporate tax rates in the 1960s incentivized business owners to shield income as retained earnings rather than disburse it.

3. Issues with the Saez and Zucman wealth tax revenue estimation are discussed in the third section of the chapter.

4. This has already begun. For example, Saez and Zucman (2019) suggest that the very wealthy pay lower tax rates than those at the bottom of the wealth distribution. This controversial finding is at odds with data from the Congressional Budget Office and the Tax Policy Center. David Splinter (2019) addresses issues in the Saez and Zucman estimation and finds that, after correction, their conclusion is reversed.

5. Specifically, to come up with a 15% avoidance number, Saez and Zucman rely on the estimates of four academic papers that report a wide range of elasticities, finding that a 1% wealth tax lowers reported wealth by between 0 and 34% (Saez and Zucman 2019d). They take 16% as the average of these estimates and then assume—contrary to the estimates that they rely on—that the change in reported wealth that will result from a wealth tax will be insensitive to the rate chosen.

References

Auten, Gerald, and Robert Carroll. 1999. "The Effect of Income Taxes on Household Income." *Review of Economics and Statistics* 81(4): 681–693.

Auten, Gerald, and David Splinter. 2019a. "Income Inequality in the United States: Using Tax Data to Measure Long-term Trends." Working paper.

Auten, Gerald, and David Splinter. 2019b. "Top 1 Percent Income Shares: Comparing Estimates Using Tax Data." *AEA Papers and Proceedings* 109: 307–311.

Auten, Gerald, David Splinter, and Susan Nelson. 2016. "Reactions of High-Income Taxpayers to Major Tax Legislation." *National Tax Journal* 69(4): 935–964.

Carroll, Robert, and David Joulfaian. 1997. "Taxes and Corporate Choice of Organizational Form." OTA Paper 73, US Department of the Treasury, Washington, DC.

Clarke, Conor, and Wojciech Kopczuk. 2017. "Business Income and Business Taxation in the United States since the 1950s." *Tax Policy and the Economy* 31(1): 121–159.

Feldstein, Martin. 1995. "Effect of Marginal Tax Rates on Taxable Income: A Panel Study of the 1986 Tax Reform Act." *Journal of Political Economy* 103(3): 551–572.

Giridharadas, Anand. 2019. *Winners Take All: The Elite Charade of Changing the World*. New York: Vintage.

Gordon, Roger H., and Joel B. Slemrod. 2000. "Are 'Real' Responses to Taxes Simply Income Shifting between Corporate and Personal Tax Bases?" In *Does Atlas Shrug? The Economic Consequences of Taxing the Rich*, edited by Joel B. Slemrod, 240–279. Cambridge, MA: Harvard University Press.

Hemel, Daniel, and Rebecca Kysar. 2019. "The Big Problem with Wealth Taxes." *New York Times*, November 7, 2019.

Kopczuk, Wojciech. 2019. "Comment on 'Progressive Wealth Taxation' by Saez and Zucman. Prepared for the Fall 2019 issue of *Brookings Papers on Economic Activity*." http://www.columbia.edu/~wk2110/bin/BPEASaezZucman.pdf.

Leonhardt, David. "The Rich Really Do Pay Lower Taxes Than You Do." 2019. *New York Times*, November 7, 2019.

Okner, Benjamin A. 1975. "Individual Taxes and the Distribution of Income." In *The Personal Distribution of Income and Wealth*, edited by James D. Smith, 45–74. NBER Working Paper, National Bureau of Economic Research, Cambridge, MA.

Piketty, Thomas, Emmanuel Saez, and Gabriel Zucman. 2018. "Distributional National Accounts: Methods and Estimates for the United States." *Quarterly Journal of Economics* 133(2): 553–609.

Plesko, George A. 1994. "Corporate Taxation and the Financial Characteristics of Firms." *Public Finance Quarterly* 22(3): 311–334.

Saez, Emmanuel, and Gabriel Zucman. 2019a. "Alexandria Ocasio-Cortez's Tax Hike Idea Is Not About Soaking the Rich. It's About Curtailing Inequality and Saving Democracy." *New York Times*, January 22, 2019.

Saez, Emmanuel, and Gabriel Zucman. 2019b. *The Triumph of Injustice: How the Rich Dodge Taxes and How to Make Them Pay*. New York: W. W. Norton.

Saez, Emmanuel, and Gabriel Zucman. 2019c. "Progressive Wealth Taxation." *Brookings Papers on Economic Activity*, BPEA Conference Draft, September 4, 2019.

Saez, Emmanuel, and Gabriel Zucman. 2019d. "Letter to Senator Warren." January 18, 2019.

Sarin, Natasha, and Lawrence H. Summers. 2019a. "A 'Wealth Tax' Presents a Revenue Estimation Puzzle." *Washington Post*, April 4, 2019.

Sarin, Natasha, and Lawrence H. Summers. 2019b. "Be Very Skeptical about How Much Revenue Elizabeth Warren's Wealth Tax Could Generate." *Washington Post*, June 28, 2019.

Sarin, Natasha, and Lawrence H. Summers. 2019c. "Shrinking the Tax Gap: Approaches and Revenue Potential." NBER Working Paper 26475, National Bureau of Economic Research, Cambridge, MA.

Sarin, Natasha, Lawrence H. Summers, and Joe Kupferberg. 2020. "Reflections on High Income Taxation." The Hamilton Project, Brookings Institution, Washington, DC.

Slemrod, Joel. 1996. "High Income Families and the Tax Changes of the 1980s: The Anatomy of Behavioral Response." In *Empirical Foundations of Household Taxation*, edited by Martin Feldstein and James Poterba, 169–192. Chicago: University of Chicago Press.

Smith, Matthew, Owen Zidar, and Eric Zwick. 2019. "Top Wealth in the United States: New Estimates and Implications for Taxing the Rich." Working paper.

Splinter, David. 2019. "U.S. Taxes are Progressive: Comment on 'Progressive Wealth Taxation.'" Joint Committee on Taxation, mimeo.

16

Should We Tax Wealth?

Emmanuel Saez

The wealth tax has burst into the US policy debate. Two major candidates in the Democratic presidential primary have proposed wealth taxes in their platforms. In January 2019, Elizabeth Warren proposed an annual progressive wealth tax of 2% on family net worth above $50 million and 3% above $1 billion (later increased to 6%). Bernie Sanders then proposed a graduated wealth tax starting at $32 million with a 1% marginal tax rate, growing by 1% increments all the way to 8% for wealth above $10 billion. The key differences relative to wealth tax experiences abroad are the high exemption thresholds proposed (less than 0.1% of US families would be liable), a comprehensive tax base including all assets, to prevent tax avoidance, and an aggressive approach to enforcement, to prevent tax evasion. In the policy debate, the US wealth tax is justified on three grounds from center-left to radical left: (1) raising more revenue from the rich, (2) restoring tax progressivity, and (3) curbing the growing concentration of wealth. Looking at data on wealth and its distribution is central to debating all three justifications.

Wealth Concentration

Aggregate US household wealth was three times annual national income around 1980. In 2018, it was about five times. This increase was driven primarily by a rise in asset prices rather than capital accumulation.[1] This implies that the weight of wealth has substantially increased. Meanwhile, wealth has become much more concentrated according to all available sources. Figure 16.1 displays the share of wealth held by the top 0.1% of families from available sources. It shows a dramatic surge in wealth concentration since the late 1970s, with the top 0.1% holding close to a 20% share of wealth today. At the very top, the share of wealth owned by the 400 richest Americans tracked by *Forbes* magazine almost quadrupled

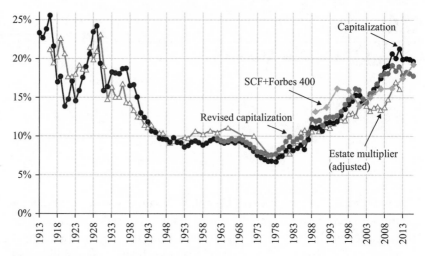

Figure 16.1
The top 0.1% wealth share, 1913–2016. The figure depicts various estimates of the share of wealth held by the top 0.1% of family tax units in the United States: (1) survey data combining the Survey of Consumer Finances (SCF) and the Forbes 400 list of wealthiest Americans; (2) the capitalization method; (3) the capitalization method with adjustments for capitalizing interest income and valuing pass-through businesses; (4) the estate multiplier method adjusted for accurate mortality differentials by wealth. *Source*: Saez and Zucman (2019a), figure 2(a).

from 0.9% in 1982 to 3.3% in 2018 (see figure 16.3). Importantly, because the United States does not yet have a wealth tax, there is more uncertainly about the distribution of wealth and its trend than for income.

Tax Revenue Potential

The combination of high aggregate wealth and high wealth concentration implies that a well-enforced wealth tax has great revenue potential. If the top 0.1% owns 20% of total household wealth, which is 100% of national income, then taxing 1% of their wealth would raise 1% of national income. The potential tax base of household wealth above $50 million (approximately the top 0.05% of families) was about $10 trillion in 2019, implying that a 2% marginal tax on this base would raise $200 billion per year, or approximately 1% of GDP.[2] Zucman (chapter 29, this volume) discusses the crucial enforcement aspects and shows that a low evasion rate of around 15% is possible with a well-designed and enforced wealth tax that learns from and hence avoids the mistakes of the European wealth tax experiences. In a nutshell, in an advanced economy with well-defined property rights and a large financial sector whose job is to value assets, the government can reliably obtain or create asset valuations.

Tax Progressivity

Figure 16.2 depicts the average tax rate relative to pretax income by income group when including all taxes at all levels of government and measuring income on a comprehensive basis consistent with national income in national accounts. The US tax system is mildly progressive below the top 0.01% but becomes regressive at the very top. In particular, we estimate that the tax rate for the top 400 richest Americans in 2018 was only 23%, lower than for any other income group (Saez and Zucman 2019b, chapter 7). There are two main reasons why. First, the individual income tax is based on realized income, but billionaires can have large economic incomes while realizing fairly small incomes. Warren Buffett provides a striking illustration. In 2015, Buffett's wealth was $65 billion, implying that his true economic income should be around $3 billion (assuming a conservative 5% rate of return on wealth), yet Buffett disclosed that his 2015 reported individual income was only $12 million, orders of magnitude smaller. Second, the corporate tax was cut significantly in 2018 and is the key backstop tax that billionaires still have to pay on the profits of their companies at the source (the estate tax has also become a very modest tax on the ultrawealthy because of a combination of large legal deductions and aggressive avoidance and evasion).

Figure 16.2 also shows how adding the initial Warren wealth tax—2% above $50 million and 3% above $1 billion—would affect the tax rates by income group (we assume an evasion rate of 15%). The tax rate for the top 0.01% would rise by 14%. Among the top 400, the tax rate would double from 23% to 46%. Therefore, the wealth tax would have a major impact and would restore tax progressivity at the top to levels last observed in 1980. The 6% billionaire rate proposed by Warren would further bump up the tax rate on the top 400 to 68%. The Sanders wealth tax would bump it up to 75%, equaling or even surpassing the top tax rates effectively applied around the middle of the twentieth century, when the US tax system was at its most progressive ever (Saez and Zucman 2019b). Interested readers can easily and interactively explore the effect of wealth taxation and other taxes on overall tax progressivity on our website, taxjusticenow.org. It shows that the wealth tax is the most powerful tool to restore tax progressivity at the very top.

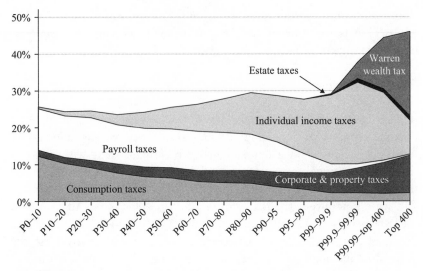

Figure 16.2
US tax progressivity and wealth taxation. The figure depicts the average tax rate (taxes divided by pretax income) by income group (P0–10 denotes the bottom 10%, etc.) and its composition by type of tax in 2018. All federal, state, and local taxes are included. The figure also depicts the effect of adding the Warren wealth tax (2% above $50 million and 3% above $1 billion). *Source*: Saez and Zucman (2019b).

Curbing Wealth Concentration

A long-standing concern with wealth concentration is its effect on democratic institutions and policy-making. Historically, wealth concentration and oligarchy—defined as power controlled by the wealthy elite—go together, as they feed each other.[3] The view that excessive wealth concentration corrodes the social contract influenced the drafting of the US Constitution. Today, US wealth concentration is high, and President Trump is a billionaire who spent $66 million of his own wealth to get elected in 2016 (Gibson and Smith 2016). Two candidates in the 2020 Democratic presidential primary, Bloomberg and Steyer, were billionaires who spent $900 million and $270 million of their own wealth in their respective campaigns. Other billionaires, most notably the Koch brothers and Sheldon Adelson, have also already spent hundreds of millions to influence US elections.[4]

In the first part of the twentieth century, the United States pioneered very progressive income and estate taxation, combined with heavy corporate taxation. This led to a large and sustained reduction in income and wealth concentration that reversed after tax progressivity went away in the last part of the twentieth century (Saez and Zucman 2019b, chapter 7). A wealth tax is a potentially more powerful tool than income, estate, or corporate taxes to address the issue of wealth concentration, as it targets the very wealthy by definition and goes after the stock of wealth directly rather than the flow of income. Therefore, it can deconcentrate wealth much faster than an income tax or the inheritance tax.

Figure 16.3 illustrates the power of the wealth tax to reduce wealth concentration. It depicts the actual share of total wealth owned by the top 400 richest Americans since 1982 from *Forbes* magazine and what their wealth share would have been if the Warren (as initially proposed, with a 2% tax on wealth above $50 million and 3% on wealth above $1 billion) or Sanders wealth taxes had been in place since 1982. The calculation uses the existing individual wealth trajectories and assumes that each year the wealth tax takes a corresponding percentage of the wealth so that it has a cumulative effect over time. Decabillionaires still emerge but do not tend to stay decabillionaires for as long. Founders of businesses (such as Jeff Bezos of Amazon) would not be able to keep a controlling stake in their business for as long.

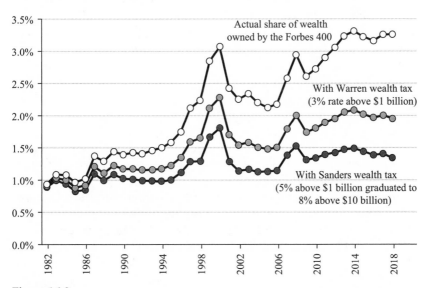

Figure 16.3
The effects of wealth taxation on top wealth holders. The figure depicts the share of total wealth owned by the top 400 richest Americans since 1982 from *Forbes* magazine. The figure also depicts what their wealth share would have been if the Warren or Sanders wealth taxes had been in place since 1982. *Source*: Saez and Zucman (2019a), figure 6.

With the Warren and Sanders wealth taxes in place since 1982, the wealth share of the top 400 would have been 2.0% and 1.3%, respectively, in 2018 instead of 3.3%. In both cases, the wealth share of the top 400 would still be higher in 2018 than it was in 1982. The wealth of billionaires has increased so quickly relative to average wealth economywide that even a radical wealth tax like the Sanders tax, which takes 5%–6% of billionaires' wealth annually on average, is not even quite sufficient to beat back the surge in billionaires' wealth.

Other Economic Effects

Would a progressive wealth tax hurt the US economy? Two main concerns have been raised. First, the wealth tax, by reducing the wealth held by the wealthiest, could end up reducing the US capital stock. This crucially depends on how wealth tax revenue is used. Using tax revenue for infrastructure or education investments, or to promote middle-class savings, could offset any loss of capital at the top. Second, it could discourage entrepreneurship. Expected financial gain is only one reason why people start businesses, and the wealth tax happens late, only after success has been achieved. Therefore, earlier interventions such as education, attracting or retaining foreign talent through immigration policy, and encouraging credit-constrained innovators are likely to have a larger impact and could offset any adverse effects from wealth taxation (Bell et al. 2019).

Notes

1. Saez and Zucman (2019a), figure 1.

2. Both the Survey of Consumer Finances (combined with the Forbes 400) and wealth inferred by capitalizing investment income on tax data generate approximately the same scoring ($9.4 and $10.9 trillion, respectively; see Saez and Zucman 2019a, table 2).

3. Acemoglu and Robinson (2012) and Piketty (2020) provide detailed historical evidence.

4. Two recent academic books by Mayer (2017) and by Page, Seawright, and Lacombe (2018) describe the influence of billionaires on US politics in recent decades.

References

Acemoglu, Daron, and James A. Robinson. 2012. *Why Nations Fail: The Origins of Power, Prosperity, and Poverty.* New York: Crown Books.

Bell, Alexander, Raj Chetty, Xavier Jaravel, Neviana Petkova, and John Van Reenen. 2019. "Do Tax Cuts Produce More Einsteins? The Impacts of Financial Incentives vs. Exposure to Innovation on the Supply of Inventors." *Journal of the European Economic Association* 17(3): 651–677.

Gibson, Ginger, and Grant Smith. 2016. "Figures Show Trump Spent $66 Million of His Own Cash on Election Campaign." Reuters, December 8, 2016.

Mayer, Jane. 2017. *Dark Money: The Hidden History of the Billionaires behind the Rise of the Radical Right.* New York: Anchor Books.

Page, Benjamin I., Jason Seawright, and Matthew J. Lacombe. 2018. *Billionaires and Stealth Politics.* Chicago: University of Chicago Press.

Piketty, Thomas. 2020. *Capital and Ideology.* Cambridge, MA: Harvard University Press.

Saez, Emmanuel, and Gabriel Zucman. 2019a. "Progressive Wealth Taxation." *Brookings Papers on Economic Activity.*

Saez, Emmanuel, and Gabriel Zucman. 2019b. *The Triumph of Injustice: How the Rich Dodge Taxes and How to Make Them Pay.* New York: W. W. Norton.

VII

Policies That Affect the Rate and Direction
of Technological Change

17

Could We and Should We Reverse (Excessive) Automation?

Daron Acemoglu

Over the past three decades, the US economy has experienced much weaker growth in labor demand than during the previous 40 years. Total spending on labor by US private businesses (the private wage bill, or the average wage multiplied by total private employment) grew 2.5% faster than the population between 1947 and 1987. This spending slowed down in the 1990s and has essentially been stagnant since 2000 (Acemoglu and Restrepo 2019b). This slowdown has also been associated with major distributional changes. Not only has the share of labor in national income fallen sharply over this period, but also inequality between workers with low and high skills has surged (Acemoglu and Autor 2011).

The standard framework economists use for thinking about changes in inequality focuses on the effects of relative supplies of different factors and technology (e.g., Tinbergen 1975; Goldin and Katz 2008). Technology, however, is conceptualized in a specific way: it is assumed to be "factor augmenting," meaning that technology directly changes the productivity (or effective supply) of some factors. Though this framework has been widely used and provides a powerful organizing framework, it is deficient in a number of ways.

First, it lacks descriptive realism. Very few technologies can be thought of as increasing the productivity of a factor across all activities. Instead, many technologies enable workers doing specific tasks to be more productive, allow some tasks to be automated (produced by capital rather than labor), or reorganize production by adding new tasks and activities. Second, the standard approach implies that, by making factors more productive, technological improvements generally increase the wages of all types of labor (whereas the data suggest major declines in the real wages of several types of labor in the US economy over the last three decades; see Acemoglu and Autor 2011). Third, it links the impact of technology to the elasticity of substitution between factors. For example, in the context of a changing labor share in national income, a capital-augmenting technological improvement will increase the labor share if the elasticity of substitution between capital and labor is less than 1 but reduce the labor share if this elasticity is greater than 1. This central role of the elasticity of substitution does not cohere with our intuitive understanding of how new technologies impact factor prices and distribution. More significantly, if the elasticity of substitution is close to 1 (as many estimates suggest; e.g., Oberfield and Raval 2014), the magnitude of the impact from technology on the labor and capital shares will be very small (Acemoglu and Restrepo 2019b).

Acemoglu and Restrepo (2019a, 2019b) proposed an alternative approach, based on tasks and the allocation of tasks to different factors of production (see also Acemoglu and Autor 2011; Zeira 1998). In addition to the standard factor-augmenting technologies, this framework allows two very different types of technological changes. The first is automation and involves the expansion of the set of tasks that can be performed by capital. Put differently, automation technologies enable tasks previously performed by labor to be reallocated to capital.

Automation always creates a powerful *displacement effect*—it displaces labor from tasks it was previously performing. This does not necessarily translate into lower labor demand, but it may. In particular, automation also reduces costs, generating a positive *productivity effect*. This productivity effect may exceed the displacement effect, in which case overall labor demand increases. But if the productivity effect is smaller than the displacement effect, overall labor demand, along with employment and wages, will decline. These observations highlight that if automation technologies are only a little more productive (or cost-effective) than traditional technologies employing labor, then they will decrease labor demand. In fact, the real threat to labor may not be the "brilliant" technologies emphasized by some commentators and technologists but instead "so-so technologies" that automate a range of tasks but are only a little more productive than labor. So-so technologies will create significant displacement effects but no positive productivity effect and will necessarily reduce labor demand, employment, and wages.

Though the implications of automation for overall labor demand are ambiguous, its impact on the labor share in value added is unambiguous and first order. By substituting capital for labor, automation always reduces the labor share in value added. In this light, if the economy is undergoing steady automation, shouldn't we expect a steadily falling labor share in national income?

The answer is no, because another type of new technology highlighted by our framework may counterbalance the impact of automation. Namely, the economy may also create new labor-intensive tasks. For example, most of the design and engineering tasks as well as myriad nonproduction, clerical tasks widespread in both the manufacturing and nonmanufacturing parts of the economy are relatively new and did not exist before the end of the nineteenth century. New tasks generate the opposite of the effects of automation. Such tasks provide new, and potentially highly productive, employment opportunities for workers. Specifically, counteracting the displacement effects of automation, they reinstate labor into the production process. Because of this *reinstatement effect*, new (labor-intensive) tasks always increase labor demand, and they raise the labor share in value added.

Acemoglu and Restrepo (2019b) developed a simple methodology for estimating the extent of displacement and reinstatement as well as the magnitude of the productivity effects on labor demand from observed changes in value added, employment, and labor share at the sectoral level. Their estimates suggest rapid displacement between 1947 and 1987—of about 0.48% a year. Remarkably, this displacement is almost exactly counterbalanced by reinstatement of the same magnitude. Without this reinstatement, labor demand would have grown only 2% a year, instead of 2.5% a year, between 1947 and 1987.

The post-1987 patterns are very different, however. Displacement accelerated, rising to about 0.7% a year between 1987 and 2017. At the same time, reinstatement slowed down to only 0.35% annually. This gap between displacement and reinstatement explains a good chunk of the slowdown in labor demand. The even larger remainder is accounted for by a slowdown in productivity growth over the last 30 years. In summary, the data suggest that the notable slowdown in the growth of labor demand from the private sector is accounted for by a combination of significantly slower productivity growth and a major shift toward faster displacement and slower reinstatement.

What explains these patterns? One obvious explanation, perhaps the most common one among economists and commentators, is that exogenous factors account for both the productivity slowdown and the faster automation accounting for displacement. But why should we expect exogenous changes to take exactly this form? After all, there are many ways to develop new technological platforms, including artificial intelligence (AI). Moreover, the last 30 years are often viewed as a period of fundamental technological breakthroughs. Why should we see slower productivity growth during such a period?

The framework in Acemoglu and Restrepo (2019a) provides an alternative interpretation. The extent of automation and the creation of new tasks are determined endogenously as the economy chooses a point along an innovation possibilities frontier linking these two types of technological changes. More automation comes at the cost of fewer new tasks and vice versa. Furthermore, for the usual reasons that underpin diminishing returns in many activities, the more heavily the economy devotes its resources to one of these activities, the lower the quality of new (marginal) technologies and the smaller the productivity gains. Hence, too much emphasis on automation generates so-so technologies that displace labor but do not create large productivity gains and misses out on low-hanging fruit from other types of technologies. The outcome is slower (total factor) productivity growth. According to this perspective, if changes in policies, institutions, or other market incentives have made us focus on automation excessively, this would be doubly costly for labor: it would reduce labor demand because of too much automation and too little reinstatement, and it would fail to realize potential productivity growth from other technologies, which would have boosted labor demand.

Why would we shift away from new tasks and other labor-complementary technologies and toward excessive automation? There are three distinct reasons.

First, tax policies subsidize capital investments, and this subsidy has increased over the last several decades. At the adoption margin, firms may have been biased toward machines instead of labor (because when they employ workers, they are taxed, and when they replace the workers with machines, they are subsidized; see Acemoglu, Manera, and Restrepo 2020). This bias toward the adoption of automation technologies naturally translates into a bias toward the invention of automation technologies. Specifically, there will be an impetus to develop fairly general platforms, such as AI, toward the single goal of greater automation instead of exploring broader avenues (Acemoglu and Restrepo 2020a).

Second, the business model of many technology firms, such as Amazon, Facebook, Google, and Netflix, which have come to play a dominant role in the direction of innovation, emphasizes automation at the expense of other technological approaches and does not involve a serious effort to reinstate labor in the production process. This not only diverts the funds that these huge companies control toward automation at the expense of other technological investments but also creates an ecosystem for innovation, in both the business world and universities, that views automation as the ultimate goal.

Third, government support for research and development has declined precipitously over the last several decades. Government funding plays a critical role not just in the quantity of research but also in its direction. Many of the most innovative and blue-sky research endeavors of the postwar era, ranging from early computers, to antibiotics, to sensors and the internet, were spearheaded by government demands and propelled by generous government support. These breakthroughs created a range of new tasks. With dwindling support from the government, it has become more likely for new research to cluster around existing paradigms and follow the path of least resistance, which may have spawned another powerful force toward automation at the expense of labor-complementing technologies.

If indeed there was a shift away from a balanced distribution of research effort toward an excessive focus on automation, this would have come with significant social costs. To start with, such a shift would have missed out on potential productivity improvements from new tasks. Equally importantly, reduced labor demand produces major economic, distributional, and social costs. On the economic front, if there are labor market imperfections creating a wedge between wages and the opportunity cost of labor, reduced employment creates greater distortions and squanders valuable economic surpluses (Acemoglu and Restrepo 2019a). On the distributional front, rapid automation creates inequality (Acemoglu and Autor 2011; Acemoglu and Restrepo 2020b). On the social front, the displacement effects of automation often create discontent and myriad social problems (Wilson 1996; Autor, Dorn, and Hanson 2019).

Can policy do anything? Yes, by redirecting technological change toward activities that are more socially valuable. Though policy can have a major impact on the direction of technological change, this issue is not on the radar of most economists and policymakers. For that reason, I want to start with a different example of successful technological redirection: innovation toward clean energy. Over the last four decades, there has been tremendous success in developing low- or zero-carbon energy sources, along with advances in carbon sequestration or carbon capture and storage technologies. The rise of these technologies was in large part a consequence of government support for clean technology, both by pricing carbon emissions (especially in Europe) and by directly supporting innovation in clean technologies.

This change was the result of a three-step transformation. First came a broad recognition that mounting fossil fuel emissions and the increasing concentration of carbon in the atmosphere was a major problem for humanity— even if this is not completely shared by the US public and policymakers. The second step was a measurement framework, which enabled policymakers to quantify the damage to the environment (via carbon emissions) and classified different technologies as clean or dirty (big engines for SUVs are not a clean technology, but solar panels are). The third step then used the broad agreement in society and the measurement framework to develop policies supporting clean technologies. I believe the same three steps are necessary to redirect technological change away from excessive automation.

The first step would again be a general agreement that automation, when not counterbalanced by other technologies, can create major social costs, and that we are on a path toward excessive automation. The second step would develop a measurement framework for quantifying the social cost of excessive automation and for classifying different types of technologies into automation versus other activities, including the creation of new labor-intensive tasks. The third step would turn the first two steps into actual policies.

The relevant policies would follow from these general principles, recognizing the possible causes of excessive automation I highlighted earlier. Reversing the excessively favorable treatment of machinery relative to labor is one obvious policy avenue. This would have a static benefit by rolling back tax-induced excessive automation at the margin and also scale back the incentives to supply further automation technologies in response to these tax incentives.

A greater role for government support and leadership in directing technological change is the second important dimension. This would both limit the dominant role of the big tech companies in shaping the direction of technological change and also create more generous funding for new, blue-sky projects that are important for producing a favorable environment for other types of technologies. If government policy can be undergirded by a broad consensus that we need more than just automation and a concrete measurement framework for distinguishing automation technologies from others, it can be used to support the creation of new tasks that will reinstate labor and generate more employment and better opportunities for workers (Acemoglu 2019).

This process needs to be accompanied by a change in general attitudes and norms both in society at large and in the corporate world. In the same way that many youths view a world in which we continue to emit huge amounts of carbon as unacceptable, they need to understand that automating much of the production process has significant social costs and that there are other ways of improving the technological frontier and our productivity. Then their values need to be implemented by the corporate world. This is a tall order, in the same way that turning away from a century of a singular focus on fossil fuels was. But it can and should be done.

References

Acemoglu, Daron. 2019. "It's Good Jobs Stupid." Economics for Inclusive Prosperity Policy Brief 13, Economics for Inclusive Prosperity, Cambridge, MA. https://econfip.org/policy-brief/its-good-jobs-stupid/.

Acemoglu, Daron, and David Autor. 2011. "Skills, Tasks and Technologies: Implications for Employment and Earnings." In *Handbook of Labor Economics*, Vol. 4, edited by Orlie Ashenfelter and David Card, 1043–1171. Amsterdam: Elsevier.

Acemoglu, Daron, Andrea Manera, and Pascual Restrepo. 2020. "Tax Policy and Excessive Automation." *Brookings Papers on Economic Activity* (forthcoming).

Acemoglu, Daron, and Pascual Restrepo. 2019a. "The Race between Machine and Man: Implications of Technology for Growth, Factor Shares, and Employment." *American Economic Review* 108(6): 1488–1542.

Acemoglu, Daron, and Pascual Restrepo. 2019b. "Automation and New Tasks: How Technology Displaces and Reinstates Labor." *Journal of Economic Perspectives* 33(2): 3–31.

Acemoglu, Daron, and Pascual Restrepo. 2020a. "The Wrong Kind of AI? Artificial Intelligence and the Future of Labor Demand." *Cambridge Journal of Regions, Economy and Society* special issue (forthcoming).

Acemoglu, Daron, and Pascual Restrepo. 2020b. "Displacement and Inequality." Manuscript in preparation.

Autor, David, David Dorn, and Gordon H. Hanson. 2019. "When Work Disappears: Manufacturing Decline and the Falling Marriage Market Value of Men." *American Economic Review: Insights* 1(2): 161–178.

Goldin, Claudia, and Lawrence Katz. 2008. *The Race between Education and Technology*. Cambridge, MA: Belknap Press.

Oberfield, Ezra, and Devesh Raval. 2014. "Micro Data and Macro Technology." NBER Working Paper 20452, National Bureau of Economic Research, Cambridge, MA.

Tinbergen, Jan. 1975. *Income Distribution Analysis and Policies*. Amsterdam: North-Holland.

Wilson, William Julius. 1996. *When Work Disappears: The World of the New Urban Poor*. New York: Knopf.

Zeira, Joseph. 1998. "Workers, Machines, and Economic Growth." *Quarterly Journal of Economics* 113(4): 1091–1117.

18

Innovation and Inequality

Philippe Aghion

Over the past 40 years, we have witnessed an accelerated increase in income inequality in developed countries between the top earners and the rest of society (e.g., see Deaton 2013; Piketty 2013). Aghion et al. (2015) argue that innovation is an unavoidable part of the story.

Why should we care that innovation partly accounts for the surge in income inequality between top earners and everyone else? As it turns out, innovation has virtues that other potential sources of this income inequality do not have. First, innovation drives productivity growth, as emphasized by the endogenous growth literature and as shown by recent empirical evidence (e.g., see Akcigit et al. 2017). But, in addition, as shown by Aghion et al. (2014), innovation fosters social mobility as a result of creative destruction, the process whereby new technologies always replace old ones.

Measuring Inequality and Innovation

There are different ways to measure inequality. First, there is the Gini coefficient, which is a global measure of how far from perfect equality a country or region is. Other global measures of inequality include the 90/10 ratio (of how much the top 10% of income earners earn compared to the bottom 10%). Second is the share of income of the top 1% or top 0.1%. This is a measure of inequality at the very top of the income distribution. Third, there is a more dynamic measure of inequality, which is the correlation between parents' income and children's income. A lower correlation reflects a higher degree of social mobility in the economy.

Chetty et al. (2014) exploit information on income inequality and social mobility across commuting zones and find a negative correlation between social mobility and broad measures of income inequality. A similar correlation was found in cross-country regressions by the Organization for Economic Cooperation and Development (OECD), referred to as the "Great Gatsby Curve." Chetty et al. (2014) also find a slightly positive correlation between social mobility and the inequality measure for the top 1%. This latter finding suggests that innovation is indeed part of the inequality story: California, the most innovative state in the United States, has a top 1% income share and level of social mobility that are both much higher than in the least innovative state, Alabama. To measure current innovation in a US state, Aghion et al. (2015) use the annual number of new patents per capita in that state and patent citations.

Three Striking Facts

The first finding of Aghion et al. (2015) is depicted in figure 18.1. It shows that the income share of the top 1% in a given US state in a given year is positively and significantly correlated with the state's degree of innovativeness, and Aghion et al. (2015) show that this correlation reflects a causal effect between innovation and inequality between those at the top of the income scale and the rest of society that is true for all measures of innovation.[1]

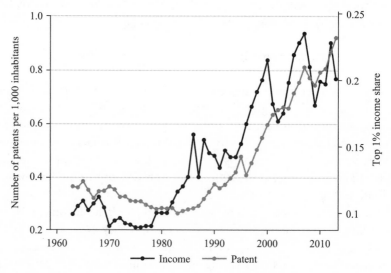

Figure 18.1
Plot of the logarithm of the number of patent applications per capita (x axis) against the logarithm of the top 1% income share (y axis). Observations are computed at the US state level from 1960 to 2010.

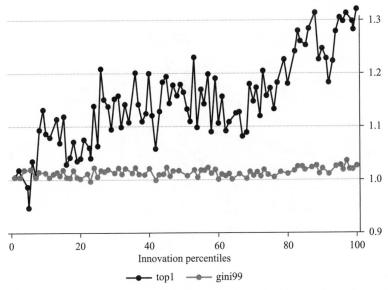

Figure 18.2
Plot of the average income share of the top 1% and the Gini index for the bottom 99% as a function of their corresponding innovation percentiles. The bottom 99% Gini is the Gini coefficient when the top 1% of the income distribution is removed. Innovation percentiles are computed using the US state-year pairs from 1975 to 2010.

Figure 18.2 shows that innovativeness is uncorrelated with the Gini. The reason is that while innovation fosters income inequality between those at the top and the rest of society, at the same time it enhances social mobility.

Indeed, Aghion et al. (2015) look at how innovativeness correlates with social mobility across US commuting zones (CZs), using the measures of social mobility from Chetty et al. (2014). Figure 18.3 shows a positive correlation between patent count and social mobility. In fact Aghion et al. (2015) show that it is "entrant" innovation (i.e., innovation by new innovators) that has a positive and significant effect on social mobility, whereas the effect of incumbent innovation on social mobility is not significant. This is in line with the view that innovation fosters social mobility when it is associated with creative destruction.

Lobbying Is a Quite Different Source of Income Inequality between those at the Top and the Rest of Society

Another source of income inequality between those at the top and the rest of society is entry barriers and lobbying, because lobbying activities typically help incumbents prevent new entry and thereby preserve their

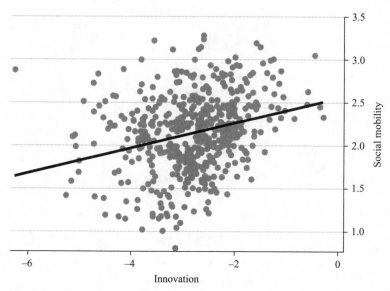

Figure 18.3
Plot of the logarithm of the number of patent applications per capita (*x* axis) against the logarithm of social mobility (*y* axis). Social mobility is computed as the probability of belonging to the highest quintile of the income distribution in 2010 (when aged 30) when parents belonged to the lowest quintile in 1996 (when aged 16). Observations are computed at the level of commuting zones (569 observations). The number of patents is the average from 2006 to 2010.

rents. But precisely because they get in the way of new entry and creative destruction, lobbying activities reduce both productivity growth and social mobility.

In fact, one can show, using panel data on lobbying across US states, that, like innovation, lobbying is positively correlated with the top 1% in income share; unlike innovation, lobbying is negatively correlated with social mobility and entrant innovation; and, unlike innovation, lobbying is positively and significantly correlated with the Gini (i.e., with broad inequality).

Should We Worry about the Rich?

It was argued earlier that innovation is a source of income inequality between the top earners and everyone else that has the virtue of enhancing social mobility, hence the absence of a correlation between innovation and broad inequality. Does this imply that we should not care about the wealthy (i.e., about the top income earners or the wealthiest)? The answer is no; we should care about the fact that the wealthy, including those that became rich by successfully innovating in the past, can use their wealth to lobby to prevent new innovators from entering the market.

Recent studies on the rise in concentration and rents and the simultaneous fall in productivity growth in the United States since the mid-2000s show how serious this latter concern is. In particular, Aghion et al. (2019) argue that the recent productivity slowdown in the United States has a lot to do with the fact that some "superstar" firms (Amazon, Facebook, Walmart, and other large firms), the so-called FAMANG (Facebook-Amazon-Microsoft-Netflix-Google), have become so prominent and have invaded so many sectors and product lines that they have discouraged other firms from entering the market and innovating.

Thus, if the average markup has gone up in the United States over the past decade, it is mainly because the superstar firms, which are also the high-markup firms, have taken over many sectors and product lines in the economy. FAMANG firms are more "efficient" than nonsuperstar firms (they are better able to network and have accumulated social capital, which is hard for other firms to imitate). Thus, when the IT revolution initially allowed those firms to expand, we observed a surge in aggregate productivity growth in the United States (during the decade 1995–2005). But the long-term effect of this market expansion has been to discourage innovation and entry by other firms, hence the decline in Total Factor Productivity (TFP) growth since 2005.

The lack of an appropriate competition policy in the United States, and in particular the absence of good regulation of mergers and acquisitions (M&As), has facilitated this expansion of superstar firms to so many local markets and product lines, and therefore it has fostered the decline in aggregate productivity growth.

Conclusion

A couple of lessons can be drawn from the preceding discussion. First, innovation is a source of income and wealth inequality between those at the top and the rest of society, but it enhances productivity growth and social mobility. Thus, we need capitalism and the protection of property rights on innovation, and we need to reward and encourage innovation, as it can bring both prosperity and social mobility. Second, yesterday's innovators have tended to become entrenched incumbents today, but with the potential to use their rents in order to deter innovation by new entrants, thereby eventually undermining productivity growth and social mobility. Capitalism thus needs to be regulated, or to use an excellent expression from Rajan and Zingales (2014), "We need to protect capitalism from the capitalists."

How can we do so? This was the whole theme of the Peterson Institute for International Economics conference (2014), "Combating Inequality: Rethinking Policies to Reduce Inequality in Advanced Economies," which led to this book. I simply want to emphasize that several instruments should be used simultaneously: progressive taxation, of course, but we also need to rethink competition policy in light of the IT and digital revolutions and the emergence of the new superstar firms and need to closely analyze the organization and functioning of the lobbying system and the interface between politicians and the private sector.

Note

1. Aghion et al. (2015) use two Instrumental Variables (IV) strategies. The first strategy uses data on the appropriations committee of the Senate, based on the view that a new appointee on the appropriations committee will push for allocating federal funds to research in their state. The second strategy uses innovating activities in other states as the instrument.

References

Aghion, P., U. Akcigit, A. Bergeaud, R. Blundell, and D. Hemous. 2015. "Innovation and Top Income Inequality." NBER Working Paper 21247, National Bureau of Economic Research, Cambridge, MA.

Aghion, P., U. Akcigit, and P. Howitt. 2014. "What Do We Learn from Schumpeterian Growth Theory?" In *Handbook of Economic Growth*, edited by P. Aghion and S. Durlauf, Vol. 2B, 515–563. Amsterdam: Elsevier.

Aghion, P., A. Bergeaud, T. Boppart, P. Klenow, and H. Li. 2019. "A Theory of Falling Growth and Rising Rents." Working paper, Stanford University, Standord, CA.

Akcigit, U., J. Grigsby, and T. Nicholas. 2017. "The Rise of American Ingenuity: Innovation and Inventors of the Golden Age," NBER Working Paper 23047, National Bureau of Economic Research, Cambridge, MA.

Chetty, R., N. Hendren, P. Kline, and E. Saez. 2014. "Where Is the Land of Opportunity? The Geography of Intergenerational Mobility in the United States." *Quarterly Journal of Economics* 129: 1553–1623.

Deaton, A. 2013. *The Great Escape: Health, Wealth, and the Origins of Inequality*. Princeton, NJ: Princeton University Press.

Piketty, T. 2013. *Le Capital au XXIeme Siecle*. Paris: Editions du Seuil.

Rajan, R., and L. Zingales. 2014. *Saving Capitalism from the Capitalists*, Collins Business.

19

Technological Change, Income Inequality, and Good Jobs

Laura D'Andrea Tyson

Introduction

Dramatic technological changes are reshaping work, the primary way most people earn their incomes. Almost daily, there are examples of how new technologies are transforming work, triggering changes in the quantity and quality of jobs. Surveys reveal deep concern among citizens about the implications of these changes for employment, wages, and living standards (Geiger 2019). Behind this concern is a fundamental question: will there be enough jobs in the future?

The history of technological revolutions indicates that the likely answer is yes (Frey 2019). Technological change drives productivity growth, and that fuels the demand for labor. There is no evidence of a long-run trade-off between productivity growth and employment growth. Many existing jobs are changed or destroyed by changes in technology, but many new ones are created. In the long run, there is no "technological unemployment." The productivity benefits of technological change, however, can take decades to arrive, and there is considerable dislocation of workers during the transition from old jobs to new ones, with significant frictional and structural unemployment along the way. For many, the destruction of jobs, industries, and even communities can last a lifetime.

History also reveals that technological change tends to increase income inequality, widening income gaps between those whose jobs are displaced and those who assume new jobs (Autor, Mindell, and Reynolds 2019). During the last half century, technological change has been both labor-saving and skill-biased. Digital technologies have reduced the demand for workers with middle skills performing routine tasks and increased the demand for workers with higher skills performing technical and problem-solving tasks (Manyika et al. 2017; Autor 2019, 2010).[1] Skill-biased technological progress is evident in the polarization of labor markets in the

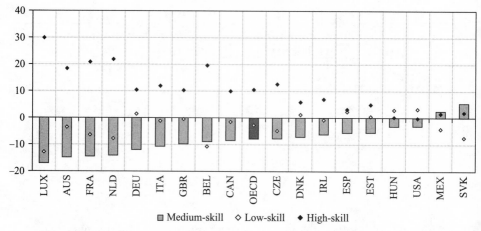

Figure 19.1
Jobs polarized across OECD countries between the mid-1990s and mid-2010s. Percentage change in share of working adults in each skill group. Results are at the individual level for working adults. *Source*: OECD staff calculations based on LIS, ECHP, and EU-SILC.

advanced economies—a decline in middle-skill jobs relative to both high-skill and low-skill jobs, with the largest gains registered by the former (see figure 19.1). Skill-biased technological change has been a factor behind widening income inequality and the falling share of labor income in national income (Tyson and Spence 2017; Berger and Woff 2017; Leduc and Liu 2019; IMF 2017). Given the current trajectory of technological progress, these trends are likely to persist for the foreseeable future.

Under these conditions, a major question is not whether there will be enough jobs but whether there will be enough good jobs—jobs that provide middle-class earnings, safe working conditions, legal protections, social protections and benefits (e.g., unemployment and disability benefits, health benefits, family benefits, pensions), and organizations to represent workers (OECD 2016). The slow growth of pretax incomes for the bottom 50% of earners has been the main driver of increasing income inequality over the past half century (Chancel 2019). Access to education, health care, and good jobs is key to lifting these incomes and making technology-enabled growth inclusive.

In the remainder of this chapter, I provide examples of four types of policies to increase the likelihood of creating good jobs in the United States: tax policies and R&D policies to affect the direction and diffusion of technological change; training policies to enable workers to meet the rising skill requirements of new jobs; direct labor market interventions to provide good jobs in nonstandard employment; and measures to strengthen workers' voice in business decisions.

Policies to Affect the Rate and Direction of Technological Progress

Tax Policy

Tax policies influence business decisions to invest in new production technologies. In the United States and other advanced economies, effective tax rates on labor greatly exceed those on physical and knowledge capital, encouraging laborsaving and capital-using investments.[2] A reduction in payroll and other employment-related taxes would moderate the resulting bias in investment incentives. So would an increase in taxes on capital, including corporate income. Recently, the US corporate tax rate was cut dramatically. Proponents argued that the cut would increase business investment and that in turn would increase employment and wages. As technology becomes more laborsaving, however, the employment effects of business investment in physical and technology capital are declining, and the new US tax law contains no links between additional business investment and the creation of good jobs.[3]

As capital has become more mobile across national borders, many multinational companies have been able to make their profits "stateless" for tax purposes by shifting them to locations where they have little or no real economic activity and pay little or no tax. Stateless corporate income erodes the tax base and reduces the capacity of individual countries to raise revenues to fund infrastructure and social protection programs. It also exacerbates the gap between the taxation of mobile profits and the taxation of immobile labor.[4] In their recent book *The Triumph of Injustice: How the Rich Dodge Taxes and How to Make Them Pay*, Emmanuel Saez and Gabriel Zucman (2019a) discuss the consequences of stateless capital income for income inequality and suggest national remedies as stopgap measures in the absence of an international agreement to tax such income (Saez and Zucman 2019b). In the long run, given the magnitude of cross-border capital flows, such an agreement is essential.

In the US, taxes on capital income should also be increased by raising the tax rate on capital gains to the tax rate on personal income and by eliminating the carried-interest loophole. Both the preferential capital gains tax rate and carried-interest feature of current tax law have encouraged technology investments favoring capital and profits over labor and wages. They have also fueled the "financialization" of the US economy and increased income inequality (Foroohar 2016).

Reductions in payroll and other direct taxes on labor, even if offset in part by higher taxes on capital, would cause significant shortfalls in government revenues to fund health care, education, and benefits for workers—all key components of good jobs. A national carbon tax should be used to offset the loss in government revenues.[5] Lower taxes on labor to promote creation of good jobs, and higher taxes on carbon to discourage carbon use, are a wise recipe for a future of good jobs and a sustainable environment.

R&D Policy

Technological change and its diffusion are not exogenous: they are path dependent and endogenous. They depend on the incentives of those who fund R&D and those who invest in and deploy the resulting technologies. As Daron Acemoglu argues, it is possible to characterize the economy as having an "innovation possibilities" frontier with trade-offs between different factor-augmenting technologies.[6] Market incentives bias investments by companies, particularly those with substantial market power, toward innovations that generate returns to capital rather than societal benefits in the form of good jobs. The result is a "tragedy of the commons" bias against investments in job-creating innovations.

In the United States and other advanced industrial countries, R&D receives substantial public support through direct government funding and tax policies. Although government (mainly federal) is the major funder of basic R&D in the United States, the business sector is both the largest funder (67%) and the largest performer (72%) of overall R&D.[7] Most business R&D focuses on product development for private returns rather than on basic science for social returns.[8] As the time horizons of US companies have shortened, business R&D has become more focused on shorter-term and lower-risk development (Hourihan and Parks 2019).

Business R&D spending is supported by the R&D tax credit, which has been effective in encouraging R&D by those companies positioned to take advantage of it (Hall 2019) and should be continued. Most of the R&D credit, however, goes to large companies, many of which also have large amounts of stateless income sheltered around the world.[9] Business R&D is heavily concentrated in five sectors,[10] accounting for 83% of the total R&D but less than 11% of employment.[11]

Federal R&D funding for defense has been a major factor in the development of the aviation, computer, and internet industries, and federal funding for health care has been a major factor in the development of the pharmaceutical/biotechnology and medical technology industries

(Mazzucato 2015). Federal R&D funding and related tax incentives have also played important roles in moving businesses along the innovation frontier toward new green technologies. Overall, there are numerous examples showing that government funding and tax incentives can "direct" technology trajectories.

New government programs and tax credits should be introduced to nudge R&D toward innovations that complement human skills in sectors of growing demand, such as health care, education, and technology itself. Allocating a share of federal R&D funds for health care to foster labor-augmenting innovations in the health care delivery system is an option worth considering. Another option is a new federal R&D program to foster investment in "intelligent infrastructure" to adapt to climate change.[12] Such investment would generate good jobs and fund necessary adaptations (e.g., port reconstruction, flood prevention, and fire prevention through the installation of underground electricity grids).

At the macro level, significant increases in federal funding for R&D and infrastructure, two public foundations of long-term economic growth and two key components of "public capital" (Council on Foreign Relations 2019),[13] are warranted.[14] The social returns on these investments far exceed the government's long-term borrowing costs. Government spending in these areas should be treated not as operational expenses but rather as investments, and should be included in a separate capital budget. Without a change in budgetary rules, government spending on them will continue to decline relative to the growing needs of the economy.[15]

Policies to Develop Worker Skills

Although skill-biased technologies are destroying middle-skill jobs and occupations, they are increasing higher-skill ones at an equal or faster pace (Manyika et al. 2017). However, there are considerable gaps between the skills required for the disappearing jobs and those required for the new ones. In response, governments are introducing new education and training programs with a focus on nonelite postsecondary educational venues.

In the United States, community colleges are the most important provider of skills at scale and are particularly important for vocational education and training for first-generation, low-income, and minority students.[16] There are substantial wage and employment benefits to completing a community college degree and lesser but still positive returns from certificate programs (Osterman 2019). Expanding funding for community college education and making it more affordable for low-income students should be key priorities for states seeking to create good job opportunities for their citizens. Thirteen states—both Republican and Democrat controlled—have implemented some form of "tuition-free" community college program, and more than nine states are working on similar legislation (Campaign for Free College Tuition n.d.).[17]

Apprenticeships combining classroom and on-the-job learning are another valuable model for skill development. Workers receive a skill-based education that prepares them and often places them directly in good-paying jobs, and employers benefit by recruiting and retaining a skilled labor force. Germany and Switzerland are well known for their successful apprenticeship programs.[18]

Apprenticeships are gaining attention in the United States. The US Department of Labor recently introduced a website and programs to encourage apprenticeships through information sharing, technical support, and small grants to employers, individuals, and educators.[19] Several states are also introducing apprenticeship initiatives. Based on the Swiss model, Colorado launched apprenticeship programs in several industries (Gunn 2018).[20] Now 28 states have joined Colorado in the Skillful network (Skillful 2019) to develop training approaches that combine classroom learning with workplace experience. Programs take a variety of forms—apprenticeships, targeted certification programs, technology "boot camps," and on-the-job classes—and target the provision of skills to the 70% of the US workforce without college degrees.

Other countries are experimenting with different approaches to lifelong learning. Singapore has established a SkillsFuture Credit of S$500 available to individuals over the age of 25 for continued education. The Federal Ministry of Labour and Social Affairs in Germany is studying "individual learning accounts" modeled on Singapore's approach.[21] An option for the United States is the creation of tax-advantaged "Lifelong Learning and Training Accounts" (Fitzpayne and Pollack 2018), funded by individual contributions, matched in part by government funds, and usable and portable by individual workers.[22] Government funding for individual learning accounts should be limited to programs that are certified for quality, designed with employer input, yield recognized credentials, and provide portable skills.

Direct Labor Market Interventions for Nonstandard Employment

The social protections associated with standard full-time employment are essential features of "good jobs." Many of these features are absent for workers in various types of "precarious" employment, including self-employment and dependent (i.e., dependent on a client or business) employment that is part-time, temporary, on call, and/or done for multiple employers and through platforms (Thelen 2019).[23] Even in Europe, where workers in standard full-time employment have legally mandated access to generous social protections that are not legally required for full-time workers in the United States, many workers in precarious and gig jobs have little or no coverage.[24] The same is true for the growing number (an estimated 57 million) of gig workers in the United States (Miklusak 2019).[25]

In Europe, several countries have created new intermediate categories of employment that extend some social protection rights to gig workers. In recent legislation, the state of California took a different approach, making it difficult for businesses to classify those who work for them as independent contractors rather than employees (Tyson 2019). The latter are covered by protections and benefits mandated by federal and state laws (including minimum wages), while the former are not.[26] Providing gig workers previously classified as independent contractors with these benefits is likely to increase labor costs between 20% and 30% (Conger and Scheiber 2019).

Individual security accounts (ISAs) that move with workers from job to job are a promising policy to provide portable benefits to workers in multiple precarious employment relationships (Hill 2015; Reder, Steward, and Foster 2019). An ISA would be established for each worker, and each business hiring that worker would be required to contribute an amount for his or her benefits prorated for the number of hours worked.[27] Workers would be able to accrue benefits even when working for and moving among multiple employers and projects. Workers would also be able to make tax-advantaged contributions into their accounts.[28] Several states are now designing portable benefit systems, and to head off other regulations, some platform companies are supporting the approach (Maxim and Muro 2018).

Worker Voice and Worker Interests

The share of workers who are members of unions and/or are covered by collective bargaining agreements has declined significantly in the United States and other advanced industrial countries (OECD 2019a). At the same time, in many industries, product market competition has eroded, concentration has increased, and there is growing evidence of monopsony power.[29] Under conditions of monopsony, unions can provide an important counterweight to employer power, fostering higher wages, more employment, and more efficient outcomes (Council of Economic Advisers 2016).

During the last 50 years, unions have atrophied in the United States for several reasons, including the misclassification of employees as independent contractors and actions by states and companies to discourage unionization. Under US federal law, independent contractors cannot form unions—a position recently affirmed by the National Labor Relations Board. Current US law also prevents the formation of work councils or other organizations to represent worker interests in nonunionized firms and hinders new forms of worker advocacy at the industry and company levels.[30]

The US system of labor relations and corporate governance is out of balance, with too much power for employers and too little power for workers. US labor law needs to be changed to strengthen the ability of workers to organize by company, by industry, and by region, and to allow companies to experiment with work councils and other institutions to provide a voice to workers as legitimate stakeholders in company decisions. In a recent statement by the Business Roundtable (2019), the CEOs of many of America's top companies explicitly identify their employees as stakeholders and commit to providing them with fair compensation and benefits and with training and education for new skills. The statement is silent, however, on unions and worker voice.

Notes

1. The founders and top managers of firms that have enjoyed market power and profitability fueled by technological change are among the "workers" who have enjoyed the largest income gains, and many of these gains show up as labor income in national accounts. Such workers are referred to as supermanagers by Piketty (2014) and as innovators, creatives, and geniuses by Benzell and Brynjolfsson (2019). The distribution of income for supermanagers and innovators/creators takes the form of a power distribution with a small number of winners capturing most of the rewards and a long tail consisting of the rest of the participants (Brynjolfsson, McAfee, and Spence 2014).

2. Direct taxation of labor constitutes the largest share of tax revenue in all these countries (Bastani and Waldenström 2018).

3. The dramatic reduction in the US corporate tax rate and the move from a worldwide to a territorial system for taxing the offshore income of US multinationals followed a series of similar actions by other advanced industrial countries as they engaged in a global race to the bottom to attract business investment. In a territorial system, a country taxes the income of its multinational companies if the income is earned at home or if it is repatriated from abroad. The race fostered the offshoring of production and the creation of elaborate supply chains to take advantage of labor arbitrage opportunities enabled

by technological changes in transportation and communication. Technology-enabled globalization in turn reduced employment and constrained wage growth for workers in the advanced economies (Milanović 2016).

4. In response to these challenges, the OECD has developed the BEPS project to forge international agreements on consistent ways to tax capital income. As a result of BEPS, individual countries now have much better information about where their multinational companies are earning or moving their profits and about the taxes they are paying in each location in which profits are made (OECD n.d.). A binding international agreement harmonizing the tax treatment of corporate income of multinational companies will take many years to realize.

5. A carbon tax would reduce the incentives for carbon-emitting activities and has widespread bipartisan support among economists as the most efficient way to cut carbon emissions and to encourage innovation to address climate change (Climate Leadership Council 2019; Tyson and Mendonca 2018).

6. His work shows evidence of such a frontier reflected in an increasing pace of technology-enabled laborsaving displacement and a decreasing pace of technology-enabled reinstatement of labor through new job and task creation (Acemoglu and Restrepo 2019). Slowing productivity growth has accompanied this shift, indicating that "overautomating" investments may be hitting diminishing returns.

7. R&D for defense purposes accounts for most federal R&D funding for both businesses and universities—accounting for about 51% of total federal R&D funding, a share that has been consistent over several decades. Health care is the second-largest area of federal R&D funding, accounting for about 53% of nondefense R&D funding.

8. Of business R&D, 80% is on development and only 20% is on basic research.

9. With the elimination of the alternative minimum corporate tax in 2016, small and medium-sized businesses with $50 million or less in gross receipts are now better positioned to take advantage of the credit.

10. The five sectors are pharmaceuticals, computers and electronic equipment, transportation equipment, information, and professional/scientific and technical services.

11. From a "good jobs" perspective, it is important to note that the credit can be applied against "qualified" R&D expenses, including spending on technical and scientific staff, which is a major share of such expenses.

12. Climate change is now recognized as a major national security risk; R&D to address this risk should be accorded the same priority as R&D for traditional national security and defense purposes and should be included in R&D spending for defense.

13. During the last several decades, the stock of public capital has declined even as the stock of private capital has soared in the United States and other advanced economies (Chancel 2019).

14. Federal funding for R&D as a share of GDP has been on a long and steady decline over the last 50 years, from 1.9% in the 1960s to a low of 0.62% in 2017.

15. Under current budgetary rules, government funding for R&D and infrastructure is contained in the "discretionary government budget," the portion of federal outlays determined annually through the appropriations process and subject to arbitrary budgetary caps and volatile rules at odds with efficient long-term investment decisions. And discretionary spending as a share of federal outlays has fallen to new lows as a result of both tax cuts that have reduced federal revenues as a share of GDP to historic lows and rising mandatory spending requirements, driven primarily by rising health care costs and demographics.

16. There are nearly 1,200 community colleges nationally that offer degrees and certificates to approximately 12 million students in credit and noncredit courses. About 6 million students are enrolled in credit courses, and another 6 million are in noncredit courses. Among the students enrolled in credit courses, 4 million are part-time, 33% work 35 or more hours a week, and 40% are over age 24.

17. In addition to legislation that expands the California College Promise program to make two years of community college free for first-time, full-time students, California recently introduced a new low-tuition online community college program that includes in-person apprenticeships and is targeted at low-wage and underemployed working adults. Calbright College was founded to improve the work prospects for approximately 8 million adult workers in California who are underemployed, working multiple part-time jobs, or in jobs that do not pay a living wage.

18. In Germany, 48% of the working-age population (age 15+) has apprenticeship and/or vocational qualification training. Apprenticeship programs exist for hundreds of occupations in Germany, and associations of employers design the training to provide the skills needed by employers. Individuals completing apprenticeships must pass rigorous exams designed and overseen by employers in order to receive certification. Young apprenticeship graduates (age 16–35) earn 46% more than similar young adults whose highest qualification is at the academic upper secondary level but 16% less than those who complete postsecondary and tertiary education (OECD 2018).

19. The Department of Labor estimates that about 655,000 individuals completed formal apprenticeship programs between January 2017 and September 2019, 94% of graduates retained a job with the organization for which they served as an apprentice, and the average salary of graduates of apprenticeship programs was $70,000 (US Department of Labor n.d.).

20. Recently, California launched a new apprenticeship program aimed at filling vacant IT jobs in California state government.

21. In addition, as part of Germany's new national skills strategy, supported by both employer associations and unions, several government agencies are working together to develop an online platform to make information about continuing education and training opportunities available to individual workers and to provide lifelong career counseling and competency assessments for them (Federal Ministry of Labour and Social Affairs and the Federal Ministry of Education and Research Information 2019).

22. An OECD paper (OECD 2018) provides policy recommendations about effective designs for individual learning systems based on assessments of the Singapore credit and several other examples of individual learning accounts, including individual training accounts recently introduced in Michigan and Washington State.

23. In the OECD, one in six workers is self-employed, one in eight dependent employees is on a temporary contract, and 16.5% of dependent employment is part-time. The comparable numbers for the United States are 6.3% self-employment, 4% temporary employment, and 13% part-time employment (OECD 2019b).

24. For a complete discussion of current social protections in the European Union for workers in standard and nonstandard employment, see Petropoulos et al. (2019).

25. This number includes independent freelancers as well as individuals working for Uber and other platform companies.

26. Employers would have the right to decide how these increased costs are shared between their owners and investors in terms of reduced profits, their workers in terms of reduced take-home pay, and their customers in terms of increased prices and reduced services. Employers' decisions would depend in part on both their market power in the product markets in which they sell their services and their monopsony power in the labor markets in which they hire workers.

27. To eliminate possible competitiveness effects of ISA costs on individual companies, all the companies in an industry could be required to make ISA contributions.

28. The portable benefits concept is attracting interest in Europe and gaining momentum in the United States. President Obama endorsed the idea in 2016 (Foster 2015), and in 2019 Senator Mark Warner introduced the Portable Benefits for Independent Workers Pilot Program Act, which would establish a $20 million fund for experimentation.

29. Together, these trends have contributed to the growing gap between wage and productivity growth, the shift in the distribution of business earnings toward profits, and the rising disparity in wages across firms and industries.

30. Under US law, the formation of a work council requires that the firm be unionized. When Volkswagen, a German company with work councils in Germany, wanted to establish a work council in its Tennessee plant, it was blocked by the state's governor, who opposed the plant's unionization.

References

Acemoglu, Daron, and Pascual Restrepo. 2019. "Automation and New Tasks: How Technology Displaces and Reinstates Labor." *Journal of Economic Perspectives* 33(2): 3–31.

Autor, David. 2010. *The Polarization of Job Opportunities in the U.S. Labor Market*. Washington, DC: Center for American Progress and The Hamilton Project.

Autor, David H. 2019. "Work of the Past, Work of the Future." *AEA Papers and Proceedings* 109:1–32.

Autor, David, David A. Mindell, and Elisabeth B. Reynolds. 2019. "The Work of the Future: Shaping Technology and Institutions." MIT Work of the Future Task Force Report, Massachusetts Institute of Technology, Cambridge, MA.

Bastani, Spencer, and Daniel Waldenström. 2018. "How Should Capital Be Taxed? Theory and Evidence from Sweden." IZA Discussion Paper 11475, Institute of Labor Economics, Bonn. http://ftp.iza.org/dp11475.pdf.

Benzell, Seth G., and Erik Brynjolfsson. 2019. "Digital Abundance and Scarce Genius: Implications for Wages, Interest Rates, and Growth." NBER Working Paper 25585, National Bureau of Economic Research, Cambridge, MA. https://www.nber.org/papers/w25585.

Berger, Bennet, and Guntram Wolff. 2017. "The Global Decline in the Labour Income Share: Is Capital the Answer to Germany's Current Account Surplus?" Bruegel Policy Contribution 12. https://bruegel.org/wp-content/uploads/2017/04/PC-12-2017-1.pdf.

Brynjolfsson, Erik, Andrew McAfee, and Michael Spence. 2014. "New World Order: Labor, Capital, and Ideas in the Power Law Economy." *Foreign Affairs* 93(4): 44–53.

Business Roundtable. 2019. "Statement on the Purpose of a Corporation." https://opportunity.businessroundtable.org/wp-content/uploads/2019/09/BRT-Statement-on-the-Purpose-of-a-Corporation-with-Signatures-1.pdf.

Campaign for Free College Tuition. n.d. https://www.freecollegenow.org/.

Chancel, Lucas. 2019. "Ten Facts about Inequality in Advanced Economies." Powerpoint presentation at the Peterson Institute for International Economics conference "Combating Inequality: Rethinking Policies to Reduce Inequality in Advanced Economies," Washington, DC, October 2019. https://www.piie.com/system/files/documents/2019-10-17-s1-chancel-ppt.pdf.

Climate Leadership Council. 2019. "Economists' Statement on Carbon Dividends." https://www.econstatement.org/.

Conger, Kate, and Noam Scheiber. 2019. "California Bill Makes App-Based Companies Treat Workers as Employees." *New York Times*, September 11, 2019. https://www.nytimes.com/2019/09/11/technology/california-gig-economy-bill.html.

Council of Economic Advisers. 2016. *Labor Market Monopsony: Trends, Consequences, and Policy Responses.* Issue Brief, October 25, 2016. https://obamawhitehouse.archives.gov/sites/default/files/page/files/20161025_monopsony_labor_mrkt_cea.pdf.

Council on Foreign Relations. 2019. *Innovation and National Security: Keeping Our Edge.* Independent Task Force Report 77. New York: Council on Foreign Relations. https://www.cfr.org/report/keeping-our-edge/.

Federal Ministry of Labour and Social Affairs and the Federal Ministry of Education and Research Information. 2019. *National Skills Strategy.* https://www.bmas

.de/SharedDocs/Downloads/EN/Topics/Initial-and-Continuing-Training/national
-skills-strategy.pdf.

Fitzpayne, Alastair, and Ethan Pollack. 2018. *Lifelong Learning and Training Accounts: Helping Workers Adapt and Success in a Changing Economy.* Issue Brief, May 2018, Aspen Institute, Washington, DC. https://assets.aspeninstitute
.org/content/uploads/2018/05/Lifelong-Learning-and-Training-Accounts-Issue
-Brief.pdf.

Foroohar, Rana. 2016. *Makers and Takers: The Rise of Finance and the Fall of American Business.* New York: Crown Business.

Foster, Natalie. 2015. "The Big Idea Buried in Obama's Speech." *Medium,* January 13, 2015. https://medium.com/ondemand/the-big-idea-buried-in-obama-s
-speech-30fe2832c0c#.yc5oujol6.

Frey, Carl Benedikt. 2019. *The Technology Trap: Capital, Labor, and Power in the Age of Automation.* Princeton, NJ: Princeton University Press.

Geiger, A. W. 2019. "How Americans See Automation and the Workplace in 7 Charts." *Fact Tank News in Numbers,* Pew Research Center, April 8, 2019. https://pewrsr.ch/2VklRnj.

Gunn, Dwyer. 2018. "The Swiss Secret to Jump-Starting Your Career." *The Atlantic,* September 7, 2018. https://www.theatlantic.com/business/archive/2018/09
/apprenticeships-america/567640/.

Hall, Bronwyn H. 2019. "Tax Policy for Innovation." NBER Working Paper 25773, National Bureau of Economic Research, Cambridge, MA. https://www
.nber.org/papers/w25773.

Hill, Steven. 2015. *Raw Deal: How the "Uber Economy" and Runaway Capitalism Are Screwing American Workers.* New York: St. Martin's Press.

Hourihan, Matt, and David Parkes. 2019. *Federal R&D Budget Trends: A Short Summary.* Washington, DC: American Association for the Advancement of Science. https://www.aaas.org/sites/default/files/2019-01/AAAS%20RD%20
Primer%202019_2.pdf.

International Monetary Fund (IMF). 2017. *World Economic Outlook: Gaining Momentum?,* chap. 3. Washington, DC: International Monetary Fund. https://
www.imf.org/en/Publications/WEO/Issues/2017/04/04/world-economic-outlook
-april-2017.

Leduc, Sylvain, and Zheng Liu. 2019. "Are Workers Losing to Robots?" *FRBSF Economic Letter,* no. 2019-25: 1–5. https://www.frbsf.org/economic-research
/files/el2019-25.pdf.

Manyika, James, Susan Lund, Michael Chui, Jacques Bughin, Jonathan Woetzel, Parul Batra, Ryan Ko, and Saurabh Sanghvi. 2017. *Jobs Lost, Jobs Gained: Workforce Transitions in a Time of Automation.* New York: McKinsey Global Institute. https://www.mckinsey.com/featured-insights/future-of-work/jobs-lost-jobs
-gained-what-the-future-of-work-will-mean-for-jobs-skills-and-wages.

Maxim, Robert, and Mark Muro. 2018. *Rethinking Worker Benefits for an Economy in Flux.* Brookings Institution, March 30, 2018. https://www.brookings.edu
/blog/the-avenue/2018/03/29/rethinking-worker-benefits-for-an-economy-in-flux/.

Mazzucato, Mariana. 2015. *The Entrepreneurial State: Debunking Public vs. Private Sector Myths*. New York: PublicAffairs.

Miklusak, Carisa. 2019. "Portable Benefits Would Provide a Safety Net for Millions of Gig Workers." *Fast Company*, April 4, 2019. https://www.fastcompany.com/90412314/portable-benefits-would-provide-a-safety-net-for-millions-of-gig-workers.

Milanović, Branko. 2016. *Global Inequality: A New Approach for the Age of Globalization*. Cambridge, MA: Belknap Press.

Organization for Economic Cooperation and Development (OECD). 2016. *How Good Is Your Job? Measuring and Assessing Job Quality*. Paris: OECD. https://www.oecd.org/sdd/labour-stats/Job-quality-OECD.pdf.

Organization for Economic Cooperation and Development (OECD). 2018. *Seven Questions about Apprenticeships: Answers from International Experience*. OECD Reviews of Vocational Education and Training. Paris: OECD Publishing.

Organization for Economic Cooperation and Development (OECD). 2019a. *Negotiating Our Way Up: Collective Bargaining in a Changing World of Work*. Paris: OECD Publishing.

Organization for Economic Cooperation and Development (OECD). 2019b. "Part-time Employment Rate (Indicator)."

Organization for Economic Cooperation and Development (OECD). n.d. "Bite-size BEPS." https://www.oecd.org/tax/beps/bitesize-beps/. Accessed November 27, 2019.

Osterman, Paul. 2019. "The Future of Work: What We Understand, What We Are Confused about, and How We Should Proceed." Powerpoint Presentation at the Institute for Research on Labor and Employment, April 15, 2019.

Petropoulos, Georgios, J. Scott Marcus, Nicolas Moës, and Enrico Bergamini. 2019. *Digitalisation and European Welfare States*, edited by Stephen Gardner. Bruegel Blueprint Series 30. https://bruegel.org/wp-content/uploads/2019/07/Bruegel_Blueprint_30_ONLINE.pdf.

Piketty, Thomas. 2014. *Capital in the Twenty First Century*. Translated by Arthur Goldhammer. Cambridge, MA: Belknap Press.

Portable Benefits for Independent Workers Pilot Program Act. 2019. S541. 116th Cong. https://www.congress.gov/bill/116th-congress/senate-bill/541.

Reder, Libby, Shelly Steward, and Natalie Foster. 2019. *Designing Portable Benefits: A Resource Guide for Policymakers*. Washington, DC: Aspen Institute. https://www.aspeninstitute.org/publications/designing-portable-benefits/.

Saez, Emmanuel, and Gabriel Zucman. 2019a. *The Triumph of Injustice: How the Rich Dodge Taxes and How to Make Them Pay*. New York: W. W. Norton.

Saez, Emmanuel, and Gabriel Zucman. 2019b. "How to Tax Our Way Back to Justice." *New York Times*, October 11, 2019. https://www.nytimes.com/2019/10/11/opinion/sunday/wealth-income-tax-rate.html.

Skillful. 2019. https://www.markle.org/rework-america/skillful/#skillful.

Thelen, Kathleen. 2019. "The American Precariat: U.S. Capitalism in Comparative Perspective." *Perspectives on Politics* 17(1): 5–27.

Tyson, Laura. 2019. "A New Approach to Protecting Gig Workers." *Project Syndicate*, October 24, 2019. https://www.project-syndicate.org/commentary/california -law-start-to-protect-gig-workers-by-laura-tyson-2019-10.

Tyson, Laura, and Lenny Mendonca. 2018. "Climate Action Trumps Trump." *Project Syndicate*, December 7, 2018. https://www.project-syndicate.org/commentary /climate-change-trump-denialism-by-laura-tyson-and-lenny-mendonca-2018-12.

Tyson, Laura D., and Michael Spence. 2017. "Exploring the Effects of Technology on Income and Wealth Inequality." In *After Piketty: The Agenda for Economics and Inequality*, edited by Heather Boushey, J. Bradford DeLong, and Marshall Steinbaum, 170–208. Cambridge, MA: Harvard University Press.

US Department of Labor, Bureau of Labor Statistics. 2019. "Employee Benefits in the United States—March 2019." News release USDL-19–1650, September 19, 2019. https://www.bls.gov/news.release/pdf/ebs2.pdf.

US Department of Labor. n.d. "Apprenticeships by the Numbers." https://www .apprenticeship.gov/. Accessed December 2, 2019.

VIII

Labor Market Policies, Institutions, and Social Norms

20

Gender Inequality

Marianne Bertrand

In a moment of deep concern about rising income inequality, the gender angle to these inequality trends provides a rare case for optimism. Throughout the developed world, gender gaps in labor force participation and labor market earnings are being reduced. As of 2018, the average difference between male and female labor force participation among workers age 25–54 across Organization for Economic Cooperation and Development (OECD) countries was 18%, whereas it had been close to 30% in 1990. The average gender difference in median full-time earnings across the OECD was 13.5% in 2017compared to close to 20% in 1995.

Despite this unambiguous progress, areas of concern remain. The declining gender gap in labor force participation masks the fact that a much larger share of women are working part-time compared to men. Also, despite the declining gender gap in median earnings, women continue to struggle to improve their representation in upper layers of the income distribution, a phenomenon commonly known as the "glass ceiling." In the United States in 2010, the share of women working full-time, full-year with earnings at or above the fiftieth percentile of the distribution of earnings for men working full-time, full-year was 25.6%, and only 2.8% of women working full-time, full-year had earnings at or above the ninetieth percentile of the men's distribution (Bertrand 2018).

What Stands in the Way of Further Progress?

First and foremost is the extreme gender asymmetry in the labor market costs of parenthood. A few recent studies have provided overwhelming evidence of the role parenthood plays in the remaining gender gaps in labor force participation and earnings. These studies adopt an event-study approach and document labor market trajectories for mothers and fathers around the birth of a first child. Kleven et al. (2019) summarize evidence from six countries: Denmark, Sweden, the United States, the United Kingdom, Germany, and Austria. In each country, trends in gross labor earnings (not conditioned on employment status) are similar for men and women prior to parenthood, but a striking divergence happens after parenthood. Mothers experience a sharp and persistent drop in earnings starting immediately after childbirth, whereas fathers' earnings are unaffected by childbirth. While the qualitative patterns are the same across the six countries, the magnitude of the long-run motherhood penalty (defined as the average annual gross labor market earnings penalty 5–10 years postparenthood) differs greatly across countries, from a low of 21% in Denmark to a high of 61% in Germany. The estimated long-run motherhood penalty in the United States is 31%.

In a companion paper, Kleven, Landais, and Søgaard (2019) further suggest that this motherhood penalty might in fact be the key remaining obstacle to full gender equality in labor market earnings in a socially advanced country such as Denmark, where gender inequality in earnings fell by half between 1980 and 2013. While the motherhood penalty could only account for 40% of the gender inequality in earnings in 1980, it accounted for 80% of the remaining gender inequality in 2013. Strikingly, the absolute size of the motherhood penalty was about the same in 2013 as it was in 1980.

The drop in earnings women experience postparenthood reflects changes both on the extensive margin (with some women leaving the workforce altogether) and on the intensive margin (reduction in hours worked). Motherhood is also associated with drops in hourly compensation, either because of a switch to lower-paying occupations that offer more of the flexibility mothers need given their caretaker role or because of a slowdown in career progression for women who remain in occupations that reward very long hours and heavily penalize taking time off. There is also evidence that mothers engage in geographically more constrained job searches because their family obligations are difficult to reconcile with longer commutes.

This asymmetry between genders in the labor market costs of parenthood demonstrates the enduring effect of norms regarding gender roles even in the most liberal societies in the world. In a 2012 Pew Research survey, only 16% of Americans said that having a mother who works full time is the ideal situation, whereas 42% said that having a mother who works part-time is ideal and 33% said the ideal situation for young children is to have a mother who does not work at all. While 71% of survey respondents found it important for a new baby to have equal time to bond with their mother and their father, 53% believed that mothers would do a better job of taking care of children, compared to 45% who believed that mothers and fathers would do about an equally good job and only 1% who said fathers would do a better job than mothers. These perceptions, tied to inaccurate beliefs that exaggerate differences between the sexes (especially with regard to warmth, empathy, and social sensitivity), need to change in order to create a path to greater gender equality in the labor market. Educators (both parents and teachers) will play a key role in fostering these changes.

In the meantime, governments should strive to design family policies that help mothers combine careers and family obligations. It is by now well understood that more generous family policies does not necessarily imply better outcomes for women. This is particularly true when it comes to the length of job-protected maternity leave. Extended maternity leave may be detrimental for women's labor market outcomes as they stay out of work for too long, accumulate less experience, and find it difficult to return to work on the track they were on prior to parenthood. Extended maternity leave mandates may also discourage employers from hiring women of childbearing age because of the costs (direct or indirect) they will experience when these women become mothers. These theoretical downsides of extended maternity leave have been empirically confirmed in country-panel data analyses that exploit within-country variation over time in the generosity of family policies (Olivetti and Petrongolo 2017). While moderate-length leave entitlements (up to about one year) are associated with higher female employment among the less skilled, longer entitlements have the opposite effect at all skill levels. Furthermore, among the more skilled, longer job-protected leave entitlements *increase* the gender gap in labor market earnings.

In contrast, the country-level evidence suggests that higher levels of government spending on child care and early childhood education have unambiguously positive effects on both female labor force participation and female earnings. This should not be surprising in that, unlike leave entitlements, these policies encourage rather than discourage young mothers' participation in the labor force and their accumulation of labor market experience. In the US context, where government spending on child care and early childhood education is very low in comparison to most other developed nations, additional investments in this area could "kill two birds with one stone." It could give women more freedom to fully realize their potential in the workplace as well as reduce some of the inequalities in early childhood that are known to hinder intergenerational social mobility.

A final aspect of the design of family policies that deserves attention is the recent effort by some OECD countries to encourage fathers', rather than mothers', leave-taking postparenthood. Several developed nations, including Sweden and Norway, and the province of Quebec, have enacted "daddy quotas" that reserve some paid parental leave for fathers; this leave time is lost if it is not taken by the father. "Daddy quotas" are a promising policy development in that they touch on the core gender asymmetry in child care responsibilities. On the positive side, studies have shown that fathers do take their reserved leave quota, even if they rarely take anything more than the quota. Peer effects have been shown to be an important force, with fathers being more willing to take their quotas if they have witnessed male family members or male colleagues doing so. Because the quotas reserved to fathers are still fairly short (a couple of months maximum), it remains to be determined whether their use will remain high as policymakers slowly increase their length. While evidence of their impact on mothers' labor outcomes is mixed so far, this is a clear example of how laws can be designed to speed up changes in gender roles. Further expansion of, and innovations in, the "daddy quota" policy seem squarely in line with the goal of further strengthening gender equality.

Besides the design of family policies, governments should also consider how the tax code may impact married mothers', and more generally married women's, labor supply. While there have been earlier explorations of the negative impact of tax progressivity on married women's work, Bick and Fuchs-Schuendeln (2017, 2018) also remind us that elements of joint taxation in the tax code might be disincentivizing work among married women. In particular, they note that in a tax system that combines joint taxation and progressivity, the marginal tax rate on the primary earner in the household (which remains the husband in a majority of households) is lower than the marginal tax rate on the secondary earner (the wife in the majority of couples). Using a calibrated model that holds the average tax burden of married households constant, they estimate substantial increases in married women's labor supply in places such as the United States and Germany were these countries to replace their current joint taxation system with a separate taxation model such as that in place in the United Kingdom or Sweden. Once elements of joint taxation are eliminated, imposing the higher average labor income tax rates of Europe in the United States would not necessarily imply lower hours worked for married women in the United States.

Another important factor holding back women in the labor market is educational choices. While women have overtaken men in the number of years of completed schooling throughout nearly all the developed world, women systematically pursue different fields of study than men. In particular, women are much less likely than men to complete tertiary degrees in STEM (science, technology, engineeering, and mathematics) fields (and more likely to complete degrees in the humanities). This is problematic in that STEM education opens the door to high-paying, high-status occupations that also offer relatively more of the workplace flexibility that mothers need (Goldin 2014). While it is difficult to predict the future of work, encouraging more women to go into STEM fields should be an important policy goal for the time being.

One of the most frequently proposed explanations for why women do not pursue STEM education at the same rate as men is that women are not good at math, but meta-analyses suggest that the gender gap in average math skills is small in comparison to the large within-gender variation in math skills (Hyde 2014). Furthermore, there is growing evidence that the (small) gender gap in math is at least in part a social construct (Guiso et al. 2008; Lippmann and Senik 2018). Again, this suggests an important role for educators (parents and teachers), who should be careful not to reinforce stereotypes surrounding women and math.

Other recent research (Breda and Napp 2019) suggests that another reason women may not pursue math-related fields might be because of their comparative advantage in verbal skills. Indeed, while the gender gap in math performance is small, there is a somewhat larger gender gap in reading and verbal skills favoring women. Breda and Napp (2019) show that the gender gap in the intention to study math could be largely explained by the fact that young people make education and career decisions based on what they enjoy rather than whether they have the skills required to succeed in a given field. If this proves correct, it implies an important role for education and career counseling in high schools so that young women (and men) are made more broadly aware of the earnings and career implications of different educational choices prior to making hard-to-reverse decisions on their future course of study.

Finally, shareholders should hold managers accountable for not running inclusive organizations. While explicit biases against women are unlikely to drive much of the gender gap in today's most advanced societies, implicit biases and inaccurate stereotypes about women can easily creep back in, especially under stress or time pressure. There is a growing battery of de-biasing tools organizations can rely on to perform less-biased job searches and conduct less-biased promotion processes (Bertrand and Duflo 2017). Organizations that succeed in implementing such inclusive practices should end up with a workforce that is not only more diverse but also more talented.

References

Bertrand, M. 2018. "Coase Lecture—The Glass Ceiling." *Economica* 85(338): 205–231.

Bertrand, M., and E. Duflo. 2017. "Field Experiments on Discrimination." In *Handbook of Field Experiments*, Vol. 1, edited by Esther Duflo and Abhijit Banerjee, 309–393. Amsterdam: North Holland.

Bick, A. and N. Fuchs-Schündeln. 2017. "Quantifying the Disincentive Effects of Joint Taxation on Married Women's Labor Supply." *AEA Papers and Proceedings* 107(5): 100–104.

Bick, A., and N. Fuchs-Schündeln. 2018. "Taxation and Labour Supply of Married Couples across Countries: A Macroeconomic Analysis." *Review of Economic Studies* 85(3):1543–1576.

Breda, T., and C. Napp. 2019. "Girls' Comparative Advantage in Reading Can Largely Explain the Gender Gap in Math-Related Fields." *Proceedings of the National Academy of Sciences* 116(31): 15435–15440.

Goldin, C. 2014. "A Grand Gender Convergence: Its Last Chapter." *AEA Papers and Proceedings* 104(4): 1091–1119.

Guiso, L., F. Monte, P. Sapienza, and L. Zingales. 2008. "'Culture, Gender, and Math." *Science* 320(5880): 1164–1165.

Hyde, J. 2014. "Gender Similarities and Differences." *Annual Review of Psychology* 65: 373–398.

Kleven, H., C. Landais, J. Posch, A. Steinhauer, and J. Zweimüller. 2019. "Child Penalties across Countries: Evidence and Explanations." *AEA Papers and Proceedings* 109(5): 122–126.

Kleven, H., C. Landais, and J. E. Søgaard. 2019. "Children and Gender Inequality: Evidence from Denmark." *American Economic Journal: Applied Economics* 11(4): 181–209.

Lippmann, Q., and C. Senik. 2018. "Math, Girls and Socialism." *Journal of Comparative Economics* 46(3): 874–888.

Olivetti, C., and B. Petrongolo. 2017. "The Economic Consequences of Family Policies: Lessons from a Century of Legislation in High-Income Countries." *Journal of Economic Perspectives* 31(1): 205–230.

21

Ownership Cures for Inequality

Richard B. Freeman

If all power be suffered to slide into hands not interested in the rights of property ... either they will ... become dupes and instruments of ambition, or their poverty and dependence will render them mercenary instruments of wealth.... In either case liberty will be subverted; in the first by *a despotism growing out of anarchy, in the second by an oligarchy founded on corruption* ... in which it may be said ... that *laws are made for the few, not for the many.*
—James Madison

What, if anything, can the United States do to reverse the upward trend in inequality and the danger that it will lead to populist despotism or a corrupt oligarchy with laws made for the few, not for the many?

I propose two sets of policies. The first requires reforms in labor laws and regulations to better enable workers to organize and bargain collectively with employers. The second requires tax and procurement policies to encourage firms to develop employment ownership programs so that workers own some of the capital that employs them and additional policies that increase worker investments in capital more broadly. By operating on ownership of both labor and capital, the policies can modernize American economic institutions to fit the coming world of artificial intelligence (AI) robotics and avoid Madison's Scylla and Charybdis choice between anarchy and corruption.

Strengthening the Voice of Labor at Work

Given the parlous state of US unions, strengthening legal protections for collective action may strike many as unrealistic and backward looking. The proportion of workers in unions has fallen for over half a century.[1] In 2018, 6.4% of private sector workers were in unions—compared to 16.5% in 1983, when the Current Population Survey began asking about unions and collective bargaining, and the 35% or so unionized in the 1950s. Public sector unionism zoomed in the 1970s but then leveled off and fell, with public sector collective bargaining coverage dropping from 45.5% in 1983 to 37.2% in 2018. The Supreme Court's (2018) *Janus* decision outlawing public sector labor contracts that require workers who are not union members to pay union fees will likely reduce unionism in the public sector.[2] When nonunion teachers in West Virginia, Oklahoma, and Arizona struck in 2018–2019 over low compensation and poor funding of education, they acted with little input from teachers unions. Supported by parents, school boards, and principals, the striking teachers won their demands without organized labor.

Given their weaknesses at the outset of the 2020s, *w*hy should anyone concerned with American workers and democracy seek ways to resuscitate trade unions? The principal reason is that unions have historically been the only institutional force in capitalist economies able to limit inequality and assure that workers share in a growing economy.[3] The inverse relation between union density and inequality is one of the strongest empirical regularities in economics, found in comparisons across countries, industries, and skilled and unskilled workers with differing levels of unionism and over time as union density changed. Unions reduce inequality *within* firms by negotiating a narrower distribution of pay among the firms' employees. Unions reduce inequality *among* firms by negotiating agreements that cover most firms in a sector—by multi-employer agreements or pattern bargaining and by inducing nonunion firms to copy union settlements to keep their workers from unionizing. The lower dispersion of wages around the average in union settings than in nonunion settings shows that the "going union wage" is closer to the "invisible hand's" single price equating supply and demand than are wages in markets without unions. Indeed, most of the increase in inequality from the 1980s to 2010s occurred between the country's more and less successful firms, as the most profitable firms shared some of their economic rents with workers while the less profitable squeezed wages to remain in business. The union decline appears to have opened the door for monopsony to play an increased role in determining pay rather than to create an ideal neoclassical market.[4]

Looking beyond collective bargaining, unions have been the major political force pressing for legislation that protects workers in all areas of workplace life: health and safety, social security and pensions, hours worked, and discrimination. Social protests—such as the 2011 Wall Street Occupiers against the financial collapse and the 2019 Extinction Resisters against the sluggish response to climate change—make headlines but rarely move policy. Rolling back inequality requires not just citizen protests but also strong bureaucratic organizations continually pressing decision makers to choose the many over the few—the trade unions of yore.

The union impact on inequality is not, however, reason enough to seek legislation that would help unions recover some of their strength. If the decline in representation reflected a growing sentiment against unions, changing laws to favor them would be an antidemocratic exercise that would almost surely end in failure. Surveys of attitudes toward unions show, however, that as inequality has grown and unions have lost their power, more Americans have come to view unions positively. In January 2019, a Rasmussen survey found that 57% of American adults favor private sector unions, while 29% oppose them. In August 2019, Gallup reported the highest rate of approval of unions since the 1970s: 64% approving compared to 32% disapproving. Responses to a question by Pew about the decline of unions tell the same story. In 2018, the proportion of respondents who viewed the decline as mostly bad exceeded the proportion who viewed it as mostly good by a greater number than in 2015 and 1994. Why the growing support for unions? The likely reason is that Americans recognize that unions, whatever their flaws, are indeed a force against inequality. If not unions of the many, who will stand up against the billionaires?

Favorable attitudes toward unions in the abstract does not, however, necessarily translate into workers voting for union representation in elections at their workplace—much less that the union would gain the majority necessary to become the legal representative of workers. Asking private sector workers how they would vote in a National Labor Relations Board (NLRB) election in a 1994 survey (when attitudes toward unions were less favorable than in the 2010s), Freeman and Rogers (1999) found that the vast majority of those with a union would vote union, while 32% of those without a union would vote union, and that the vast majority of those who would vote union believed that their co-workers would also support the union. The reason is that workers who seek unions are concentrated in companies with bad labor practices, low pay, and poor conditions. If it were the workers' choice and theirs alone, these voting patterns imply a union density two to three times the current 6.4% in the private sector. Massive employer opposition to organizing, often led by union-busting firms that specialize in persuading workers to reject unions, is prima facie evidence that there is indeed a substantial desire for unions at some nonunionized workplaces.

Labor Law Reform to the Rescue?

So what can the United States do to give American workers the representation they want and that the country needs to roll back the tide of inequality? In 2019, Harvard Law School's Labor and Worklife Program initiated the Clean Slate for Worker Power project, "to elicit the best ideas from a broad array of participants including advocates, activists, union leaders, labor law professors, economists, sociologists, technologists, futurists, practitioners, workers, and students from around the world." Groups of industrial relations experts and law professors worked with others to examine how the United States might modernize labor law to resuscitate trade unions and collective bargaining.[5] The Clean Slate for Worker Power project examined a far-ranging set of policy reforms to make the NLRB Act work better for workers and to strengthen the ability of unions to gain representation rights and bargaining power with employers. These reforms included: expanding labor law protection to workers historically left out—agricultural and domestic service workers, supervisors, and low- and middle middle-level managers; tightening the definition of employer and employee to prevent firms from evading the law by hiring workers under the guise of their being independent contractors or by subcontracting or franchising work; raising penalties on firms for violating the law; expanding the ways unions and community organizations can press firms to accept unions, including increasing the scope for secondary boycotts; while reducing management's ability to pressure workers to reject the union. In an ideal world, labor and management would come together to discuss these proposed reforms and to consider changes in the law that might ease the administrative burden on management of following the law and/or of enhancing the ability of the NLRB to carry out its legal duties. But in a world where a large proportion of the business community seeks to be "union free" and where most Republicans view unions as a political enemy Democrats view them as a political ally, even modest reforms could create a political war.

The most far-reaching change in the United States' labor relations system examined by Clean Slate for Worker Power were policies designed to widen the scope of United States collective bargaining and wage-setting from its historic reliance on agreements between local unions and individual establishments or firms to agreements between higher-level union groups and employer associations that would cover many firms in a market at once as in many European Union countries. Government agencies have a substantial role in developing and buttressing such arrangements. Legislature can give them legal rights to extend agreements to firms that were not party to the agreement, and to institute industry and/or regional boards that could legally determine pay for all workers in specified domains—say all persons cleaning buildings or houses in a given city—in the absence of a collective bargaining agreement covering those workers. By establishing a going rate of pay and work conditions, this centralized mode of pay setting would reduce inequality in pay and conditions among firms and lessen the willingness of firms to fight unions: why spend money fighting union organizing efforts if your firm will have to pay the union or government agency determined wages and benefits in any case?

But placing government in a key role in determining pay would surely touch off a firestorm of opposition in the United States. It would risk continual political conflict over workplace issues, with policies and practices depending more on who won the last election than the logic of economic rationality. Such has been the experience of the National Labor Relations Board (NLRB) the agency that oversees current labor law. When a Democrat is in the White House, the NLRB generally favors workers and unions. When a Republican is in the White House, the NLRB generally favors firms and management.

The European Union's centralized bargaining arrangements work in part because firms voluntarily join employer associations that bargain for them, in the belief that "social partnership" is the best way to solve labor disputes. These firms want a level playing field in pay and work conditions so they can compete in other dimensions of business performance. The US's weak employer associations and large number of businesses that survive via low wages suggests that any effort to move pay setting to higher-level bodies would meet massive employer opposition.

Finally, there is a chicken and egg problem in trying to change labor laws to strengthen unions without already having a more centralized wage setting system that reduces employer opposition since all firms will pay similar centralized wages and of trying to centralize the collective bargaining system without a stronger union movement to favor centralizing wage setting. Moving from a world of weak unions and decentralized wage-setting to one of strong unions and centralized wage-setting would require a simultaneous reform on both fronts at once against the opposition of the vast bulk of businesses and management. Historically, unions have grown in the United States and elsewhere in sudden sharp spurts when workers are sufficiently disgruntled with their economic lives to "go to war" against employers. Union growth during the Great Depression was sparked by sit-down strikes and protests not the legal reform of the Wagner Act, which the US government developed to offer a more orderly way for workers to unionize. The legal changes followed worker initiated mass actions rather than precipitated those actions.

If it were my choice and mine alone and everyone would go along with it, I would reform the US labor system in a different way—from the bottom up, albeit with some legal changes to encourage workers and firms to experiment with new modes of organizing labor-management relations. I would allow firms to set up committees of workers and managers to discuss labor issues (currently outlawed by section 8a3 of the National Labor Relations Act to prevent company-dominated unions) and would mandate that firms establish works councils when workers want one, as many European countries have done. I would expect unions to provide bargaining and other services to the councils, and for centralized agreements to emerge naturally from that bargaining. But while my reforms would not, I believe, lead to the opposition that the Clean Slate for Worker Power would almost surely arouse, I doubt that Congress will seek to reform the labor system even along the more consensual lines that I favor until an economic crisis brings workers "into the streets" demanding change.

Increasing Worker Ownership of Capital

My second set of policies, designed to increase worker ownership of firms, has a better chance of being enacted in non-crisis times, even though those policies could create more revolutionary democratic change in our economy than resuscitating unions and collective bargaining. Ownership policies have a better chance of being enacted because nearly everyone across the political spectrum considers employee ownership "a good thing." On the worker side, the 2019 National Opinion Research Center survey of Americans found that 72% of workers said they preferred to work for an employee-owned firm rather than for a firm owned by a private investor or for a government agency.[6] On the business side, many business leaders with an ownership or profit-sharing scheme in their firm favor employee ownership because their experience says that it works to raise productivity and profits. Others favor giving some ownership to workers in the belief that worker-owners will shift their politics to the right. Progressives generally favor worker ownership as a way to expand democracy at the workplace and reduce pay inequality within firms.

Thanks in part to the 1974 Employee Retirement Income Security Act (ERISA), which regulates private pension plans, the United States has a strong base on which to expand employee ownership. ERISA established Employee Stock Ownership Plans (ESOPs) that give workers collective ownership of shares in their employer via a trust fund and gives tax breaks to firms that set up such funds. Today, about 10% of all private sector workers are in ESOP firms, with shares of ownership that range from a modest proportion to 100%. Beyond ESOPs, many workers have an ownership stake in their firm via stock options or share purchase plans. And many more have profit- sharing, which gives them a stream of income from profits without capital ownership. In 2019, 47% of US workers had some form of ownership or profit-sharing at their workplace, though many had small stakes that did not add much to their income. Finally, US workers also have substantial pension fund equity in businesses outside of their employer. The growth of pension fund investment equity was so rapid in the 1970s that Peter Drucker (1976) famously declared that "If 'socialism' is ... ownership of the means of production, ... the United States is the first truly Socialist country."

Socialism or workers' capitalism, all of these forms of ownership supplement wages and salaries with income from capital, which is sorely needed in an era when the distribution of national income has shifted from labor to capital. With capital earning more of national income than ever before and with capital income being far more unequally distributed than labor income, it is exceedingly difficult to see a path forward to reducing inequality without raising workers' ownership of capital and capital income.

So what can the United States do to expand employee ownership?

A natural first step is for government to spread knowledge of what the ESOP business form can do and how employees and business owners can shift business ownership toward ESOPs or other forms of ownership or profit-sharing. Some states, such as Massachusetts and Ohio, have developed worker ownership offices or centers to help retiring small business owners sell their companies to employees and to spread best practices among ESOPs.[7] The federal government could designate the Small Business Administration or some group in the Department of Commerce to undertake such a role nationally. A presidential candidate could commit his or her administration to tilt economic decisions toward employee owned firms and to press Congress for new laws that would put employee ownership at the heart of a new economic order.

For its part Congress to could increase the tax breaks for worker-owned firms. Currently, an owner who sells his/ or her firm to employees pays no capital gains tax on the sale. And the profits the ESOP uses to buy shares of the firm are also tax-free. ESOP advocates favor giving more tax advantages to retiring owners in S corporations (closely held corporations that do not pay corporate taxes but pass profits to owners, who pay taxes) by excluding them from capital gains taxes when they sell to the workers, in the belief that this would substantially increase the number of ESOPs. In considering such a policy or others, economics points to the central importance of the incidence of the tax break. The nominal gain goes to the owners, which presumptively increases inequality in the short run, but the workers who buy the firm benefit by being able to buy at a lower price and receive higher income and wealth in later years. Artful design of the tax break can assure that it accomplishes its objective.

Using the tax system to spur the growth of employee ownership, however, need not be limited to ESOPs. The United Kingdom gives substantial tax breaks for workers to purchase and hold shares as individuals in employee stock purchase plans, which has spurred UK firms to develop share purchase plans more extensively than US firms. In the 2016 US presidential race, the Hillary Clinton campaign proposed giving a tax break for firms without profit-sharing to introduce such a program. Senator Sanders's 2020 presidential campaign proposed creating a bank to give "low-interest loans, loan guarantees, and technical assistance" to workers who want to purchase firms and has also proposed taxing large firms to shift 2% of shares to a fund run by worker-elected trustees that would pay dividends to workers.[8]

On the notion that positive incentives work better (and are easier to enact) than taxes, I favor government procurement policies that would give preference to enterprises that meet some employee ownership or profit-sharing criterion. Current procurement policies give preference to small businesses, (guaranteed 23% of federal contracts), to businesses owned by disabled veterans, to businesses owned by women, and to businesses with economically or socially disadvantaged owners. Why not include employee-owned businesses as well? But any such preference for worker owned firms ought to go beyond small businesses. A program for employee-owned or profit-sharing firms should include large firms, whose choice of such an ownership form would benefit large numbers of workers.

Finally, since workers should diversify ownership of capital beyond their own firm to avoid taking on too much risk, any major reform should consider ways to assure that ESOPs and other ownership forms offer 401k pension funds, as well (which most do). Alaska's Provident Fund and other sovereign wealth funds in which the government establishes a trust/mutual fund that pays dividends to workers offers another potential way to increase capital income going to workers.[9]

All of these schemes have weaknesses as well as strengths that merit investigation by economics, legal, and business experts as well as input from workers and firms experienced with or considering introduction of worker ownership or profit-sharing schemes akin to the Clean Slate for Worker Power analysis of labor laws. Given widespread nonpartisan support for employee ownership, policies to increase ownership could be the first step to improving the state of labor in the United States (and other countries) and creating a more favorable environment from which to approach the more contentious path to reforming labor laws and regulations.

Notes

1. Union and collective bargaining data are from http://www.unionstats.com /. For views on unions, see https://news.gallup.com/poll/265916/labor-day -turns-125-union-approval-near-year-high.aspx; http://www.rasmussenreports .com/public_content/business/econ_survey_questions/january_2019/questions _unions_january_14_15_2019; https://www.pewresearch.org/fact-tank/2018/06 /05/more-americans-view-long-term-decline-in-union-membership-negatively -than-positively/. For recent evidence on unions reducing inequality, see https:// www.nytimes.com/2018/07/06/business/labor-unions-income-inequality.html.

2. *Janus v. American Federation of State, County, and Municipal Employees, Council 31*, No. 16-1466, 585 U.S. (2018).

3. For recent evidence on unions reducing inequality, see https://www.nytimes .com/2018/07/06/business/labor-unions-income-inequality.html.

4. A growing literature has found evidence of monopsony in US labor markets, see José Azar Ioana Marinescu and Marshall I. Steinbaum, "Labor Market Concentration," NBER Working Paper 24147, revised February 2019; Arindrajit Dube, Jeff Jacobs, Suresh Naidu, and Siddharth Suri, "Monopsony in Online Labor Markets," NBER Working Paper No. 24416, issued March 2018; and Brad Hershbein (W. E. Upjohn Institute), Claudia Macaluso—(FRB Richmond), and Chen Yeh (FRB Richmond), "Monopsony in the U.S. Labor Market," December 31, 2019.

5. For information on the Clean Slate for Worker Power project, see https://lwp .law.harvard.edu/clean-slate-project.

6. For information on the National Opinion Research Center survey, see https:// www.fiftybyfifty.org/2019/06/three-quarters-of-americans-prefer-to-work-for-an -employee-owned-company/.

7. For the Ohio program, http://www.oeockent.org/about/; for the Massachusetts program, see https://www.bostonglobe.com/business/2019/04/02/mass -lawmakers-revive-effort-spur-employee-ownership/c2j95QZssyPyeYYyN5hfAI /story.html. For the Ohio program, see http://www.oeockent.org/about/.

8. For Sanders's proposals, see https://berniesanders.com/issues/corporate -accountability-and-democracy/.

9. For a summary analysis of the Alaska fund, see https://www.sciencenews.org /article/alaska-free-money-residents-hints-how-universal-basic-income-may-work.

References

Drucker, Peter. 1976. *The Unseen Revolution: How Pension Fund Socialism Came to America.* New York: Harper and Row.

Freeman, Richard B., and Joel Rogers. 1999. *What Workers Want.* Ithaca, NY: Cornell University Press.

Madison, James. 1788. "Observations on the 'Draught of a Constitution for Virginia.'" October. https://founders.archives.gov/documents/Madison/01-11-02-0216.

IX

Labor Market Tools

22

Guaranteeing Employment for All

William Darity Jr.

A federal job guarantee is a macroeconomic policy that will ensure that all adult Americans can find employment at a decent level of compensation and under safe work conditions. To be clear at the outset, the federal job guarantee can reduce income inequality but will have little effect on wealth inequality. It will affect income inequality by raising the incomes of persons at the lowest level of the earnings distribution. Furthermore, it has a long history in the United States. It's very much an American idea. The major American precedents for a federal job guarantee are the Civilian Conservation Corps and the Works Progress Administration (WPA) during the Great Depression. The current proposal differs from those initiatives insofar as it will be a permanent and universal program of job assurance (Darity 2010; Aja et al. 2013).

Franklin Roosevelt's Second Bill of Rights (Roosevelt 1944) claimed that every American should have the right to "a useful and remunerative job in the industries or shops or farms or mines of the nation" and the right "to earn enough to provide adequate food and clothing and recreation for their family members." Harry Truman's Fair Deal in 1949 echoed the same theme. Bayard Rustin prepared a Freedom Budget for the A. Philip Randolph Institute in 1967, which included a provision for a job guarantee. Both Martin Luther King Jr. and his wife, Coretta Scott King, endorsed a federal job guarantee. The Caucus of Black Economists, the predecessor of the National Economic Association, advocated a federal job guarantee in 1972 (Darity and Hamilton 2017).

Economist Sadie Mossell Alexander, who was the first black PhD recipient in economics, gave a 1945 speech at Florida A&M University in which she talked about the implications of a federal job guarantee in promoting greater racial economic equality in the labor market. Idiosyncratic economist Hyman Minsky, who introduced the financial instability hypothesis, was an advocate of having the federal government serve as an employer of last resort (Darity and Hamilton 2017). However, the type of federal job guarantee proposed here is not an employer of last resort program; no proof of denial of private sector employment would be required in order to take a position under the federal job guarantee.

Additional supporters include an important cadre of economists associated with the Levy Economics Institute at Bard College and the University of Missouri at Kansas City–including Randall Wray, Mathew Forstater, Stephanie Kelton, Michael Murray, and Pavlina Tcherneva. They have placed a special emphasis on what can be learned from non-US precedents for a job guarantee, particularly the Jefes y Jefas program in Argentina and the Rural Employment Job Guarantee in India (see especially Tcherneva 2018). Moreover, there is already a legal basis for the federal job guarantee, in the form of the unfunded mandate of the Humphrey-Hawkins Act of 1978. Essentially, a federal job guarantee would make Humphrey-Hawkins a funded mandate.

A federal job guarantee would establish—in Roosevelt's words in his 1944 declaration for an Economic Bill of Rights—a universal right "to a useful and remunerative job" and "to earn enough to provide adequate food and clothing and recreation." The specific form of job guarantee proposed here would create the National Investment Employment Corps (NIEC) to assure every American adult employment from the public sector. It would be a federally funded and federally managed project. As noted, strictly speaking, it would not be an employer of last resort program, insofar as individuals would always have the option of taking these jobs regardless of their current employment status. It would be a permanent option or a permanent alternative to private sector employment, and it would be a large-scale direct hiring program by the federal government.

Compensation would include nonpoverty wages, so that the lowest-paid jobs would be salaried at approximately $25,000, and a benefits package similar to the one offered to all federal civil servants, including medical insurance. In addition, there would be job safety provisions and advancement opportunities built into the program.

A federal job guarantee would enable the nation to meet the physical and human infrastructure needs of the society in a direct way through this public employment program. The human infrastructure dimensions will include the professionalization of child and elder care. This would be of particular significance to women workers in the US economy, because they bear a disproportionate burden of caring for both the elderly and young children.

A team of teacher aides that could be part of the federal employment program and employees under the federal job guarantee could perform work on repairing school facilities simultaneously. The postal system in the United States could be rejuvenated by an influx of additional personnel. "Solarization," or greening of the nation's economy, could be pursued by employees of the NIEC. With sufficient imagination, an individual's skills and talents could be matched with the particular types of jobs that they might pursue. In the 1930s, for example, under the Works Progress Administration, people were employed as muralists, actors, and writers. In fact, it was during those years that the slave narratives that we have access to today were gathered by employees of the WPA.

Furthermore, a "permanent" staff could be combined with a fluid or cyclical staff to conduct the program. The federal job guarantee would function as an automatic stabilizer; it would expand during downturns and contract during upturns, producing a countercyclical accordion effect. It would moderate the impact of recessions and in fact provide some insulation from their effects because it could help maintain household incomes during economic downturns.

The effect of this type of program would be to create a floor on compensation and job quality. This would be somewhat different from relying exclusively on minimum wage or living wage laws. Wage floors are only useful to individuals who actually have work, and even if you have a job, wage floors do not ensure enough hours to qualify for benefit packages.

A key goal of a federal job guarantee is to wipe out bad jobs. The premise behind the job guarantee is that everyone should have a viable exit option from a bad job, whether it is bad because of low pay, uncertain hours, low or no benefits, or unsafe work conditions.

The Earned Income Tax Credit (EITC) or a universal basic income actually *could* subsidize the private sector's continued creation of bad jobs. However, some form of the EITC may need to be retained in a world with a federal job guarantee in order to address the limitations generated by earned incomes above the poverty line that are still associated with familial deprivation. But generally, antipoverty measures require that people be exposed to poverty before income-support mechanisms are activated. The federal job guarantee is predicated on the view that people should be protected from experiencing poverty in the first place.

In addition, existing levels of antipoverty expenditures could be reduced significantly, since the federal job guarantee could function simultaneously as a full-employment program as well as an antipoverty program. Indeed, it could be the case that, in many years, the federal job guarantee will be virtually revenue neutral. The best available estimates indicate that the upper bound on the annual cost of the program would be in the vicinity of $1.5 trillion to $2 trillion (Paul et al. 2018). These sums will be roughly equivalent to the costs of antipoverty programs at times when the number of unemployed and underemployed who would take NIEC jobs is high enough to correspond to federal job guarantee expenses at those levels (Paul et al. 2018).

Ultimately, the federal job guarantee would produce less inflationary pressure than a pure income-transfer program such as a universal basic income, because there would be actual production of goods and services associated with the public job system. As I said, it addresses income inequality by lifting the bottom of the earnings distribution. It ensures decent employment for groups who have been subjected to discriminatory exclusion or underpayment.

This would include folks who are excluded on the basis of race, veteran status, gender, disability, or ex-felon status. In effect, we would assure employment for all categories of individuals. They would always be able to get a job. Therefore, the Federal Reserve could deemphasize its dual mandate of price stability and full employment. It could focus more intensively on fighting inflation if so desired, because the federal job guarantee would preserve full employment.

A federal job guarantee has substantial political support, so much so that it is baffling that during the campaign for the presidency now under way, very little attention has been given to the policy. In fact, an October 2019 national poll (The Hill 2019) indicates that 70% of eligible American voters are in favor of the federal government ensuring that everyone has a job. It would therefore seem to be to the advantage of the candidates to voice enthusiastic support for a federal job guarantee. Paradoxically, they have not.

A final benefit of the federal job guarantee mentioned here is the relief it would grant economists, who would no longer have to worry about determining the natural rate of unemployment (or the nonaccelerating inflation rate of unemployment, for that matter). After all, the federal job guarantee would make the Phillips curve vertical at a zero rate of unemployment.

References

Aja, Alan, Daniel Bustillo, William Darity Jr., and Darrick Hamilton. 2013. "Jobs Instead of Austerity: A Bold Policy for Economic Justice." *Social Research* 80(3): 781–794.

Darity, William, Jr. 2010. "A Direct Route to Full Employment." *Review of Black Political Economy* 37(3): 179–182.

Darity, William, Jr., and Darrick Hamilton. 2018. "Full Employment and the Job Guarantee: An All American Idea." In *Full Employment and Social Justice: Solidarity and Sustainability*, edited by Michael J. Murray and Mathew Forstater, 195–204. New York: Palgrave Macmillan.

The Hill. 2019. "Majority of Voters Support a Federal Jobs Guarantee Program." *The Hill*, What America's Thinking, October 30, 2019. https://thehill.com/hilltv /468236-majority-of-voters-support-a-federal-jobs-guarantee-program.

Paul, Mark, William Darity Jr., Darrick Hamilton, and Khaing Zaw. 2018. "A Path to Ending Poverty by Way of Ending Unemployment: A Federal Job Guarantee." *Russell Sage Foundation Journal of the Social Sciences* 4(3): 44–63.

Roosevelt, Franklin D. 1944. "The Economic Bill of Rights." USHistory.org. https://www.ushistory.org/DOCUMENTS/economic_bill_of_rights.htm.

Tcherneva, Pavlina. 2018. "The Job Guarantee: Design, Jobs and Implementation." Working Paper 902, Levy Economics Institute of Bard College, New York.

23

Making Work Work

David T. Ellwood

Two graphs haunt me. All by themselves, they seem to explain much of the anger, the desperation, the partisanship, the racial animosity, the anger toward immigrants, and the utter disdain for elites (and perhaps especially economists) that one sees in the United States today.

The first graph, which is actually a pair of figures done separately by sex, traces the earnings of *full-year, full-time* "prime age" men (figure 23.1a) and women (figure 23.1b). We set 1961 as the baseline year and then graphed the percentage change in real earnings for each group relative to 1961. If all our fates were tied together, these lines would rise and fall together, and for a time that is what happened. Looking first at men, during the 1960s and into the early 1970s, real earnings for each group rose by roughly 30%. But then the wages began to diverge. In 2018, the median male still earned no more than his counterparts from 45 years earlier! Meanwhile, the earnings of workers at the seventy-fifth and ninetieth percentiles kept growing into the twenty-first century, while those of fully employed men in the twenty-fifth and tenth percentiles fell back to 1960s levels. For women who started at a much lower level, the picture is one of modest and fairly similar growth for those at the median and below, and even sharper rises at the upper ends.[1]

The consequences of slow and sometimes collapsing earnings growth for so many workers can be vividly seen in a graph produced by Raj Chetty and his colleagues (figure 23.2). This graph captures a notion at the heart of the "American Dream": do children earn more than their parents did? Chetty et al. (2017) show that children who were born in the early 1940s (who came of age in the 1960s and early 1970s) had a 90% chance of earning more than their parents. By contrast, children born in the 1980s, who are coming of age today, have roughly a 50/50 chance of doing better than their parents. And when sons alone were compared to their fathers, well over half the sons earned less than their fathers did at the same age.

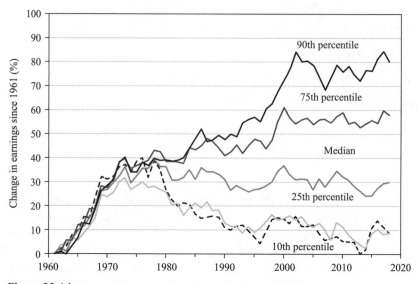

Figure 23.1A
Distribution of real wage and salary earnings of male workers age 25–54 working full-year, full-time in 2018 compared to 1961. *Source*: Author's tabulation from Current Population Survey data. Earnings are deflated by the CPI-U-RS, the Bureau of Labor Statistics price index for urban consumers adjusted to current methods.

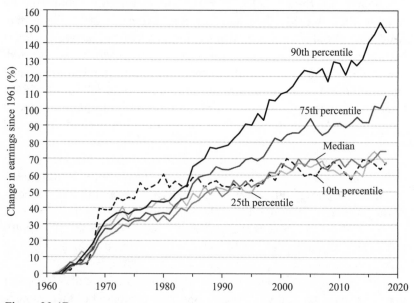

Figure 23.1B
Distribution of real wage and salary earnings of female workers age 25–54 working full-year, full-time in 2018 compared to 1961. *Source*: Author's tabulation from Current Population Survey data. Earnings are deflated by the CPI-U-RS.

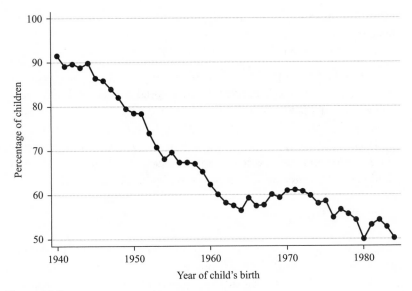

Figure 23.2
Percentage of children earning more than their parents did at age 30. *Source*: Chetty et al. (2017).

Hard work was supposed to pay off. Elites seemingly promised that trade, immigration, and technology would create short-term turmoil but that eventually nearly everyone would share in the benefits. The rewards to the upper reaches of society soared, but very many people, particularly men, have still been left behind, even after 40 or 50 years. So, many citizens blame immigrants, people of color, free trade, Republicans, Democrats, government, business, and/or the elites.

The other contributors to the rather spectacular conference that led to this volume offer many diagnoses for the dramatic growth in inequality. The solutions that have been offered have often been large, systemic ones, such as providing a universal basic income, transforming education and training, a massive public jobs program, or reshaping the nature of labor-management relations. Many of these are worthy and important, but they stumble on both the question of whether they can ever be achieved politically and whether the scale and speed of the changes are sufficient to achieve real changes in inequality. Meanwhile, the two charts continue to haunt.

This brief chapter is focused primarily on where we might look for credible and immediate solutions tied closely to work. In most countries and certainly in the United States, people believe that work helps define and sustain them. One's job and its monetary and personal rewards and costs carry messages about dignity, meaning, and belonging.

Let me offer three ideas about moving forward.

- First, "making work pay" is an essential strategy for combating inequality.
- Next, we need to move beyond the traditional "make work pay" strategies toward a larger focus on turning "bad jobs" into "good jobs."
- Finally, the low-skill job market seems to function poorly and is probably getting worse over time. Understanding and correcting the flaws in this marketplace may be essential to permanently reduce inequality and achieve greater opportunity and prosperity for the nation.

Making Work Pay

"Making work pay" describes strategies designed to ensure that all paid work offers a reasonable level of compensation. Reasonable is in the eye of the beholder, of course, but there are plenty of quite practical strategies that can make work more financially rewarding for those at the lower end of the wage and earnings distribution.

A favorite strategy of economists is a wage or earnings subsidy. In the United States, this has mostly taken the form of the Earned Income Tax Credit (EITC). The EITC is an earnings subsidy administered through the tax system. For every dollar low-income workers earn up to a maximum, they get an additional fully refundable tax credit, which varies by their family situation. For a tax filer with two children earning up to $14,570 in 2019, the credit amounts to a 40% pay raise.[2] And since the credit is refundable, even people who owe little or no taxes get the full benefit.

Economists appreciate the fact that the EITC increases the rewards for working while not raising, and potentially lowering, the cost of hiring workers for employers. Politicians in both major parties support it precisely because it recognizes the dignity of work and rewards low-income *working* persons and families. Unlike a universal basic income, the money goes only to those who work, and the more you work at a low-paying job, the more you get, up to a point. Sociologist Jennifer Sykes and her colleagues (Sykes et al. 2015) report that low-income persons themselves like it far better than other forms of public assistance because, far from creating a stigma or forcing people into a frustrating bureaucracy, it is administered within the tax system and recipients get a tax refund. The impact of the EITC dwarfs that of all employment and training programs combined without interfering with them in any way.

Another strategy to make work pay is to raise the minimum wage. That is much more controversial because it more directly interferes with the labor market and forces employers to pay more. It is very popular politically in the United States. For example, a spring 2019 poll by the Pew Research Center showed two-thirds of Americans favoring a $15 per hour minimum wage (David and Hartig 2019). Many economists have been concerned about the potential reductions in employment that might result. Recently, however, a growing body of literature suggests that monopsony (a case where employers enjoy sizable market power) may be more common in the low-wage labor market than was previously recognized (Council of Economic Advisers 2016). When a market is characterized by monopsony, a minimum wage can actually increase employment. A combination of the two can be particularly attractive.

Finally, discussions on making work pay are increasingly focusing on benefits, not just pay. Laura Tyson (chapter 19, this volume) discusses a number of them, as have others. Expanding the likelihood that working people get child care, maternity leave, sick leave, health care, pensions, and other supports also helps make work pay.

In sum, if one wants to make a serious difference in inequality, in a way that is politically popular, economically sound, fast acting, and already practical, making work pay is the place to start.

Turning "Bad Jobs" into "Good Jobs"

I very much doubt that we will ever have a shortage of jobs, despite numerous claims about robotic capabilities and self-driving vehicles. As a grandparent with aging parents, I cannot imagine the day when I would be comfortable with child care or elder care by robot or computer screen. We do and we will have a shortage of "good jobs." Pay is clearly part of the picture, but so are issues such as predictable and relatively stable hours, learning and growing on the job, having job ladders to create a career path, being treated with dignity, and having a job that society values.

Ironically, some of the lowest-paid and most unstable jobs in America are almost certainly some of the most important. Care workers are an obvious example: they care for our children and our grandchildren, and in this increasingly aging society, us. They are good at what they do, many love caring for others, but they are often exploited. They are paid poorly, they often have unpredictable hours, and there is rarely an obvious career ladder. Perhaps worst of all, we often treat such workers as if they should be invisible.

The relegation of such workers to obscurity and poverty is troubling not only on human grounds but also because it quite possibly robs us of far better outcomes for us all. In 1982, a General Accounting Office report on the child care centers serving 53,000 military dependents stated simply that "many child care centers currently in use" were "neither safe nor suitable" (General Accounting Office 1982). It is hard to ask parents to deploy or redeploy when they are worried about the safety and development of their children, so, over the years, the US military embarked on a dramatic improvement. They set high standards for leaders in their centers, improved facilities, trained their workers to deal with the unique challenges facing children with a parent who may be away for extended periods and often in harm's way, and, to retain these newly trained workers, raised pay considerably. Now US military child care is regarded as the "gold standard" (Lucas 2001).

This solution cost resources, no doubt. Yet it certainly seems to have been a high-value investment, for this transformation was a win in four ways: it improved the effectiveness of the military, it improved the situation for their soldiers, it improved things for the children, and it improved the situation for the care workers. This extended example illustrates that there are potential win-win strategies that can apply to many other "bad jobs" that we cannot live without. A fraction of the kind of money that universal basic income advocates push for might be far better invested in win-win strategies for turning "bad jobs" good.

The Broken Lower-Skill Labor Market

This final section is short and speculative. Over the years, I have come to believe, as others do, that the "low skill" labor market is a classic example of market failure. I already discussed the growing evidence of monopsony, which would lead to artificially low prices for labor. Information is essential to a well-functioning labor market—even more than in product markets. Information is critical on both sides: employers need to know how likely a candidate is to perform well in a myriad of tasks, and workers need to know what the work involves, how they are likely to be treated, and whether the job is likely to lead to better jobs in the future.

In the upper parts of the labor market, information is plentiful and becoming more so. Employers check references, they can tap their own networks to learn about past performance, conduct interviews, and use extensive recruiting network services. Workers can tap into their own social networks and employer rating sites. New platforms, such as LinkedIn, give both employers and employees the ability to search for opportunities and find just the right match. Turnover often lets workers move up rapidly or find jobs that offer far greater satisfaction.

At the other end, however, there is often almost no reliable information. No employer would call a big box retailer or a fast food establishment to see if someone was a good worker there. Work is tenuous. Even at major discount retailers, three days of absence (say because a brother neglected to mention he returned the borrowed truck empty of gas) can lead to immediate dismissal, even if a worker has been reliable for years. There is almost no information about which jobs are more likely to lead to better ones or even what a career ladder looks like. Turnover is not a stepping-stone to success; it is yet another moment when labor market information is lost and workers face greater and greater insecurity.

The situation is probably getting worse. Larger firms used to hire a far wider range of workers, from janitors to executives. It was theoretically possible to rise from the mailroom to the CEO because information was in-house. Now, lower-skilled work is increasingly contracted out. Larry Katz and Alan Krueger demonstrate rises in such alternative work, defined as "temporary help agency workers" and "independent contractors or freelancers" (Katz and Krueger 2019).

Thus, at the upper end, where workers and jobs are seen with greater and greater clarity, opportunities grow. Workers and employers have enormous incentives to invest in attractive qualities and to take advantage of highly differentiated capacities. Meanwhile, absent information at the lower levels, workers and work itself become commoditized, routine, and interchangeable. A lack of information can kill job ladders, dampen incentives to invest in oneself, and reduce the payoff to employers to offer jobs with a real future or an environment of learning. The market may settle into a terrible equilibrium with low rewards and prestige begetting weaker service and performance and justifying low pay.

There are rays of hope. Even though educational institutions for this group are highly variable, with community colleges often suffering from very low graduation rates and limited direct links to employers or higher education, a rare few offer real paths to success. So-called sectoral (in effect, industry-specific) training also offers promising results. A few entrepreneurs are looking for ways to provide better information to employers and employees in low-wage markets. What is missing is a comprehensive and coherent examination of the overall lower-skill market and a strategy for improving its functioning.

Work and its rewards, financial, personal, and societal, lie at the heart of growing inequality. In the near term, we can find ways to make work pay. We can expand that work into looking for ways to turn "bad" jobs into good ones, and the longer-term solution may lay in part in gaining a far greater understanding of why the low-skill labor market is collapsing under the weight of limited information and opportunity.

Notes

1. The higher percentage growth for women has helped close the gender gap, but the gap remains sizable for all percentiles. Note also that since women work considerably more on average than they did in earlier decades, some of their wage growth can be traced to their having greater years of experience in the labor market.

2. Once family income reaches roughly $25,000, the credit begins to phase out, being reduced by 21% per dollar earned above that level.

References

Chetty, Raj, David Grusky, Maximilian Hell, Nathaniel Hendren, Robert Manduca, and Jimmy Narang. 2017. "The Fading American Dream: Trends in Absolute Income Mobility since 1940." *Science* 356 (6336): 398–406.

Council of Economic Advisers. 2016. "Labor Market Monopsony: Trends, Consequences, and Policy Responses." Issue Brief, October 25, 2016. https://obamawhitehouse.archives.gov/sites/default/files/page/files/20161025_monopsony_labor_mrkt_cea.pdf.

David, Leslie, and Hannah Hartig. 2019. "Two-Thirds of Americans Favor Raising the Minimum Wage to $15 an Hour." *Factank*, Pew Research Center, July 30, 2019. https://www.pewresearch.org/fact-tank/2019/07/30/two-thirds-of-americans-favor-raising-federal-minimum-wage-to-15-an-hour/.

General Accounting Office. 1982. "Military Child Care Programs: Progress Made, More Needed." GAO/FPCD-82–30, General Accounting Office, Washington, DC.

Katz, Lawrence, and Alan Krueger. 2019. "The Rise and Nature of Alternative Work Arrangements in the United States, 1995–2015." *ILR Review* 72: 382–416.

Lucas, M.-A. 2001. "The Military Child Care Connection." *The Future of Children, Caring for Infants and Toddlers* 11(1): 128–133.

Sykes, Jennifer, Katherine Kriz, Kathryn Edin, and Sarah Halpern-Meekin. 2015. "Dignity and Dreams: What the Earned Income Tax Credit (EITC) Means to Low-Income Families." *American Sociological Review* 80: 243–267.

24

The Importance of Enforcement in Designing Effective Labor Market Tools

Heidi Shierholz

A sometimes overlooked but critical component of any labor and employment protection is its enforcement. Even the most perfectly designed protections will not be effective if employers have little incentive to comply with them because of lax enforcement.

To motivate this discussion, I first provide examples of violations of worker protections and what is known about how prevalent these violations are. The data suggest that violations are quite prevalent, and I examine potential reasons why they are so widespread. Finally, I discuss what a more effective enforcement system might look like, one that would incentivize more employers to comply with worker protections rather than shirk their responsibilities. I frame the discussion in terms of violations of wage and hour laws, or "wage theft." The discussion, however, also largely applies to safety and health standards, protections against employment discrimination, and labor law.

The following are some examples of the form that wage and hour violations typically take:

- A worker being paid below the minimum wage. This can also include workers who are misclassified as independent contractors by their employers, who then fail to comply with wage and hour laws such as the minimum wage as a result.
- A worker not being paid for all hours worked. For example, consider a late-shift convenience store worker whose supervisor says "clock out and then clean up." That's a form of wage theft.
- An overtime-eligible worker not being paid time and a half when they work more than 40 hours in a week.
- Illegal deductions from a worker's pay. For example, under federal law, an employer cannot legally deduct the cost of a uniform if that results in the worker making less than the minimum wage. If the employer does, that's a form of wage theft.

- Tip theft by employers or supervisors. Tips are legally the property of workers, not their supervisors or employers. If they end up in the wrong hands, that is wage theft.

How extensive are these violations? There are not a lot of empirical studies on this issue, but what is available shows that the problem is pervasive. For example, a survey of 4,300 workers in low-wage industries in Chicago, Los Angeles, and New York found that two-thirds of the workers surveyed experienced at least one pay-related violation in any given week. On average, the violation amounted to 15% of their earnings. Thus, looking at all workers surveyed—including those who did not face a pay-related violation—low-wage workers in these places reported losing about 10% of their earnings to wage theft on average (Bernhardt et al. 2009). Another study looked at Bureau of Labor Statistics (BLS) Current Population Survey data and, by comparing the wages received by workers who are eligible for the minimum wage to the minimum wage the worker is subject to, found that total wages stolen from workers as a result of minimum-wage violations alone exceeds $15 billion annually (Cooper and Kroeger 2017).

Extrapolating from existing studies, a back-of-the-envelope estimate suggests that in the aggregate, low-wage workers lose on the order of $50 billion annually to all forms of wage theft (McNicholas, Mokhiber, and Chaikof 2017). As a point of comparison, according to the FBI, the total value of all robberies, burglaries, larcenies, and motor vehicle thefts is $13 billion annually (Cooper and Kroeger 2017). Federal, state, and local governments spend tremendous resources to combat property crime. As I will discuss, lawmakers allocate surprisingly few resources to combat wage theft, despite the problem being much larger in magnitude than property crime.

Why is wage theft so prevalent? One reason is workers' diminished bargaining power relative to their employers. The fact that this unlawful employer behavior is not being "competed away" underscores that, for a variety of reasons, workers do not have the ability to quit these jobs as a de facto form of enforcement. Moreover, there are simply not enough government resources devoted to combating violations of workplace protections. For example, federal resources for the enforcement of worker protections have declined, while at the same time the US workforce has grown. In 1978, there were 69,000 workers per wage and hour investigator on average, but today that ratio is 175,000 to one (Hamaji et al. 2019). This means there is an extremely low chance that any violator will be caught. Furthermore, even when violators are caught, penalties are surprisingly low, and there are well-documented problems with collection of payments from employers found to be in violation (Cho, Koonse, and Mischel 2013). The very low chance of getting caught combined with extremely low penalties and the ease of avoiding paying them mean that there are almost no financial incentives for companies to comply with the law. In other words, our system of worker protections relies largely on managerial goodwill for its enforcement.

At the same time that government resources for enforcement are dwindling, an increasing number of corporations are forcing their employees to sign away their right to pursue justice in court if their employer violates their workplace rights. They are doing this through forced arbitration, a controversial practice in which businesses require employees to agree to arbitrate any legal disputes with the business. In forced arbitration, the employer requires the worker to agree to a contract that says that if the employer violates their rights—if the employer does not pay the worker the wages they are owed under the law, if it doesn't follow safety regulations, if it sexually harasses workers, or if it discriminates against workers on the basis of their race or sex—the worker cannot take them to court. Instead, disputes must be resolved by a private arbitrator that may be chosen by the employer, where the arbitrator typically knows that a favorable ruling for the employer will increase their likelihood of getting work from that employer in the future. Unsurprisingly, the outcomes for workers in this setting are much worse than they are in a court, with employees winning less often and receiving much lower awards in forced arbitration than they do in court (Stone and Colvin 2015). But forced arbitration is widespread and growing. Survey data show that today *more than half* of private sector nonunion employees are subject to forced arbitration agreements—up from less than 8% 25 years ago (Colvin 2018). Using a simple extrapolation, I project that, within five years, over 80% of private sector nonunion employees will be subject to forced arbitration (Hamaji et al. 2019).

Furthermore, recent Supreme Court decisions gave the green light to forced arbitration agreements with class and collective action waivers (McNicholas 2018). Why is this a problem? Class actions are an essential component of private enforcement, because individual lawsuits are often unrealistic for low- and even moderate-wage workers given that the cost of legal representation typically exceeds their lost wages. Class and collective actions allow workers to aggregate claims, making litigation cost-effective and accessible. To underscore the importance of class action lawsuits in our enforcement framework, in 2015 and 2016, the top 10 private wage and hour class action settlements alone exceeded the *combined* total wages recovered by all state and federal enforcement agencies (McNicholas, Mokhiber, and Chaikof 2017). Forced arbitration with class action and collective action waivers makes it virtually impossible for low-wage workers to get any meaningful type of remedy. Given the low *government* funding for enforcement, forced arbitration combined with class waivers essentially removes any remaining *financial* incentive companies have to comply with the law.

Another contributor to pervasive violations is workplace "fissuring," a term coined by David Weil of the Heller School for Social Policy and Management at Brandeis University and also known as "domestic outsourcing" (Weil 2014). An example he uses to explain the phenomenon is the fact that it used to be that essentially everyone working in a hotel was working for the company whose name was on the front of the building, but starting in roughly the 1980s, employers began contracting out many services, particularly labor-intensive ones. As a result, instead of the housekeepers, janitors, landscapers, laundry workers, and human resource workers being employed by the hotel, the hotel contracts out those services. This means that where there used to be just the lead firm—the hotel—setting the wages of all workers, there are now a host of satellite wage setters *that are all competing for contracts on the basis of price.* For most of these contractors, their main cost is labor, which means contractors face great pressure to cut corners on labor costs, including through violating labor and employment laws.

A final reason for prevalent violations of worker protections is declining unionization. Unionized workers are much less likely to be victims of wage theft and other violations because unions provide support, leverage, and representation to workers in claiming their rights, along with protections against retaliatory firing. But over the last 40 years, the share of workers covered by a collective bargaining agreement dropped by more than half, from over 25% to less than 12% (Shierholz 2019). This means fewer workers receive the protections unions provide in combating violations.

What do we need to put in place to have an enforcement system that would incentivize employers to comply with worker protections rather than violate the law? The first step would be to allocate more resources to the enforcement of worker protections, on both the state and federal levels. In addition to obvious—and crucial—changes, such as increasing the number of investigators, there are other important measures that can be taken. For example, enforcement dollars can be employed more efficiently through strategic enforcement efforts that target investigations in industries where workers are most likely to experience violations but are often unlikely to report them and by taking into account industry-specific dynamics, with the goal of creating ripple effects that will influence the compliance behavior of a number of employers at once (Weil 2018). In addition, some offices of state attorneys general have set up labor units and are using their authority to enforce state laws, investigating and filing suit against companies that cheat their workers (Gerstein and von Wilpert 2018). Evidence suggests that it is also important to publicize when firms are found to be in violation, because publicizing firms' socially undesirable actions may increase their incentive not to engage in such actions. For example, a recent study found that when the Occupational Safety and Health Administration began issuing press releases about workplaces that were found to be violating safety and health regulations, the publicity led *other* workplaces to substantially improve their compliance and experience fewer occupational injuries (Johnson 2019).

Forced arbitration and class action and collective action waivers in labor and employment matters must be banned. It should not be legal for employers to ask workers to sign away their right to a crucial layer of enforcement: the courts. A ban on forced arbitration and class action and collective action waivers could be done through federal legislation. In the meantime, states can and are enacting "whistleblower enforcement" laws that allow workers who are subject to forced arbitration to sue lawbreaking employers *on behalf of the state*, given that states haven't agreed to arbitration (Hamaji et al. 2019).

The impact of workplace fissuring on wage theft can be counteracted by strong joint employer standards. As employers outsource various functions to contractors and subcontractors, it has become more and more possible for lead firms to evade liability for violating labor standards. One solution would be for all firms who share control over the terms and conditions of a worker's job—such as pay, schedules, and job duties—to be considered employers of that worker, or "joint employers." For example, lead firms who are legally joint employers with their contractors would then be unable to put pressure on contractors to cut corners with labor costs while facing no liability for violations themselves. They would also be incentivized to affirmatively ensure compliance by their contractors.

Another way to boost enforcement is to pass laws that will boost unionization so that more workers get the protections that unions provide against workplace violations. It is important to note here that the decline of unions has not been a "natural" phenomenon. More people report that they want to be in unions than was the case 40 years ago (Shierholz 2019), so it's not that workers don't want unions. Furthermore, the decline in unionization within sectors has been much more important in the erosion of union coverage than changing industry composition (Nunn, O'Donnell, and Shambaugh 2019), so it has not been the shift to services that's been driving it. The decline of unionization in large part has been the result of massively increased employer aggressiveness in fighting union organizing and the fact that labor law has not evolved to counteract that (Bronfenbrenner 2009). This must be corrected.

Another relatively simple step to boost enforcement would be for federal law to require, as some states do, that all employers provide workers with a statement of pay, including, among other things, the name of the worker's legal employer or employers, rate of pay, hours worked, and all deductions from pay. When employers are required to provide workers with written notice of their terms of employment—which in most places they currently are not—it helps reduce the noncompliance that results from employers being able to easily hide violations. It also provides workers with necessary documentation to pursue a claim in the event of a violation.

Lastly, it is important to note that, every year, the federal government spends hundreds of billions of dollars on contracts for everything from building interstate highways to serving concessions at national parks. The Office of Federal Contract Compliance Programs at the Department of Labor estimates that around a quarter of all US workers work at firms that receive one or more government contracts (US Department of Labor 2016). Currently, there is no effective system to ensure that taxpayer dollars are not awarded to contractors who are chronic violators of workers' rights. The law should require that companies competing for federal contracts disclose previous workplace violations, with agencies independently confirming the disclosure, and those violations should be considered when new contracts are being awarded. In other words, government procurement should be leveraged as an enforcement tool.

The prevalent violations of worker protections described here are a sign that our system of enforcement has far too many holes in it. Even the most perfectly designed worker protections will not be effective if employers have little incentive to comply with them. In considering a framework of labor market tools to halt and reverse rising inequality in the United States, strong enforcement should be prioritized through measures such as allocating more government resources to enforcement, banning forced arbitration, strengthening joint employer standards, passing laws that will boost unionization, and leveraging government procurement for enforcement.

References

Bernhardt, Annette, Ruth Milkman, Nik Theodore, Douglas Heckathorn, Mirabai Auer, James DeFilippis, Ana Luz González, Victor Narro, Jason Perelshteyn, Diana Polson, and Michael Spiller.2009. *Broken Laws, Unprotected Workers: Violations of Employment and Labor Laws in America's Cities.* Center for Urban Economic Development, National Employment Law Project, and UCLA Institute for Research on Labor and Employment. https://s27147.pcdn.co/wp-content/uploads/2015/03/BrokenLawsReport2009.pdf.

Bronfenbrenner, Kate. 2009. *No Holds Barred—the Intensification of Employer Opposition to Organizing.* Washington, DC: Economic Policy Institute.

Cho, Eunice Hyunhye, Tia Koonse, and Anthony Mischel. 2013. *Hollow Victories: The Crisis in Collecting Unpaid Wages for California's Workers.* Los Angeles and New York: National Employment Law Center, UCLA Labor Center.

Colvin, Alexander J. S. 2018. *The Growing Use of Mandatory Arbitration.* Washington, DC: Economic Policy Institute.

Cooper, Dave, and Teresa Kroeger. 2017. *Employers Steal Billions from Workers' Paychecks Each Year: Survey Data Show Millions of Workers Are Paid Less Than the Minimum Wage, at Significant Cost to Taxpayers and State Economies.* Washington, DC: Economic Policy Institute.

Gerstein, Terri, and Marni von Wilpert. 2018. *State Attorneys General Can Play Key Roles in Protecting Workers' Rights.* Washington, DC: Economic Policy Institute.

Hamaji, Kate, Rachel Deutsch, Elizabeth Nicolas, Celine McNicholas, Heidi Shierholz, and Margaret Poydock. 2019. *Unchecked Corporate Power.* Washington, DC: Center for Popular Democracy, Economic Policy Institute.

Johnson, Matthew S. 2019. "Regulation by Shaming: Deterrence Effects of Publicizing Violations of Workplace Safety and Health Laws." Working paper for *American Economic Review.*

McNicholas, Celine. 2018. *In Epic Systems Corp. Decision, the Supreme Court Deals a Significant Blow to Workers' Fundamental Rights.* Washington, DC: Center for Popular Democracy, Economic Policy Institute.

McNicholas, Celine, Zane Mokhiber, and Adam Chaikof. 2017. *Two Billion Dollars in Stolen Wages Were Recovered for Workers in 2015 and 2016—and That's Just a Drop in the Bucket.* Washington, DC: Economic Policy Institute.

Nunn, Ryan, Jimmy O'Donnell, and Jay Shambaugh. 2019. *The Shift in Private Sector Union Participation: Explanations and Effects.* Washington, DC: Brookings Institution.

Shierholz, Heidi. 2019. *Working People Have Been Thwarted in Their Efforts to Bargain for Better Wages by Attacks on Unions.* Washington, DC: Economic Policy Institute.

Stone, Katherine V. W., and Alexander J. S. Colvin. 2015. *The Arbitration Epidemic*. Washington, DC: Economic Policy Institute.

US Department of Labor. 2016. "Workplace Rights." Fact sheet. Office of Federal Contract Compliance Programs, US Department of Labor, Washington, DC.

Weil, David. 2014. *The Fissured Workplace: How Work Became So Bad for So Many and What Can Be Done to Improve It*. Cambridge, MA: Harvard University Press.

Weil, David. 2018. "Creating a Strategic Enforcement Approach to Address Wage Theft: One Academic's Journey in Organizational Change." *Journal of Industrial Relations* 60(3): 437–460.

X
Social Safety Net

25

Enhancing Micro and Macro Resilience by Building on the Improvements in the Social Safety Net

Jason Furman

The United States has greatly expanded the social safety net over the past 50 years. As a result, more people are lifted out of poverty by social programs today than ever before. This expansion of the social safety net has generally followed the path of least political resistance, which has typically meant programs that require work or that are for children. Fortunately, there are substantial economic benefits from focusing on children and work. The biggest remaining gaps in the system are for politically less sympathetic groups, creating a political obstacle to further progress. However, overcoming these obstacles would yield broad benefits. It would not only directly help the individuals falling through the gaps of the current system but also have spillover benefits by enhancing automatic fiscal stabilizers and thus contribute to macroeconomic stability.

The expansion of the social safety net can be understood using an anchored version of the supplemental poverty measure (SPM), which shows the poverty rate after fully accounting for taxes and transfers, including noncash transfers.[1] The impact of this expansion has been considerable, with the SPM falling by about 10 percentage points since the late 1960s (figure 25.1). On the other hand, market income poverty has basically remained unchanged, reflecting the well-known lack of real wage growth at the bottom of the distribution and the withdrawal of less-skilled men from the labor force.

In 1965, the poverty rate after taxes and transfers was almost exactly the same as the market income poverty rate. That's because some people were lifted above the poverty line by transfers, but a lot of people were taxed below the poverty line. In 1965, a family of four that earned a little above the poverty line was effectively taxed into poverty. This has changed dramatically over time, and today nearly half the people in market poverty are lifted above the poverty line, all else equal, by the social safety net. This reflects the establishment and expansion of the Child Tax

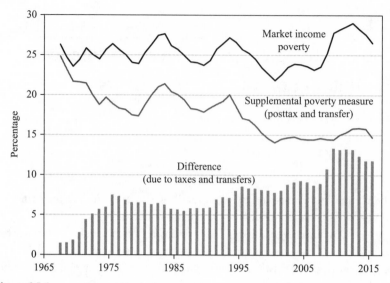

Figure 25.1
Trends in market income poverty and poverty after taxes and transfers, 1967–2015.
Source: Based on Wimer et al. (2013), updated in November 2016 as reported in Furman (2017).

Credit, Earned Income Tax Credit (EITC), Medicaid, and the Supplemental Nutrition Assistance Program (SNAP), which was previously known as the Food Stamps program.

The largest expansions in public programs have involved programs that target children (e.g., the Children's Health Insurance Program, or CHIP) or programs that target both work and children (e.g., the EITC). The biggest source of this shift is the EITC—available only to those with earnings—which was created in 1975 and was expanded multiple times over the following decades. It was most recently expanded in 2009, as part of the Recovery Act, with those improvements being extended in 2010 and 2013. Reflecting this growing emphasis on work, since 1996 the EITC has accounted for more support for low-income households than traditional cash welfare. In fiscal year 2019, the refundable portions of the EITC and the partially refundable Child Tax Credit (also available only to those with earnings) totaled roughly $88 billion, nearly six times federal expenditures on Temporary Assistance for Needy Families (TANF), which is a more traditional cash welfare program.

As a result, the United States has effectively stopped taxing families with children into poverty. It is still the case, however, that a single person making about $14,000 annually with no qualifying children will pay enough in taxes that it will move her or him below the poverty line. These workers without qualifying children are a major hole in the current social safety net, which could be addressed with a modest reform that expanded the currently tiny EITC for workers without qualifying children or with a more significant reform that separated the two components of the EITC into two different programs, a child allowance and a separate tax credit for lower-earning workers. Further investments in children also can have substantial returns and even potentially pay for themselves in present value (Hendren and Sprung-Keyser forthcoming).

One way to understand the impact of the social safety net is to examine what the poverty rate would be in the absence of various programs by "zeroing out" their contributions to income. The overall percentage of people lifted out of poverty by these different programs in 2018 is shown in figure 25.2. Social Security benefits had the largest effect on the poverty rate, especially for those age 65 and older, a third of whom were lifted out of poverty by these payments. Among children, refundable tax credits had the largest impact, reducing their poverty rate by over 6%.

The expansion of the social safety net has also reduced the cyclicality of poverty. For example, from 2007 to 2010, the market poverty rate rose 4.8 percentage points amid the worst recession since the Great Depression, but the poverty rate after taxes and transfers only rose 0.4 percentage point because of the combination of the existing social safety net and temporary expansions under the Recovery Act (Furman 2017). Overall, the expansion of the safety net represents a big improvement in the

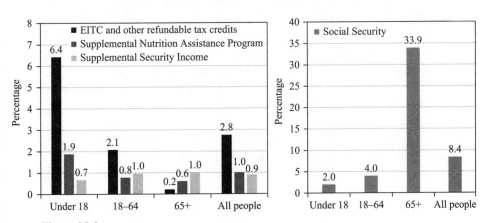

Figure 25.2
Reduction in poverty rate by program, 2018. *Source*: Fox (2019).

overall fairness of the fiscal system if judged by a criterion like Rawls's difference principle (Rawls 1971).

All these estimates are based on a direct mechanical counterfactual that takes income as given and then adds or subtracts taxes and transfers. They do not reflect how the absence of these taxes and transfers might affect market income by changing behavior. Examining a wide range of studies, Ben-Shalom, Moffitt, and Sholz (2012) conclude that the labor supply incentives of antipoverty programs have "basically, zero" effect on overall poverty rates—at least in the short run. Going program by program, they conclude that TANF does not meaningfully alter incentives to work and that the work disincentives induced by disability insurance, Medicare, and unemployment insurance might reduce the estimated static antipoverty effects of those programs by one-eighth or less. Other programs, such as the EITC, increase work incentives.

This assessment of the programmatic evidence is consistent with the fact that broader trends are not consistent with the belief that the expanded social safety net has led to a reduction in work and thus in market incomes. Although the social safety net has expanded overall, it *increased* for groups that have seen *increased* participation in the workforce (e.g., prime age women) and *decreased* for groups that have seen *decreased* participation in the workforce (e.g., prime age men, who saw their rate of cash benefit receipt fall from 20% in 1975 to 9% in 2018[2]).

The traditional economics literature has focused on the short-term effects of the safety net, the trade-off between providing support and discouraging work. A rapidly expanding body of literature is adding a critically important new perspective: the long-term impact of social safety programs on children in households that receive benefits. This literature has found that programs, including preschool, Medicaid, SNAP, the EITC, and housing vouchers, can have long-term benefits for the children who receive them, including higher earnings, better health, greater likelihood of graduating from college, and reduced likelihood of being incarcerated (for reviews, see Furman 2017; Hoynes and Schanzenbach 2018; Hendren and Sprung-Keyser forthcoming).

Steps that could further reduce risk for families at the microeconomic level will also help reduce macroeconomic risks, by improving the system of automatic stabilizers. This is particularly important because of the constraints on conventional monetary policy, which is likely to hit the effective lower bound in future recessions, increasing the need for, and benefit from, fiscal policy.

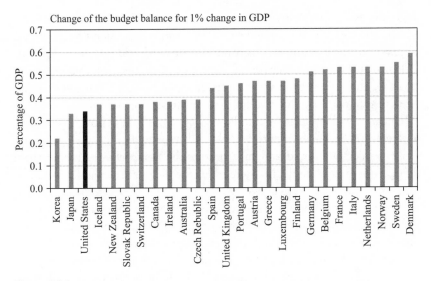

Figure 25.3
Automatic stabilizers in advanced Organization for Economic Cooperation and Development (OECD) countries. *Source*: International Monetary Fund (2015).

The United States has comparatively weak automatic stabilizers, as shown in figure 25.3. This is because the most important determinant of the magnitude of automatic stabilizers is the size of government, and the second most important determinant is the degree of progressivity of the overall fiscal system. The United States has a relatively small government that is less progressive than those of other advanced economies, and as a result it has smaller automatic stabilizers.

The potency of any degree of automatic stabilizers is related to their design. For example, transfers to low-income households, which have a higher marginal propensity to consume and less ability to smooth consumption in the face of shocks, will likely have a higher multiplier than other policies.

A larger or more progressive fiscal system would result in larger automatic stabilizers, but absent consensus on that, the automatic stabilizers could be improved by adding more contingencies to the current system. For example, the optimal length of unemployment insurance is longer in a recession than it is in a boom because the importance of consumption smoothing rises relative to the moral hazard (Baily 1978; Chetty 2006). This is why it would make sense to build in automatic triggers that would expand and extend unemployment insurance in states that have high or rising unemployment even for purely microeconomic reasons (Chodorow-Reich and Coglianese 2019). Similarly, expanding Medicaid support to states in downturns could reduce Medicaid cutbacks at a critical time, preventing a negative fiscal externality and negative spillovers to other states that result when states cut spending on Medicaid and that are compounded by the resulting cuts in federal matching spending on Medicaid (Fiedler, Furman, and Powell 2019). All these policies could be designed to be budget neutral while still improving the safety net from both a microeconomic and macroeconomic perspective. Making them budget increasing could be preferable if policymakers wanted more of these programs on average over the cycle.

Over the last 50 years, essentially all progress in reducing poverty has been through the social safety net, not through improvements in market incomes. To make substantial progress on poverty over the next 50 years, we should continue to build on the social safety net, but that may not be enough. Higher market incomes will likely be necessary as well. Well-designed safety net expansions can actually help in both these regards. Through the longer-term benefits they have for children and the ways they could ameliorate business cycles, further expansions have the potential to raise the average level of GDP, and the wages of workers at the bottom, in the process.

Notes

1. The official poverty measure reflects an incoherent hybrid of market income and income after taxes and transfers in that counted income includes cash transfers but omits taxes—including refundable tax credits—and also noncash transfers. As a result, it doesn't accurately capture market developments or reflect the effects of the major expansions in the social safety net over the last 50 years.

2. Calculations based on Flood et al. (2020).

References

Baily, Martin Neil. 1978. "Some Aspects of Optimal Unemployment Insurance." *Journal of Public Economics* 10(3): 379–402.

Ben-Shalom, Yonatan, Robert Moffitt, and John Karl Scholz. 2012. "An Assessment of the Effectiveness of Antipoverty Programs in the United States." In *The Oxford Handbook of the Economics of Poverty*, edited by Philip N. Jefferson, 709–749. New York: Oxford University Press.

Chetty, Raj. 2006. "A General Formula for the Optimal Level of Social Insurance." *Journal of Public Economics* 90(10–11): 1879–1901.

Chodorow-Reich, Gabriel, and John Coglianese. 2019. "Unemployment Insurance and Macroeconomic Stabilization." In *Recession Ready: Fiscal Policies to Stabilize the American Economy*, edited by Heather Boushey, Ryan Nunn, and Jay Shambaugh, 153–179. Washington, DC: Brookings Institution.

Fiedler, Matt, Jason Furman, and Wilson Powell III. 2019. "Increasing Federal Support for State Medicaid and CHIP Programs in Response to Economic Downturns: Unemployment Insurance and Macroeconomic Stabilization." In *Recession Ready: Fiscal Policies to Stabilize the American Economy*, edited by Heather Boushey, Ryan Nunn, and Jay Shambaugh, 93–127. Washington, DC: Brookings Institution.

Flood, Sarah, Miriam King, Renae Rodgers, Steven Ruggles and J. Robert Warren. 2020. Integrated Public Use Microdata Series, Current Population Survey: Version 7.0 [dataset]. Minneapolis, MN: IPUMS.

Fox, Liana. 2019. "The Supplemental Poverty Measure: 2018." Current Population Reports P60-268 (RV), US Census Bureau, Washington, DC.

Furman, Jason. 2017. "Reducing Poverty: The Progress We Have Made and the Path Forward." Speech, Washington, DC, January 17, 2017. https://obamawhitehouse.archives.gov/sites/default/files/page/files/20170117_furman_center_on_budget_poverty_cea.pdf.

Hendren, Nathaniel, and Ben Sprung-Keyser. Forthcoming. "A Unified Welfare Analysis of Government Policies." *Quarterly Journal of Economics*.

Hoynes, Hilary W., and Diane Whitmore Schanzenbach. 2018. "Safety Net Investments in Children." *Brookings Papers on Economic Activity* (Spring): 89–132.

International Monetary Fund. 2015. "Can Fiscal Policy Stabilize Output?" In *April 2015 Fiscal Monitor: Now Is the Time*, 21–48. Washington, DC: International Monetary Fund.

Rawls, John. 1971. *A Theory of Justice*. Cambridge, MA: Harvard University Press.

Wimer, Christopher, Liana Fox, Irv Garfinkel, Neeraj Kaushal, and Jane Waldfogel. 2013. "Trends in Poverty with an Anchored Supplemental Poverty Measure." Working Paper 13–01, Columbia Population Research Center, New York.

26

The Social Safety Net for Families with Children: What Is Working and How to Do More

Hilary Hoynes

In 2018, 14.5% of children lived in families with incomes below the federal poverty line (Fox 2019). This sets us apart from other advanced economies with similar or lower per capita income but that have lower levels of poverty. Stagnating wages for low-skill workers (Autor 2014), taken in isolation, put upward pressure on child poverty rates. Social safety net programs, on the other hand, can help to combat these labor market pressures. What is the net effect of the forces of the labor market along with the evolving US social safety net? What changes to the social safety net could yield larger reductions in child poverty?

In this chapter, I discuss child poverty and potential policy changes in four parts. First, I summarize the state of the current social safety net for families with children and its effectiveness in reducing child poverty. Second, I look backward and summarize how the social safety net has changed, describing the net impact of welfare reform and the rise of a largely work-contingent social safety net. From this, I identify where our policies are working and where we need to do more. Third, I present two packages of policy changes that could dramatically reduce child poverty. I conclude by highlighting new research that shows that social safety net spending on children yields large benefits in the long run through changing the life trajectories of children.

Before proceeding, it is useful to step back and ask why I focus on child poverty. First, in the United States, children have among the highest poverty rates of any demographic group. Second, and more importantly, concern about child poverty relates to issues around intergenerational mobility, what private and public costs result from low incomes at this age, and what the potential returns from more spending and investment for this group might be. Third, US safety net policies directed at families with children have changed dramatically over the decades.

The Social Safety Net for Families with Children: Current Policies and Recent Changes

Figure 26.1 provides a snapshot of the antipoverty effectiveness of the current social safety net in the United States. This is a static calculation—zeroing out one program at a time with no change to labor supply or to other behavior—starting from the baseline where all programs for children remain intact. The baseline child poverty rate (for 2015) is 13%.[1] Figure 26.1 shows that the largest antipoverty program for children in the United States is tax credits (the Earned Income Tax Credit, or EITC, and the refundable portion of the Child Tax Credit); the child poverty rate would be 5.9 percentage points higher (18.9%) in the absence of these programs. The second-largest antipoverty program for children is Food Stamps (now known as the Supplemental Nutrition Assistance Program, SNAP); without it, poverty rates would increase by 5.2 percentage points. Other programs yield moderate effects—eliminating disability benefits received through the Supplemental Security Income (SSI) program would raise poverty rates by 1.8 percentage points and eliminating social security benefits would raise child poverty by 2.3 percentage points. Smaller impacts are found for housing benefits and other programs, with almost no reductions in poverty coming from cash welfare (Temporary Assistance

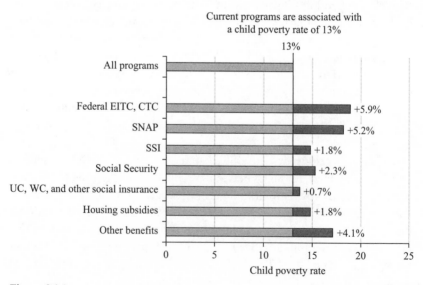

Figure 26.1
Effects of social safety net on child poverty, 2015. *Source*: National Academies of Sciences, Engineering, and Medicine (2019).

for Needy Families, TANF). When looking at deep child poverty rates (the incidence of having posttax and transfer income below 50% of the poverty line), SNAP becomes the most important program with regard to cash welfare benefits.

Figure 26.2 presents the trend in child poverty from 1967 to 2016, with separate plots for *market income* poverty (pretax and pretransfer) and *posttax and transfer* poverty (the Supplemental Poverty Measure, SPM). The figure shows that SPM child poverty declined substantially between the early 1990s and around 2000, and has been relatively constant since then. In contrast, market income poverty is highly cyclical and increased substantially in the Great Recession. The contrast between these two series highlights one aspect of the "safety net" feature of our tax and transfer programs. Despite the reductions in child poverty in the 1990s, poverty rates remain high in absolute terms or in comparison to those of other rich countries.

How has the social safety net changed over this period? Figure 26.3 plots the share of the social safety net going to different subgroups across the period 1990–2015.[2] Figure 26.3(a) apportions total spending into four bins of posttax and transfer income relative to the SPM poverty threshold (less than 50%, 50%–99%, 100%–149%, and 150%–199%).

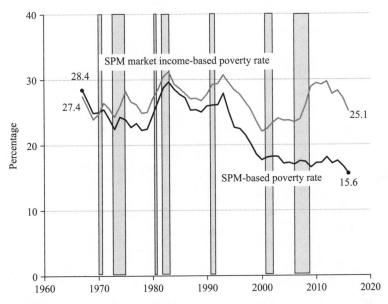

Figure 26.2
Child poverty rates before and after taxes and transfers, 1967–2016. *Source*: National Academies of Sciences, Engineering, and Medicine (2019).

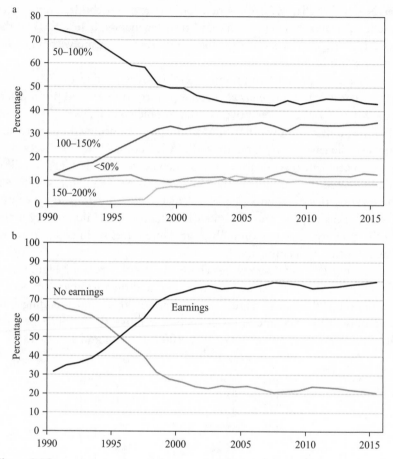

Figure 26.3
Trend in share of state and federal spending on children by group: (a) by income relative to SPM poverty threshold; (b) by presence of earnings. *Source*: Hoynes and Schanzenbach (2018).

Figure 26.3(b) apportions the safety net spending to families with earnings versus families without earnings. The two graphs illustrate a dramatic evolution of policies for poor families in the United States. First, the safety net for families with children has almost completely shifted to *work-contingent* assistance. In 1990, 70% of the social safety net targeted at children went to families that didn't have earnings. By 2015, this had completely reversed—with less than 30% of spending going to children in families with no earnings. Second, and relatedly, essentially all growth in the social safety net over this 25-year period went to the more advantaged part of the disadvantaged population. In contrast, a shrinking share went to those with the lowest income levels. This is the result of welfare reform and the decline of cash assistance for those out of work. Additionally, the expansions to the social safety net have largely taken the form of work-contingent benefits (the tax credits) or Medicaid (not included in figure 26.3).

An implication of this shift is less protection from negative (labor market and other) shocks. The research confirms this; studies examining the Great Recession showed that the social safety net did quite a good job of protecting those with income around the poverty line (as shown in figure 26.2), but incomes at lower levels were more volatile than we would have expected from the experience of earlier recessions (Bitler and Hoynes 2015; Bitler, Hoynes, and Kuka 2017). This is directly connected to the decline in cash assistance (Bitler and Hoynes 2016).

Policies to Reduce Child Poverty

What can we do to reduce child poverty and deep poverty? Table 26.1 summarizes two packages of policies that achieve a 50% reduction in both poverty and deep poverty. The estimates are based on a National Academies of Sciences, Engineering, and Medicine (2019) report panel that I was part of. These simulations are based on the Urban Institute's TRIM3 model and include adjustments for behavioral responses of labor supply (sometimes positive, sometimes negative) based on estimates from the literature. The table presents a description of the policy changes as well as the total cost and the change in the number of workers.

These simulations illustrate two ways to try to get to the 50% reduction. The first column expands preexisting policies, including the EITC, SNAP, housing vouchers, and child care tax benefits. The second column includes some of these expansions (the EITC, child care tax benefits, and others) but also introduces new policy—a child allowance. The child allowance provides $2,700 per year to families, including those with no earnings. It is essentially an extension of the current Child Tax Credit, which gives $2,000 per child up to about $400,000, but does not extend to the lowest-income families (including those with no earnings).

These two combinations of policies achieve the 50% reduction in child poverty and deep poverty. They include a combination of programs that induce more work (the EITC and the child and dependent care tax credit) and programs that induce less work (SNAP, housing vouchers, and child allowance). On balance, however, the policy expansions lead

Table 26.1
Policy packages meeting goal of 50% reduction in 100% and 50% child poverty

	Using preexisting policies only	Introducing child allowance
Expand EITC (40% expansion)	X	X
Expand Child and Dependent Care Tax Credit	X	X
Increase the minimum wage		X
Expand housing voucher program (extend to 70% eligible)	X	
Expand SNAP benefits (35% expansion)	X	
Begin a child allowance ($225/month/child)		X
Begin child support assurance		X
Eliminate 1996 immigration eligibility restrictions		X
Percentage reduction in the number of poor children	−50.7%	−52.3%
Percentage reduction in the number of children in deep poverty	−51.7%	−55.1%
Change in the number of low-income workers	+404,000	+611,000
Annual cost, in billions	$90.7	$108.8

Note: Adjusts for underreporting and includes behavioral changes in labor supply.
Source: National Academies of Sciences, Engineering, and Medicine (2019).

to a net increase in employment (400,000 to 600,000 new workers). The expansions come at a cost of $90–100 billion per year.

The Social Safety Net as an Investment

So there are policies that can be deployed to reduce child poverty and increase work. It is important to point out that spending to reduce child poverty isn't just a single-period benefit. Recent research documents that more social safety net spending when children are young yields returns, both private and public, in the long run. We have substantial evidence from Medicaid, the EITC, and SNAP that more spending when children are young leads to increases in economic and health outcomes for them in adulthood (Hoynes and Schanzenbach 2018). For example, more access to public health insurance when children are young increases their years of education completed and future earnings and lowers their mortality in adulthood. Access to SNAP in childhood leads to improvement in completed education, adult health, lower mortality, and, for African American men, lower incarceration rates (Hoynes, Schanzenbach, and Almond 2016; Bailey et al. 2020). These long-run gains are also found for the Earned Income Tax Credit and cash welfare. The challenge is that the costs for these programs appear today but the benefits take decades to develop (and require good causal identification to estimate them).

In sum, our social safety net needs to do more to reduce child poverty and deep poverty. Reducing poverty is feasible, and we have programs and policies in place that we could expand to meet these goals. Additionally, there is growing evidence that social safety net spending on children—Medicaid, SNAP, EITC, and cash welfare—leads to reductions in child poverty today as well as leading to improvements in adult human capital and health in the longer run. Therefore, spending more on poverty reduction today provides benefits—both private and public—in the next generation.

Notes

1. The figure comes from the National Academies of Sciences, Engineering, and Medicine (2019) and adjusts for underreporting of benefits using the Urban Institute's TRIM3 model. The adjustment for underreporting leads to smaller poverty rates than the unadjusted numbers reported in figure 26.2.

2. The social safety net programs included in figure 26.3 include AFDC/TANF, Food Stamps, the Earned Income Tax Credit, and the Child Tax Credit. We only measure spending in families up to 200% of poverty. This cuts off a significant portion of the Child Tax Credit spending, which extends quite high into the income distribution. For more information, see Hoynes and Schanzenbach (2018).

References

Autor, David. 2014. "Skills, Education, and the Rise of Earnings Inequality among the 'Other 99 Percent." *Science* 344(6186): 845–851.

Bailey, Martha, Hilary Hoynes, Maya Rossin-Slater, and Reed Walker. 2020. "Is the Social Safety Net a Long-Term Investment? Large-Scale Evidence from the Food Stamps Program." NBER Working Paper 26942, National Bureau of Economic Research, Cambridge, MA.

Bitler, Marianne, and Hilary Hoynes. 2015. "Heterogeneity in the Impact of Economic Cycles and the Great Recession: Effects within and across the Income Distribution." *AEA Papers and Proceedings* 105(5): 154–160.

Bitler, Marianne, and Hilary Hoynes. 2016. "The More Things Change, the More They Stay the Same? The Safety Net and Poverty in the Great Recession." *Journal of Labor Economics* 34(S1, Pt 2): S403–S444.

Bitler, Marianne, Hilary Hoynes, and Elira Kuka. 2017. "Child Poverty, the Great Recession, and the Social Safety Net in the United States." *Journal of Policy Analysis and Management* 36(2): 358–389.

Fox, Liana. 2019. *The Supplemental Poverty Measure: 2017.* Current Population Report P60–268, US Census Bureau, Washington, DC.

Hoynes, Hilary, and Diane Whitmore Schanzenbach. 2018. "Safety Net Investments in Children." *Brookings Papers on Economic Activity* (Spring): 89–132.

Hoynes, Hilary, Diane Whitmore Schanzenbach, and Douglas Almond. 2016. "Long-Run Impacts of Childhood Access to the Safety Net." *American Economic Review* 106(4): 903–934.

National Academies of Sciences, Engineering, and Medicine. 2019. *A Roadmap to Reducing Child Poverty.* Washington, DC: National Academies Press.

XI

Progressive Taxation

27

Reflections on Taxation in Support of Redistributive Policies

Wojciech Kopczuk

The fundamental role of tax policy is to raise revenue to finance expenditures. This may seem like a truism, but much discussion nowadays is framed around an alternative, corrective role for taxation. In this chapter, I discuss what (I believe) focusing on the revenue role of taxation implies for policy instruments that US policymakers should consider when embarking on funding any expansion of the welfare state.

The line between spending and taxation is not always bright—the Earned Income Tax Credit operates through the tax code but is a form of transfer program, and "tax expenditures" encompass many types of tax breaks that are economically close (and sometimes equivalent) to direct spending. The United States falls on the side of strong reliance on tax expenditures. For example, a tax preference for employer-sponsored health insurance appears to be a tax break but subsidizes health spending in a manner similar to how direct subsidies might.

Issues like this make looking at the progressivity of the tax code in isolation, without thinking about the spending side, incomplete and potentially misleading. Even more so, focusing on the progressivity of any single tax instrument is not particularly appealing. For example, a carbon tax by itself is likely mildly regressive, but a carbon tax coupled with a carbon dividend is progressive. A carbon tax compensated by changes in income taxation to offset its regressivity could be even more progressive. For these reasons, I (and many other economists) tend to think about progressivity of the tax and transfer system as a whole rather than considering the progressivity of each individual piece separately.

With that in mind, I will take as given that there are desirable ways to spend that would have a strong progressive aspect to them. Some that I find particularly appealing include investments in children, especially in early childhood interventions; direct (preferably with no strings attached) transfers to the most needy; or addressing the looming problems with financing Social Security and Medicare. Such progressive forms of spending require financing.

Taxation Elsewhere

One way to think about how to raise funds is to think about taxes that don't yet exist. The other way is to look at what countries that raise more money and spend it much more progressively than the United States do. These two approaches happen to lead to the same place: the value-added tax (VAT).

I will rely on the data from the Organization for Economic Cooperation and Development (OECD 2019) for 2016 (see figure 27.1). It will not surprise anyone that the United States collects less revenue than the OECD average, 25.9% of GDP (accounting for all layers of the government), compared to 34% on average among the OECD countries. Neighboring Canada collects 32.7%. What accounts for this 8.1% difference compared to the OECD or 6.8% difference compared to Canada? The elephant in the room is the VAT. OECD countries collect on average 6.8% of GDP using this tax. Canada relies on it relatively weakly at just 4.4%. Some countries, including Denmark, New Zealand, Hungary, Sweden, and Finland, collect more than 9%.

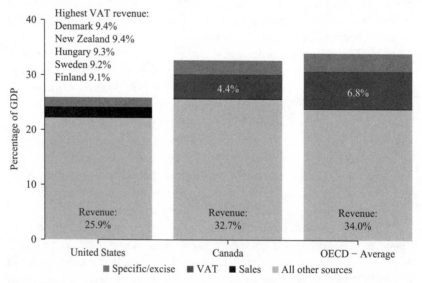

Figure 27.1
The role of VAT, sales, and excise taxation. *Source*: Data for 2016 from the OECD (2019).

This is interesting by itself because a VAT is not a very progressive instrument. It is a tax on consumption, imposed mostly at a flat rate, though often accompanied by preferential rates on some goods and by exemptions. A flat tax on consumption might be neither progressive nor regressive if the base is comprehensive and one takes a very long-term view (a short-term perspective would render consumption taxes less progressive than an income tax, because the propensity to consume varies with income). Practical implementations, however, often leave out some forms of consumption for various administrative and policy reasons. Often (though to a varying degree) this includes health care, education, parts of housing consumption, and charity, all of which likely push toward regressivity. Such exemptions are not inevitable—New Zealand taxes over 90% of consumption at the statutory rate through its VAT (OECD 2018, table 2.A.7)—but are common (the average OECD country collects 55% of what a hypothetical comprehensive consumption tax would collect at a statutory rate). Exemptions of necessities may partially compensate for that, but there is obviously a trade-off between base and revenue. At the end of the day, VATs are at best mildly progressive, yet countries with much more progressive spending patterns than the United States rely on them heavily.

If not a VAT, are there perhaps other components of the tax system that are much more progressive? As figure 27.2 illustrates, the United States raises more revenue through personal income and corporate taxes than the OECD average and a little bit less than Canada. This suggests that there may be opportunities to raise more through these taxes, and I will comment on some priorities here. Nevertheless, the United States is not out of line in its reliance on personal income and corporate taxes, and even the reductions after the 2017 reform will not change this pattern.[1]

The third large category of taxes, next to consumption and income taxes, is payroll taxes, which predominantly fund social insurance programs. Relative to the OECD average, the United States relies less on payroll taxes, and it uses them a bit more than Canada does. Payroll taxes are a close cousin of consumption taxes—in fact, there is a theoretical similarity between the two because both are imposed on the present value of earnings and consumption, which should be equal to each other absent additional considerations. The "additional considerations" here are interesting though. A new tax on consumption taxes consumption out of preexisting wealth, so it is effectively a one-time tax on wealth. A tax on consumption taxes consumption out of supernormal returns, whereas a payroll tax does not. Both these facts suggest that payroll taxes are even less progressive than

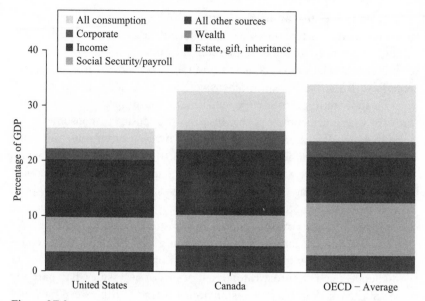

Figure 27.2
Composition of revenue as a percentage of GDP. *Source*: Data for 2016 from the OECD (2019).

consumption taxes, yet countries with much more progressive policies than the United States rely heavily on this form of taxation.

Finally, the newcomer on the US political agenda—a wealth tax—plays virtually no role anywhere.

Clearly, pursuing redistributive policies does not necessarily require that all sections of the tax code be progressive. In fact, I hope that this discussion makes it clear that countries that pursue policies that are much more redistributive than those of the United States get there by raising a lot of revenue through means that are at best mildly progressive and rely on very broad bases involving taxing all individuals. Given that the United States already has a decent reliance on the payroll tax, that leaves a VAT as the major revenue source that could bring the country in line with patterns seen elsewhere.

Why are VAT and payroll taxes so important as revenue raisers? Economists (with some notable exceptions) traditionally have not been too concerned with administrative issues, but this is exactly where these revenue sources shine. By involving businesses and leveraging arm's length transactions either between employers and employees or between businesses, these are contexts that naturally give rise to an ability to institute well-functioning information reporting regimes that make tax evasion hard. Furthermore, by taxing well-defined and broad bases, policymakers reduce opportunities for tax avoidance.

Fixes to Existing US Taxes

The VAT is the missing piece of the US puzzle of tax policy that, in my view, is necessary to consider as a way of financing any large increases in government spending. It is not, of course, the only reform worth considering. Given the political focus on inequality between those at the top of the wealth ladder and the rest of society, what are the options there?

The 2017 reform had a number of provisions that were questionable. I will highlight one that was costly, regressive, and with little economic justification: a 20% income tax deduction for qualifying pass-through businesses. Repealing this one provision should make a bucket list of immediately possible tax changes. Beyond fixing some of the most egregious loopholes and tinkering with marginal tax rates, what are the other major reform directions?

I doubt that a wealth tax is a good idea, for both economic and administrative reasons. I'm skeptical about its revenue-raising possibilities, especially given the experience elsewhere. I am not convinced that it's the best tool (or even a good one) for addressing political power, dynastic wealth, monopoly power, or other sources of rents. In each of these cases, there are alternative direct instruments—political reform, the estate tax, antitrust policy, or capital taxation. Elsewhere, I provide a longer discussion of these issues (Kopczuk 2019).

Although I am skeptical of the desirability of a wealth tax, the estate and gift tax system is important for limiting intergenerational transfer of inequality. Broadly speaking, weaknesses of the existing estate and gift tax system follow from four problems. First, valuation is difficult and uncertain.[2] Second, its interaction with income and especially capital gains taxation has major problems. Third, its treatment of charity creates avoidance opportunities. Fourth, gift and estate taxes are integrated, but in a very imperfect fashion.

The estate tax is not, and is unlikely to ever be, a major source of revenue. Still, addressing some of the valuation problems and better integration of gift and estate taxes are important issues if one wants to make this particular part of the tax system work better.

Problems with capital gains taxation and charity, on the other hand, extend well beyond the estate and gift tax context. In my view, these are two of the largest weaknesses in the existing US personal income tax system. The fundamental problem with capital gains taxation as currently implemented is that it is based on realization: capital gains are taxed when the asset is sold. Deferral by itself creates a disparity between capital gains and other forms of capital income that are taxed on accrual and thus creates an advantage to represent income in tax-advantaged form.

A particularly pernicious form of deferral is the step up in basis at death: assets held until a taxpayer's death avoid capital gains taxation altogether (see Kopczuk 2017 for a discussion). This is not a rational policy—in fact, it appears that it originally happened without much foresight, effectively by administrative mistake (Zelenak 2018)—and it has obvious alternatives: constructive realization of capital gains at death or carryover of the original basis. The availability of step up makes capital gains' revenue-maximizing rate lower than it would be otherwise, partially explaining why taxing them at rates equal to or at least much closer to personal income tax rates is controversial. Eliminating step up is an obvious first step up in improving taxation of capital gains.

The second direction is to weaken the deferral advantage. There are ways to defer taxation even when there are natural realization events (e.g., like-kind exchanges) that serve no good economic purpose. Separately, some assets can be relatively easily taxed on an accrual basis. The difficulty and the reason for taxing realizations is twofold: lack of valuation and liquidity. Most obviously, publicly traded assets can be taxed on accrual (mark to market), because regular valuation is straightforwardly possible. Extending accrual-based taxation to assets where regular valuation is possible is a natural reform direction. When valuation is not possible or when liquidity is an issue, there are two alternative solutions. One is to accrue a notional tax liability to be settled at realization. The other is to implement a form of "retrospective capital gains taxation" (Auerbach 1991) that eliminates the deferral advantage.

The existing capital gains tax rules also interact with charity. A gift of appreciated capital gains to a charity has two tax benefits. First, it is another way to escape capital gains taxation. Second, despite the lack of tax recognition of income, it can still be used to claim a charitable deduction for personal income tax purposes. This is an egregious policy with no good purpose.

However, beyond this particular issue, there are many other questionable aspects of the treatment of charitable contributions. On the tax side, charitable contributions give rise to personal income and estate tax deductions. The value of these deductions is a function of marginal tax rates so that higher-income taxpayers receive a higher marginal tax subsidy for their contributions to charity. It is hard to think why a subsidy for contributions to a public good should depend on who makes the gift (Schizer 2015). A more rational system, which would still subsidize giving, would replace a deduction by a tax credit. This does not exhaust tax-related problems with charity, however. Some income and estate tax planning involves structuring gifts to charity in a tax-advantaged fashion (e.g., charitable remainder trusts). Many charitable gifts blur a line between private and public because they involve benefits to donors—applying to gifts that come with influence over the future direction of a charity (e.g., board memberships), nonpecuniary benefits from controlling a foundation, gifts to universities that may involve prestige or benefits to children, conservation easements that may benefit neighboring properties, and others. It is also not clear why society should direct its scarce subsidy dollars to particular (even if desirable) pet causes favored by rich donors. Finally, and going beyond charity to a more general ecosystem of tax-exempt entities, the existence of tax-exempt entities creates arbitrage opportunities (e.g., in the context of carried interest) and potential tax responses (e.g., one reason for having an entity-level corporate tax is to guarantee taxation of otherwise nontaxable investors). I do not have answers for exactly how charity should be reformed in the United States, but we are long overdue for rethinking this important aspect of public policy.

Conclusion

Financing redistributive policies is done elsewhere by relying heavily on taxes that are not very progressive: payroll taxes and a VAT. The United States does not have a VAT, and I find it hard to imagine significant increases in government spending without introducing it. There is also, obviously, room for some changes in the rates of existing taxes. What I find more appealing, however, are changes to existing taxes that would simultaneously raise revenue and improve the fairness and coherence of the US tax system. Chiefly, these changes involve reforming how capital gains are taxed to reduce possibilities for deferral and changing the treatment of charity.

Notes

1. As an aside, thinking about income and corporate taxes together for the purpose of such comparisons is appropriate because countries vary with respect to the breadth of their corporate income taxes. In particular, the United States taxes an unusually large share of business income through a personal income

tax (passthrough businesses), making its corporate tax appear smaller than such taxes elsewhere.

2. This weakness is shared with wealth taxation, too, though taxation at death, when assets change hands anyway, should make valuation easier because estate disposition often involves valuation anyway.

References

Auerbach, Alan J. 1991. "Retrospective Capital Gains Taxation." *American Economic Review* 81(1): 167–178.

Kopczuk, Wojciech. 2017. "U.S. Capital Gains and Estate Taxation: A Status Report and Directions for a Reform." In *The Economics of Tax Policy*, edited by Alan Auerbach and Kent Smetters, 265–291. Oxford: Oxford University Press.

Kopczuk, Wojciech. 2019. "Comment on 'Progressive Wealth Taxation.'" *Brookings Papers on Economic Activity*, forthcoming. http://www.columbia.edu/~wk2110/bin/BPEASaezZucman.pdf.

Organization for Economic Cooperation and Development (OECD). 2018. *Consumption Tax Trends 2018: VAT/GST and Excise Rates, Trends and Policy Issues.* Paris: OECD Publishing.

Organization for Economic Cooperation and Development (OECD). 2019. Revenue Statistics. https://stats.oecd.org/Index.aspx?DataSetCode=REV.

Schizer, David M. 2015. "Limiting Tax Expenditures." *Tax Law Review* 68: 275–354.

Zelenak, Lawrence. 2018. "The Tax-Free Step-Up in Basis at Death and the Charitable Deduction for Unrealized Appreciation: The Failed Reforms." In *Figuring Out the Tax: Congress, Treasury, and the Design of the Early Modern Income Tax*, 110–132. Cambridge Tax Law Series. Cambridge: Cambridge University Press.

28

Why Do We Not Support More Redistribution? New Explanations from Economics Research

Stefanie Stantcheva

Rising Inequality but Stagnating Support for Redistribution

Understanding the connection between citizens' information, beliefs, and political support for redistributive and progressive policies that can affect their lives in profound ways is both critical and difficult. Amid rising inequality and political polarization, uncovering citizens' (mis)perceptions, views on fairness, and economic circumstances is an important first step in addressing problems that currently weaken US democracy. A central puzzle is why so many voters seem to vote against redistributive policies that would benefit them, such as more progressive income taxes, taxes on capital income or estates, or more generous transfer programs, and why voters have tolerated policies that have contributed to a stark rise in inequality over the past few decades (Bartels 2008).

The median voter model predicts that an increase in inequality, as captured by the gap between median and average income, should lead to an increase in support for redistribution and an increase in actual redistribution as policymakers cater to the median voter's preferences (Meltzer and Richard 1981). Yet, as shown by Kuziemko et al. (2015), using the General Social Survey, there has been no increase at all in stated support for redistribution in the United States since the 1970s, even among those who say they have below average income.

A New, Innovative Research Tool

A promising way to answer these questions is through large-scale online surveys and experiments with methodology I have developed and pushed forward over the years and that reveal what's obscured in other datasets. My guiding principle here is that we need to listen more to people, not in an idealistic or wishful way but rather through the better use of surveys and online experiments as rigorous research methods. A survey means directly asking people for answers rather than trying to infer them indirectly from observational data. An experiment means controlling part of the perception or information to see the effect it has on policy outcomes or attitudes.

Surveys have been used for a long time in political science and sociology. In addition, "traditional" surveys were used for tangibles that are now much better recorded in high-quality administrative datasets, such as earnings, demographics, or program eligibility. The online surveys and experiments I create and run improve on earlier work in many important ways: they leverage new design and large-scale diffusion methods, they are quantitative and calibrated so they can be rigorously analyzed using econometric and machine-learning methods, and they present respondents with carefully designed, intuitive, and interactive questions. They allow me to reach a large number of people quickly and either target specific harder-to-reach subgroups (such as minorities, younger people, or residents of particular geographic areas) or collect substantial nationally representative samples in one or several countries. The most valuable contribution of such surveys is to reveal three types of intangibles that cannot be seen in other types of data, even high-quality administrative datasets or other "big data."

Perceptions

The first of these intangibles is perceptions. What are the perceptions that people have about themselves, others, the economic system, and economic policies? Misperceptions may push people to wrongly vote in favor of or against certain policies, render them vulnerable to further misinformation, and damage democracy. Detecting misperceptions is the first step toward fixing them and creating better-informed citizens. Caplan (2007), for instance, writes: "The greatest obstacle to sound economic policy is not entrenched special interests or rampant lobbying, but the popular misconceptions, irrational beliefs, and personal biases held by ordinary voters."

Views on Fairness

When people decide which policies to support, they weigh views on fairness, equity, and justice that are much more complex and context-specific than we have grasped until now. Views on fairness may be more important than gaps in knowledge and may interact with them; understanding these views and their interplay is key for preventing dangerous slides into populism caused by feelings of unfairness or injustice.

People's Own Economic Circumstances

We can learn a lot about economic circumstances from administrative records, yet much still remains unknown, and the most direct way of uncovering it may simply be to ask people: Along which margins do people adjust to economic policies? How exactly do people benefit or suffer from policies? As Enrick (1963) wrote, "Every man is 'aware' of taxes, especially in this year of 1963. The extent of this awareness has rarely been examined, despite the ever-increasing importance of the public sector. Given our ignorance about tax awareness or tax consciousness, it is surprising that some economists are so willing to predict the effects of changes in the tax structure on individual behavior. If we do not know people's tax consciousness, how can we know the extent to which changes in their tax burden will affect their behavior?" Policymakers often must operate with limited data that obscure specific circumstances. This may render policies ineffective or, worse, hurt vulnerable groups.

Findings

These types of surveys and online experiments have already yielded interesting answers to the question of why people support or oppose redistribution.

A lack of information about the level or rise of inequality does not seem to be the culprit for the lack of support for redistribution. Kuziemko et al. (2015) use a series of randomized online survey experiments to show respondents' personalized information on US inequality, such as where people are in the US income distribution and where they would have been if growth had been equally distributed. They find that respondents' concern about inequality strongly increases in response to seeing this information, yet this has only a small effect on their support for more progressive policies.

It is worth noting that some type of targeted information about policies does work. For instance, respondents starkly overestimate the share of estates subject to the estate tax. Providing information about the extremely small true share strongly improves support for the estate tax.

Trust in government (or lack thereof) also seems to be a critical element in driving support for redistribution. When faced with negative information about inequality (i.e., that it is high and has increased), respondents tend to say that they trust the government less. This may stem from the belief that if it is politicians who let inequality become this bad, they should not be trusted to remedy it. In all surveys described in this chapter, trust in government in the United States in general is abysmally low. Over 89%

of respondents agree that "politicians in Washington work to enrich themselves and their largest campaign contributors, instead of working for the benefit of the majority of citizens." In addition, priming respondents to think about topics that they dislike about the government (such as asking them about their opinions on lobbyists or the Wall Street bailout) lowers their trust in the government experimentally. This significantly lowers support for most redistribution policies and increases support for "private charity" over government policies as a better way to reduce inequality.

Being able to connect the concern for inequality with concrete public policy measures is critical as well. This idea, raised by Bartels (2008), can be explored experimentally, too. One experiment consisted in showing respondents the budget constraint and spending of a household at the poverty line. The experiment was interactive and customized so that the household had the same composition as the respondent's household. Then, respondents were shown concretely how different government programs (e.g., the minimum wage and food stamps) would alleviate the budget constraints of that household. Such an experiment did improve support for the policies that were shown but not for other redistributive policies that were not specifically mentioned. Taken together with the previous findings, this suggests that when trust in government is so low, the only way to move people's views on a given policy is to explicitly tell them about their impact on specific families.

Fourth, it appears as if John Steinbeck was at least partially correct in his conjecture made in 1966 that Americans do not support that much redistribution because the working poor perceive themselves as "temporarily embarrassed millionaires." It does appear to be the case that people are willing to tolerate high levels of inequality if they think that opportunities are relatively equally distributed and that everyone has a chance at climbing the social ladder. Alesina, Stantcheva, and Teso (2018) show that more optimistic beliefs about intergenerational mobility reduced support for redistribution in five countries, but beliefs about mobility are not in line with reality. American respondents are in general too optimistic about the "American Dream," the likelihood of making it from the proverbial rags to riches. On the contrary, Europeans are too pessimistic, specifically about the likelihood of staying stuck in poverty. There is also stark political polarization: even when shown pessimistic information about mobility, right-wing respondents do not want to support more redistribution policies, because they see the government as a "problem" and not as the "solution."

Furthermore, inside the United States, there is widespread geographical variation in perceptions of national intergenerational mobility, and these perceptions correlate negatively with the actual state levels of mobility. The South, for instance, has the lowest actual rates of intergenerational mobility in the United States, yet respondents there paradoxically have the most optimistic perceptions.

It does seem that generosity travels less well across ethnic, national, and religious lines and that people dislike redistributing toward people who are different from themselves. One such group is immigrants. Using large-scale survey experiments in six countries, France, Germany, Italy, Sweden, the United Kingdom, and the United States, Alesina, Miano, and Stantcheva (2018) show experimentally that simply making respondents *think* about immigrants in a randomized manner (which is achieved by asking them questions about immigrants without providing any information) before asking them questions about redistribution lowers support for redistribution. But, importantly, people seem to have strikingly large biases in their perceptions of the number of immigrants, their social and economic characteristics, and their reliance on government transfers. In all countries in the sample, respondents think there are more immigrants than there actually are and that those immigrants are less educated, more likely to be unemployed, more reliant on government transfers, and more likely to benefit from redistribution than is the case. Respondents also think there are many more Muslim immigrants and many fewer Christian immigrants than there really are. It also appears that, in this instance, providing factual information does not have much power to convince people. Showing information about the actual shares and origins of immigrants to a subgroup of people merely makes the immigration issue more salient to them and further reduces support for redistribution. Telling people an anecdote about the day in the life of a very hardworking immigrant does somewhat better. On balance, it appears that, when it comes to immigration, narratives are more powerful than hard facts in shaping people's views.

What Can Be Done? The Role of Economists

The first critical thing to clarify is what our goal here is. My strong conviction is that the aim is to give citizens the best tools to understand policies and the economic environment so they can make better decisions for themselves when it comes to policy choices and voting. The goal is by no means to push people in one direction or the other. On the contrary, it is to give them the means to think for themselves. The way forward, in my view, is through better, broader, and earlier economics education.

We need outreach and education on economic policy issues for a much broader public, including for young people. This is a long, uphill battle and by no means a quick fix.

There are two main challenges to overcome. First, it is clear from this new body of research evidence that hard facts and pure information do not always work to correct misperceptions or improve understanding. Narratives sometimes have a strong hold, too. Hence, education must go beyond facts and explain workings, mechanisms, causes, and consequences in balanced, understandable ways (Stantcheva 2019).

Second, "experts" appear to be mistrusted more and more. Economists are no exception. Many scientists face large obstacles in getting through to the public, on issues such as climate change, vaccines, or evolution. Economists are perhaps in an even more difficult position because we do not always have perfect empirical evidence and randomized experiments to answer pressing questions. We are also particularly at risk of being considered biased and partisan. The fault is not wholly ours; "TV economists," who are often quite nonrepresentative of academic economists, attract more attention in the media than do rigorous researchers. Although there are examples of stellar economic journalism out there, more often than not, the media takes up simple messages, which may be misleading and quite far from the nuanced view an academic economist would hold. But much of it is our responsibility; by not reaching out to a broader public, we are leaving the stage to self-proclaimed, partisan experts. By letting ideologies or political views slant our results, we are imposing a negative externality on all economists, as we hurt their future credibility, too.

References

Alesina, Alberto, Armando Miano, and Stefanie Stantcheva. 2018. "Immigration and Redistribution." NBER Working Paper 24733, National Bureau of Economic Research, Cambridge, MA.

Alesina, Alberto, Stefanie Stantcheva, and Edoardo Teso. 2018. "Intergenerational Mobility and Support for Redistribution." *American Economic Review* 108(2): 521–554.

Bartels, Larry M. 2008. *Unequal Democracy: The Political Economy of the New Gilded Age*. Princeton, NJ: Princeton University Press.

Caplan, Bryan. 2007. *The Myth of the Rational Voter: Why Democracies Choose Bad Policies*. Princeton, NJ: Princeton University Press.

Enrick, Norbert Lloyd. 1963. "A Pilot Study of Income Tax Consciousness." *National Tax Journal* 16(2): 169–173.

Kuziemko, Ilyana, Michael Norton, Emmanuel Saez, and Stefanie Stantcheva. 2015. "How Elastic Are Preferences for Redistribution? Evidence from Randomized Survey Experiments." *American Economic Review* 105(4): 1478–1508.

Meltzer, Allan H., and Scott F. Richard. 1981. "A Rational Theory of the Size of Government." *Journal of Political Economy* 89(5): 914–927.

Stantcheva, Stefanie. 2019. "Understanding Economics: What Do People Know and How Can They Learn?" Working paper, Harvard University, Cambridge, MA.

Steinbeck, John. 1966. *America and Americans*. New York: Viking Press.

29

Can a Wealth Tax Work?

Gabriel Zucman

There is a demand for progressive taxation among the American electorate. According to Gallup, 62% of Americans say that upper-income people pay too little in taxes (Levitz 2019). Two major presidential candidates, Senator Elizabeth Warren and Senator Bernie Sanders, have proposed to create a federal wealth tax, an idea that according to a number of surveys seems to have broad support among voters.[1]

The centrality and popularity of the idea of wealth taxation raises the question of its feasibility. One frequent objection is that wealth taxes have not fared well in Europe. France, Germany, and Sweden all used to have progressive wealth taxes before repealing them. Although in these three countries the tax was abolished by conservative governments (Helmut Kohl's conservative party in Germany in 1995, an alliance of center-right parties in Sweden in 2007, and Emmanuel Macron's center-right government in France in 2017), a frequent interpretation of these episodes is that European wealth taxes were abolished because progressive taxation is inherently unworkable.

This interpretation, however, is based on a superficial reading of European history. Taxes are neither bound to fail nor guaranteed to succeed: governments can choose to make them work or to make them fail. European governments made a number of wrong choices, allowing tax avoidance and evasion and failing to modernize their taxes, which in many cases had been created decades ago. The progressive taxes discussed in the US context today could be shielded from the key pitfalls that undermined wealth taxation on the other shore of the Atlantic (Saez and Zucman 2019).

To understand this, one needs to delve into the reality of how wealth was (and in some countries, such as Norway, Switzerland, and Spain, still is) taxed in Europe. Although there are some differences across countries, these various attempts share three distinctive—but preventable—flaws.

The first is the choice to tolerate tax competition. In Europe, rich tax-payers can avoid taxation by moving abroad. A tax-averse Parisian can move his tax residence to Brussels to become immediately free from taxation in France; his friends and business partners remain a mere 90-minute train ride away. The European Union has never put restrictions on tax competition. Any common tax policy requires the unanimity of all member states, which in practice means there's no common tax policy. Moreover, individual member states do not attempt to tax their nationals living abroad. In principle, France could choose to continue taxing its expatriates, at least for a few years—for a system where one can become very rich thanks to French infrastructure, markets, and schools and then move abroad without paying taxes seems hard to justify—but, like other European countries, France does not choose to do so.

The situation in the United States is the opposite: moving abroad does nothing to reduce one's tax duties. US citizens are taxable in the United States no matter where they live. The only way to escape the IRS is to renounce citizenship—a move that triggers exit taxes on unrealized capital gains today and could trigger exit taxes on the stock of wealth itself should a wealth tax exist, making renouncing citizenship costly in practice. Europe embraces tax competition; the United States refuses it.

Tax competition almost single-handedly killed European wealth taxes. In Sweden, the country's wealthiest man—the founder of Ikea, Ingvar Kamprad—moved to Switzerland to avoid the wealth tax and only returned to Sweden after the wealth tax was abolished in 2007. In France, the threat of expatriation was one of the key arguments put forward by Macron's government to abolish the wealth tax in 2018.

The second pitfall of European wealth taxes has been the weakness of European governments when it comes to fighting wealth concealment in tax havens. Until 2018, there was no exchange of information between banks in Switzerland (and other secrecy havens) and European tax authorities. When no information is exchanged, hiding assets and evading taxes on portfolios of stocks and bonds is easy. Based on leaks from offshore banks (the "Swiss Leaks" from HSBC Switzerland and the Panama Papers), the wealthiest Scandinavians evaded close to 20% of their taxes through hidden offshore accounts in 2007 (Alstadsæter, Johannesen, and Zucman 2019).

Over the last few years, however, there has been substantial progress in the fight against offshore tax evasion. In 2010, the US Congress passed and President Obama signed into law the Foreign Account Tax Compliance Act (FATCA). The law compels foreign financial institutions to automatically send detailed information to the IRS about the accounts of US citizens each year. Under the threat of economic sanctions, almost all foreign banks have agreed to cooperate. Emulating the United States, other countries have secured similar agreements, and the exchange of bank information has become the global standard. Properly funded tax authorities, drawing on the reports they receive each year from foreign financial institutions, could do a better job enforcing taxes on offshore accounts than was the norm in Europe.

The third flaw of European wealth taxes is their many loopholes, exemptions, and deductions. Consider the case of the French wealth tax abolished in 2017. Paintings were exempt, shares in businesses owned by their managers were exempt or taxed at lower rates, homes that were primary residences enjoyed a 30% deduction, and shares in small or medium-size enterprises benefited from a 75% exemption. The list of tax breaks kept growing year after year.

These exemptions had been created over time under the pressure of lobbying groups. In Europe, progressive wealth taxes typically exempt or used to exempt only the first $1 million or so in net wealth. This means that the "merely rich" owners of valuable houses and burgeoning businesses were liable for the tax. They lobbied to obtain exemptions from it, claiming they faced liquidity constraints (which in some cases might have been true).

The progressive taxes currently discussed in the United States are different in that they start much higher in the wealth distribution and would fall on a different population. In Warren's plan, all net wealth below $50 million is exempted; in Sanders's version, the exemption is $32 million. It would be harder for taxpayers to claim they face liquidity problems; starting above $32 million or $50 million may protect these taxes from the type of lobbying that eventually undermined European wealth taxes.

Tax avoidance is not a law of nature; it is a policy choice. In Europe, a choice was made to let wealth taxes fail—not a conscious or democratic choice or the product of a rational deliberation by an informed citizenry but a choice nonetheless. Other choices can be made. By systematically collecting data on wealth (including from foreign banks), by taxing all assets above a high wealth level at their market value, by refusing tax competition, and by giving the tax authority the resources to enforce the law, a progressive tax on net wealth could collect sizable sums, increase the progressivity of the US tax system, and curb the rise of wealth concentration.

Figure 29.1 illustrates the effect of a wealth tax. It shows the effective tax rate paid by each group of the population—from the 10% of

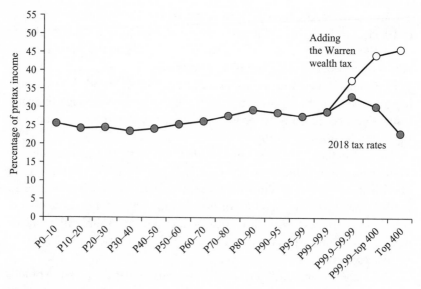

Figure 29.1

Total tax rate (percentage of income) by income group. *Source*: Saez and Zucman (2019).

Americans with the lowest incomes up to the 400 richest Americans—in 2018, in the aftermath of the Tax Cuts and Jobs Act, when taking into account all taxes paid at all levels of government. When all taxes are included, the US tax system looks roughly like a flat tax: every social group pays roughly the same tax rate, close to 28% (the macroeconomic rate of taxation in the United States). The only exception is the top 400 richest Americans, who according to these estimates pay 23%. With a wealth tax at a rate of 2% above $50 million and 3% above $1 billion (labeled "Warren wealth tax" in figure 29.1), the effective tax rate paid by the ultrawealthy would double from 23% to 46%.

There are, of course, other ways to increase tax progressivity. The website http://taxjusticenow.org allows anyone to assess the impact of possible tax reforms (such as creating a wealth tax, increasing the top marginal income tax rate, or better enforcing corporate tax laws) on the progressivity of the US tax system and government revenue. Increasing the progressivity of the income tax and taxing multinational companies better would be powerful steps, but because the truly rich can own a lot of wealth while realizing little taxable income, these reforms would not be enough to impose significant effective tax rates on billionaires—as a wealth tax could.

Note

1. About 60%–70% of Americans say they favor a tax of 2% above $50 million in net wealth, according to surveys. See Casselman and Tankersley (2019) and Sheffield (2019).

References

Alstadsæter, Annette, Niels Johannesen, and Gabriel Zucman. 2019. "Tax Evasion and Inequality." *American Economic Review* 109(6): 2073–2103.

Casselman, Ben, and Jim Tankersley. 2019. "Democrats Want to Tax the Wealthy. Many Voters Agree." *Nytimes.com*, February 19, 2019. https://www.nytimes.com/2019/02/19/business/economy/wealth-tax-elizabeth-warren.html.

Levitz, Eric. 2019. "Voters Aren't Moving Left on Taxes. Democrats Are Moving Towards Voters." *Nymag.com*, February 2019. http://nymag.com/intelligencer/2019/02/wealth-tax-warren-polls-media-public-opinion-democrats.html.

Saez, Emmanuel, and Gabriel Zucman. 2019. "Wealth Taxes Often Failed in Europe. They Wouldn't Here." *Washington Post*, October 25, 2019. https://www.washingtonpost.com/outlook/wealth-taxes-often-failed-in-europe-they-wouldnt-here/2019/10/25/23a59cb0-f4ff-11e9-829d-87b12c2f85dd_story.html.

Sheffield, Matthew. 2019. "New Poll Finds Overwhelming Support for an Annual Wealth Tax." *TheHill.com*. February 6, 2019. https://thehill.com/hilltv/what-americas-thinking/428747-new-poll-americans-overwhelmingly-support-taxing-the-wealth-of.

Contributors

Daron Acemoglu, Massachusetts Institute of Technology

Philippe Aghion, College de France

Danielle Allen, Harvard University

Ben Ansell, University of Oxford

David Autor, Massachusetts Institute of Technology

Sheri Berman, Barnard College

Marianne Bertrand, University of Chicago

Olivier Blanchard, Peterson Institute for International Economics

Lucas Chancel, Paris School of Economics

William Darity Jr., Duke University

Peter Diamond, Massachusetts Institute of Technology

Christian Dustmann, University College London

David T. Ellwood, Harvard University

Richard B. Freeman, Harvard University

Caroline Freund, The World Bank

Jason Furman, Harvard University

Hilary Hoynes, University of California, Berkeley

Lawrence F. Katz, Harvard University

Wojciech Kopczuk, Columbia University

N. Gregory Mankiw, Harvard University

Nolan McCarty, Princeton University

Dani Rodrik, Harvard University

Jesse Rothstein, University of California, Berkeley

Emmanuel Saez, University of California, Berkeley

T. M. Scanlon, Harvard University

Tharman Shanmugaratnam, Monetary Authority of Singapore

Heidi Shierholz, Economic Policy Institute

Stefanie Stantcheva, Harvard University

Michael Stynes, Jain Family Institute

Lawrence H. Summers, Charles W. Eliot University Professor and President Emeritus at Harvard University

Laura D'Andrea Tyson, University of California, Berkeley

Philippe Van Parijs, Université catholique de Louvain

Gabriel Zucman, University of California, Berkeley

Index

A. Philip Randolph Institute, 213
Acemoglu, Daron, xiv, xvii, 164–166, 180
Adelson, Sheldon, 156
Aghion, Philippe, xiv, xviii, 171–175
Alesina, Alberto, 266–267
Alexander, Sadie Mossell, 213
Allen, Danielle, xv, 88
Amazon, 166, 175
American exceptionalism, 85
American National Election Survey, 69
Anderson, Elizabeth, 41–42
Ansell, Ben, xvi, 69
Aristotle, 41
Artificial intelligence (AI), 99, 104, 122, 165–166, 201
Atkinson, Anthony B., 4, 33
Atwater, Lee, 80n2
Australia, 12, 94
Auten, Gerald, 142
Auto industry bailout, 132
Automatic stabilizers, 237–240
Automation, xvii, 24, 26n17, 164, 166–168, 185n6
Autor, David, xiv, xviii

Bartels, Larry, 44, 266
Base Erosion and Profit Shifting (BEPS), 185n4
Battisti, Michele, 120
Ben-Shalom, Yonatan, 240
Benzell, Seth G., 184n1
Berlin, Isaiah, 43

Berman, Sheri, xvi
Bertrand, Marianne, xiv
Bick, Alexander, 198
Blair, Tony, 78
Blanchard, Olivier, 31, 114
Blanchet, Thomas, 4, 56
Bloomberg, Michael, 156
Bonica, Adam, 88
Breda, Thomas, 199
British Household Panel Survey, 68–69
Brynjolfsson, Erik, 184n1
Buffett, Warren, 155
Bush, George H.W., 80n2
Bush, George W., 70
Business Roundtable, 184

California College Promise program, 186n17
Callahan, Gene, 264
Campaign finance, 88–90
Canada, 15, 22, 36, 46, 94, 126, 256–257
Caney, Simon, 50
Capitalism and Freedom (Friedman), 140
Case, Anne, 19
Caucus of Black Economists, 213
Chancel, Lucas, xi–xii, 4, 31–32, 35, 51, 55n6, 56n10, 85
Chetty, Raj, 14, 18–19, 171–173, 219
Child care
  benefits of quality, 197–198, 223
  military reforms, xviii, 224

Children's Health Insurance Program
(CHIP), 238
Child Tax Credit (CTC), 94, 237
China. *See also* Trade shock
manufacturing advantage, 109, 111,
113
Permanent Normal Trading Status,
109
Citizens United v. Federal Election
Commission, 89
Civic participation, 46
Civilian Conservation Corps, 213
Clean energy, 167–168
Climate change
carbon tax, 185n5
effect on inequality, 24
national security risk, 185n12
revenue needs for, 35–36
"solarization" federal employees,
215
Clinton, Hillary, 79, 208
Commitment for Equity Institute
(CEQ), 25n3
Congressional Budget Office (CBO),
145, 149n4
Conservative Party, 79
Constant, Benjamin, 42
Current Population Survey, 201, 228

Dalton, Hugh, 33
Danish People's Party (DPP), 72
Darity, William, Jr., xiv
Dauth, Wolfgang, 118
Deaton, Angus, xviii, 19
Democracy in America (Tocqueville),
49
Democratic Party (American), 77,
79, 86–88, 138, 148, 153, 156,
204–205
Denmark, 16, 22, 26n16, 68, 72, 104,
130, 196, 256
De Ruijter, Stan, 119
Diamond, Peter, xix, 140
Distribuendum, 50–51
Distributional national accounts
methodology (DINA), 5, 26n11
Distributive justice, 50, 55n4

Dodd-Frank bill, 144
Drucker, Peter, 207
Dustmann, Christian, xiv, xvii,
119–120

Earned Income Tax Credit (EITC)
bad job subsidies, 215
earnings subsidies, 222
family supports, 94–95, 226n2
postproduction policies, xiv, xviii
poverty reduction, 249
social safety net, 238, 250–251
spending and taxation, 255
workers without children, 239
work incentives, 240
Economist, The, 78
Education
apprenticeships, xvii, 120–121, 182,
186nn18–20
community colleges, 181–182,
186nn16–17
current labor markets and, 99
early interventions, 100
leveling up, 100–101
lifelong learning, 104, 182, 186n21,
187n22
science, technology, engineering and
mathematics (STEM), 46, 129,
132, 199
social engineering and, 100
teacher aides, 215
technology, influence of, 99
tertiary education, 101, 103
training and retraining programs,
120–122, 130–131, 178, 181
uniformity of curriculum, 102–103
well-functioning public school
systems, 101–102
women's choices, 198–199
Egalitarian ideas, 43–44, 49–50,
54–55, 55nn1–2, 59, 62
Egalitarianism, 43–44, 50, 61
Egger, Peter H., 23
Ellwood, David, xiv, xviii
Employee ownership, 201, 206–208
Employee Retirement Income Security
Act (ERISA), 206

Employee Stock Ownership Plans
(ESOPs), 206–208
Enrick, Norbert Lloyd, 265
Extinction Resisters, 202

Facebook, xviii, 166, 175
Fair Deal, 213
Federal Bureau of Investigation (FBI),
228
Federal job guarantee. *See also* Earned
Income Tax Credit (EITC);
National Investment Employment
Corps (NIEC)
antipoverty expenditures, 215–216
history of, 213
political support, 216
supporters, 213–214
Feldstein, Martin, 140
Findeisen, Sebastian, 118
Flinn, Christopher J., 26n15
Forbes, 153, 157
Forbes 400, 88, 142
Forbes 500, 10
Foreign Account Tax Compliance Act
(FATCA), 272
Forstater, Mathew, 214
France
education, 19
gender data, 16
immigration and bias, 267
income distribution, xii, 5, 9, 11–12
inequality data, 17
trade shock, 120
wealth taxes, 271–272
workers' data, 17, 20
Freedom Budget, 213
Freeman, Richard B., xiv, 203
Friedman, Milton, 140
Fuchs-Schuendeln, Nicola, 198
Furman, Jason, xiv

Gallup, 203, 271
Garbinti, Bertrand, 11
Garnero, Andrea, 14, 26n15
Gates Foundation, 144
Gender gap
bias and stereotypes, 199

glass ceiling, 195
motherhood penalty, 195–197
STEM education, 199
wage growth, 226n1
General Accounting Office, 224
General Agreement on Tariffs and
Trade (GATT), 126
General Social Survey, 263
Germany. *See also* Trade shock
apprenticeship system, 121–122,
182
China trade relations, xvii,
123n3
corporate boards, 46
education, 130
flexible industrial relations, 120
gender data, 196
high export industries, 118–119
immigration and bias, 267
income distribution, 12–13
technological and organizational
change (T&O), 120–121
trade surplus, 118, 125–127
vocational education, 120
Volkswagen unionization, 187n30
wealth distribution, 129
wealth taxes, 271
workers' data, 17, 19–20, 22
Gethïn, Amory, 4, 56n10
Gig workers. *See* Precarious
employment
Gini coefficient, 25n6, 32–33, 54–55,
60, 86, 171, 173–174
Giridharadas, Anand, 144
Google, 166, 175
Goupille-Lebret, Jonathan, 11
Government policies
child care, 197
father's leave postparenthood,
198
maternity leave, 197
Great Depression, 205, 213, 239
"Great Gatsby Curve," 172
Great Recession, 3, 11–12, 72, 114n2,
247, 249
Greenberg, Stanley, 78
Greenspan, Alan, 32

Harrison, Allan J., 4
Harvard University
  Clean Slate for Worker Power
    project, 139, 206, 209
  Labor and Worklife Program, 204
  wealth transfer survey, 139
Health care, 45, 255
Higher education
  college premium, 103
  income growth and, 18–19, 26n19
Hijzen, Alexander, 14
Housing. *See also* British Household
    Panel Survey; International Social
    Survey Program
  effect on politics, 71–72
  price data, 68–70
Hoynes, Hilary, xiv
Human motivation
  liberties, negative and positive,
    42–43
  policies for well being, 45–46
  purposiveness, 42–44
Humphrey-Hawkins Act of 1978, 214
Hungary, 256

Immigration, 45–46, 55n10
Income and wealth, 61, 126–129
Individual security accounts (ISAs),
    183, 187n27
Inequalities
  European and American, xi–xii
  full time or part time, 53
  importance of, xii–xiii, xv–xvi, 59
  justifiable, 49–50
  maximin and leximin, 50, 55, 55n3
  middle-class jobs, xv
  negative effects, 75
  objectionable, 44, 49, 51, 59–61, 63
  opportunities, xii, xiii, 44, 52,
    54–55, 61
  outcome or opportunity, 54
  policy considerations, 54
  political preferences and, 68–69
  postproduction policies, xiv
  preproduction policies, xiii–xiv
  production policies, xiv
  proposals and ideas, xix

support for redistribution, 265
  within and between countries,
    51–53, 55n7, 55n9, 55n10
Inequality data. *See also* Gini
    coefficient
  Census Bureau, 75
  class and, 12–13
  earnings comparisons, 219–221
  education, 17–20, 26n19
  gender and racial, 15–16, 26n16
  geographic view, 6–9, 12, 25n6,
    26n11, 51, 55n6
  health systems, 19–20
  historical view, 5–7
  household surveys, 4
  innovation correlation, 172–173
  labor market institutions, 20–21
  measurements of, 171
  patents, 172
  scarcity of, 3–4
  statistical overview, xi, 3
  tax data, 4, 25n2
Innovation, xviii, 24, 166, 171–172,
    175–176, 176n1. *See also*
    Automation
International Social Survey Program,
    70
Italy, 12, 16–17, 19, 120, 267

*Janus v. American Federation of
    State, County, and Municipal
    Employees, Council,* 31, 202
Japan, 12, 26n8, 125–127, 129–131
Jefes y Jefas program (Argentina), 214
Justice by Means of Democracy
    (Allen), 43

Kamprad, Ingvar, 272
Katz, Lawrence F., xiv, 225
Kelton, Stephanie, 214
Kemp-Roth bill, 32
Keynes, John Maynard, xvii
King, Coretta Scott, 213
King, Martin Luther, Jr., 213
Klein, Michael W., 118
Kleven, Henrik, 195–196
Koch brothers, 144, 156

Kopczuk, Wojciech, xiv, 14, 142
Krueger, Alan, 225
Kupferberg, Joe, 148
Kuziemko, Ilyana, 263, 265
Kuznets, Simon, 4

Labor law, 204–205. *See also*
    National Labor Relations Act
Labor market. *See also* Gender gap;
    Trade Adjustment Assistance
    (TAA)
    college education and, 112
    commuting zones (CZ), 111–112,
        171, 173
    displacement and reinstatement, 165
    earnings decline, 109, 114nn1–2,
        117
    job losses, 113, 125
    labor-intensive manufacturing, 109,
        111, 113, 115n6, 165
    local labor markets, 110
    low-skilled workers, 17, 126,
        224–225
    low wage countries and, 113
    manufacturing employment, 111,
        113, 119, 123n2
    non-college education and,
        110–112, 115n5
    problems of, xiii
    supermanagers, 177, 184n1
    urban wage premiums, 110–111
    weak growth, 163
Labor unions. *See also* Germany;
    Wage theft
    apprenticeships, xvii
    attitudes toward, 203
    decline of, xix, 62, 96, 187n30,
        201–202
    European, 20–21
    history of, 205–206
    monopsony power, 183–184,
        187n29, 202
    New Deal and, xvii
    policy changes, 204–206
    political clout, 89, 205
    regional differences, 111
    usefulness, 202–203

Labour Party, 78–79
Lakner, Christoph, 26n11
Landais, Camille, 196
Levy Economics Institute (Bard
    College), 214
Lewis, Arthur, 104
Liberalism, 43
Lifelong Learning and Training
    Accounts, 182
Lifetime earnings, 14–15
LinkedIn, 224
Luxembourg Income Study (LIS), 25n3

Macron, Emmanuel, 103, 271–272
Madison, James, 32, 201
Mankiw, N. Gregory, xiv
Marshall, George, 45
Marshall Plan, 45
Martin, Sébastien, 14
McCarty, Nolan, xvi, 44, 85
McGovern, George, 148
Medicaid, 143, 238, 240, 242,
    249–250
Medicare, 143, 240, 256
Meritocratic systems, 99
Mexico, 126
Miano, Armando, 267
Milanovic, Branko, 26n11, 51
Minimum wage, 16, 20, 215, 223,
    227–228
Minsky, Hyman, 213
Moffitt, Robert, 240
Moser, Christoph, 118
Murray, Michael, 214

Nagel, Thomas, 50
Napp, Clotilde, 199
National Academies of Sciences,
    Engineering, and Medicine, 249,
    251n1
National Economic Association, 213
National Industrial Recovery Act of
    1933 (NIRA), xvii
National Investment Employment
    Corps (NIEC), 214–216
National Labor Relations Act, 204,
    206

National Labor Relations
    Board (NLRB), 184, 203–205
National Opinion Research Center, 206
Netflix, 166, 175
Netherlands, 21
New York Times, 35, 143
New Zealand, 12, 256–257
Nigai, Sergey, 23
North American Free Trade
    Agreement (NAFTA), 126
Nozick, Robert, 62

Obama, Barack, 187n28, 272
Occupational Safety and Health
    Administration (OSHA), 231
Office of Federal Contract
    Compliance Programs, 232
Oikonomika (Aristotle), 41–42
Organization for Economic
    Cooperation and Development
    (OECD). *See also* Programme for
    International Student Assessment
    (PISA)
    BEPS project, 185n4
    commuting zones comparisons, 172
    gender gaps, 195
    inequality of earnings, 14, 75, 85
    labor policy comparisons, 130
    revenue collection comparisons, 256
    union density, 20

Parijs, Philippe Van, xv, 55nn3–4
Peterson Institute for International
    Economics, xi, 176
Pettit, Philip, 41–42
Pew Research Center, 196, 203, 223
Piketty, Thomas, 11, 23, 68, 86, 184
Polarized America (Poole, Rosenthal,
    McCarty), 85
Politics. *See also* Housing
    doubt in government, 76
    economic interests, 76–77
    influence of wealthy, 143–144
    Left leaning parties, 77–80
    non-economic issues, 78
    polarization, 67, 71, 85–87
    populism, 70–71, 77

Right leaning parties, 77, 79–80
    taxation reform proposals, 147–148
    views on welfare state, 70
Polls and surveys. *See* American
    National Election Survey;
    British Household Panel Survey;
    Current Population Survey;
    Gallup; General Social Survey;
    International Social Survey
    Program; Rasmussen survey
Poole, Keith, 85
Portable benefits, 183, 187n28
PovCalNet database, 25n3
Poverty
    antipoverty programs, 246
    childhood, 245, 249–251
    poverty rate, 240–241, 246–247
    shame and, 60–61
Precarious employment, 182–183,
    187n23, 187nn25–26
Prioritarians, 59
Programme for International Student
    Assessment (PISA), 101–102, 130
Provident Fund, 208
Purchasing power parity (PPP), 52,
    56n8

R&D funding, 180–181, 185nn7–15
Race
    economic questions of, 44–45
    inequality data, 15–16, 26n16
Rajan, Raghuram G., 176
Ramsey, Frank P., 33
Rasmussen survey, 203
Rawls, John, xv, 41, 43, 49–50, 55n3,
    62, 240
Reagan, Ronald, 76
Recovery Act (2008), 238–239
Redistribution policies
    immigration and bias, 267
    intergenerational mobility, 26n15,
    266–267
    international comparisons, 18
    politics and, 87, 89
    predistribution, 21
    support for, xviii, 68–70, 263, 266
    trust in government, 265–266

Republican Party, 77, 80n2, 86–87, 89, 147, 204–205
Restrepo, Pascual, 164–166
Retirement finance, 36, 68, 208. *See also* Social Security
Rodrik, Dani, 31, 114
Rogers, Joel, 203
Ronglie, Matthew, 68
Roosevelt, Franklin D., xvii, 213–214
Rosenthal, Howard, 85, 88
Rothstein, Jesse, xiv
Rural Employment Job Guarantee (India), 214
Russia, 4
Rustin, Bayard, 213

Saez, Emmanuel
  earnings inequality, 14, 142–143
  estate and gift tax, 146
  international agreements, 179
  preproduction policies, xiv
  private wealth, 11
  tax credits, 26n21
  tax rates, 23, 86, 145, 149nn4–5
  wealth taxation, 141, 147–148
Safety net
  benefits of, 250–251
  child care, 93–94
  expansion and decline of, 237–240, 242, 247–249
  job loss, 95
  programs, 245, 251n2
  welfare, 95–96
  work supports, 94
Samuelson, Paul, 140
Sanders, Bernie, 138, 153, 157–158, 208, 271, 273
Sarin, Natasha, 145, 148
Savings rate, 10–11
Scanlon, Thomas M., xv, 43–44
Schönberg, Uta, 120
Second Bill of Rights, 213–214
Sen, Amartya, 41–42
Senate Finance Committee, 32
Shanmugaratnam, Tharman, xiv
Shierholz, Heidi, xiv
Sholz, John Karl, 240

Singapore, 101–102, 187n22
Singer, Peter, 50
Skillful network (Colorado), 182
SkillsFuture Credit (Singapore), 182, 187n22
Small Business Administration, 207
Smith, Adam, 41, 60
Smith, Matthew, 142, 145
Social mobility, 13–14, 26n13, 26n15, 173, 175
Social Security, 35–36, 69, 143, 202, 239, 256
Social Security Trust Fund, 36
Social welfare, 33–34
Søgaard, Jakob Egholt, 196
Song, Jae, 14
Splinter, David, 142
Stantcheva, Stefanie, xiv, 266–267
Steinbeck, John, 266
Steyer, Tom, 156
Strecker, Nora M., 23
Stynes, Michael, xiv
Südekum, Jens, 118
Summers, Lawrence H., xiv, 145, 148
Superstar effect, 21
Supplemental Nutrition Assistance Program (SNAP), 238, 240, 246, 250–251
Supplemental poverty measure (SPM), 237, 242n1, 247
Supplemental Security Income (SSI), 246
Surveys, 264–265
Sweden, 9, 21, 36, 68, 102, 196, 198, 256, 267, 271–272
Switzerland, 22, 182, 271–272
Sykes, Jennifer, 222

Tariffs, 117, 123n1, 125–127
Taxation. *See also* Earned Income Tax Credit (EITC); Value-added tax (VAT); Wealth tax
  attitudes toward, 32, 35, 69
  global taxation of multinationals, 184nn3–4
  married women and, 198

Taxation (cont.)
  policy effects, 179–180, 184n2
  progressive and regressive, 24,
    255–256, 259, 261, 271, 273
  tax rates, 274
Taxation, studies of, 33–35, 142,
    148n2, 274
Tax Cuts and Jobs Act, 274
Tax evasion, 4–5, 50, 153, 259,
    272
Tax revenue
  capital gains taxation, 259–260
  charitable contributions, 259–261
  economic outcomes, 31–33
  income taxes, 257, 261n1
  labor supply effects, 34
  payroll taxes, 143, 257–258
  public spending, 31
  stateless corporations, 179
Tcherneva, Pavlina, 214
Technology
  productivity and, 163–164, 171
  redirection toward clean energy,
    167
  skilled jobs and, 177–178, 181
Temporary Assistance for Needy
    Families (TANF), 238, 240
Teso, Edoardo, 266
Thatcher, Margaret, 70
Theil index of pretax national income
    inequality, 12–13, 26n11, 51
Thrift Savings Plan, 36
Tobin, James, 140
Tocqueville, Alexis de, 46
Total Factor Productivity (TFP), 175
Trade, international, 118, 123n2,
    125–127
Trade Adjustment Assistance (TAA),
    114, 130–131
Trade shock, xvii, 109–111, 113,
    114n3, 118, 120, 122, 132
TRIM3 model (Urban Institute), 249,
    251n1
Triumph of Injustice, The (Saez and
    Zucman), 179
Trotsky, Leon, 76
Truman, Harry S., 213

Trump, Donald and Trump
    administration, 77, 79, 123n1,
    123n3, 147–148, 156
Tyson, Laura, xiv, xvii, 223

UN Comtrade data, 118
Unemployment Insurance, 95–96,
    114, 130, 240–241
United Kingdom
  children in, 94
  education, 130
  employee ownership, 208
  gender data, 15, 26n16, 196, 198
  housing and wealth, 69
  immigration and bias, 17, 267
  income tax rates, 22–23, 208
  job losses, 125–127, 129
  minimum wage, 20
  private wealth, 128
  trade shock, 132
  wealth distribution, 4, 9, 12
United Nations International Labor
    Organization, 119
Universal basic income (UBI), xviii, 33,
    138–140, 215–216, 221–222, 224
UN System of National Accounts, 5
Urban, Dieter M., 118
Uruguay Round, 126

Value-added tax (VAT), xiii, 138, 140,
    256–259, 261

Wage theft
  declining unionization, 230–232
  enforcement, 230–232
  examples, 227–228
  motivation for, 228–229
  surveys of, 228
  whistleblower enforcement laws,
    231
Wagner Act, 205
Wall Street Occupiers, 202
Warren, Earl, 37
Warren, Elizabeth, 138, 153, 155,
    157–158, 271, 273
Wealth, government, 7–9, 31–32, 181,
    185n13

Wealth, private, 7–12, 25n7, 26n8, 68, 142–143, 149n4, 153–154, 156. *See also* Housing
Wealth, public. *See* Wealth, government
Wealth tax
  Americans offshore, 272–273
  effect on US economy, 158
  effect on wealth holders, 157–158
  estate and gift tax, 146–147, 149n5, 259, 262n2, 265
  European experience, 271–273
  influence of wealthy, 141–144
  policy debate, 153
  political proposals, 271
  progressive tax rates, 3, 22–24, 26n20, 36, 46, 141, 155
  revenue from, 145–147, 149n5, 154, 158n2, 258–259
  tax credits, 26n21
Weil, David, 230
Welfare state, 68, 70, 76, 255
Work, value of. *See also* Earned Income Tax Credit (EITC)
  benefits, 223
  low-paying jobs, 223–224
  low-skilled workers, 224–225
Worker ownership. *See* Employee ownership
Worker protection, 96–97
  forced arbitration, 229–231
  government contracts and, 232
workplace fissuring, 230–231
Works Progress Administration (WPA), 213, 215
World Bank's Ease of Doing Business list, 130
World Inequality Database (WID), 5
World Input Output Database, 118
World Top Incomes Database, 4
World Trade Organization (WTO), xviii, 109, 126
Wray, Randall, 214

Yang, Andrew, 138, 140

Zidar, Owen, 142, 145
Zingales, Luigi, 176
Zucman, Gabriel, xiv
  earnings inequality, 142–143
  estate and gift tax, 146
  international agreements, 179
  private wealth, 11
  tax credits, 26n21
  tax rates, 23, 145, 154
  wealth taxation, 141, 147–148
Zwick, Erick, 145